Papers of the Fifty-First Algonquian Conference

Actes du cinquante-et-unième Congrès des Algonquinistes

PAPERS OF THE ALGONQUIAN CONFERENCES
ACTES DU CONGRÈS DES ALGONQUINISTES

51

Papers of the Fifty-First Algonquian Conference

Actes du cinquante-et-unième Congrès des Algonquinistes

EDITED BY Monica Macaulay and Margaret Noodin

MICHIGAN STATE UNIVERSITY PRESS | EAST LANSING

♾ The paper used in this publication meets the minimum requirements of ANSI/NISO Z39.48-1992 (R 1997) (Permanence of Paper).

Michigan State University Press
East Lansing, Michigan 48823-5245

Library of Congress Cataloging-in-Publication Data is available
ISBN 978-1-61186-424-3 (Paper)
ISBN 978-1-60917-691-4 (PDF)

Cover design by Erin Kirk
Cover detail of a quill box is used courtesy of Julie L. Loehr

green press INITIATIVE

Michigan State University Press is a member of the Green Press Initiative and is committed to developing and encouraging ecologically responsible publishing practices. For more information about the Green Press Initiative and the use of recycled paper in book publishing, please visit *www.greenpressinitiative.org*.

Visit Michigan State University Press at *www.msupress.org*

CONTENTS

Preface

Initial organization for the Fifty-First Algonquian Conference was done by Janine Metallic, assistant professor in the Department of Integrated Studies in Education at McGill University, with Jessica Coon (McGill University), Amy Dahlstrom (University of Chicago), Monica Macaulay (University of Wisconsin–Madison), and Margaret Noodin (University of Wisconsin–Milwaukee) assisting. Angela Mesic of the University of Wisconsin–Milwaukee did a beautiful job preparing the program.

The conference was held from October 25 to 27, 2019, at McGill University in Montreal, Quebec, Canada. A large group of wonderful students stepped up to help onsite, including Vanessa Racine (undergraduate student), Kanontienentha Brass (undergraduate student), Tarynne Pachano (MA in Indigenous language revitalization), and Marie-Eve Senecal (University of Victoria student), who were all participating in an Indigenous Languages Reading Group/independent study that semester led by Jessica Coon and Janine Metallic. Colin Jacobs (undergraduate student), Clara Saliba (undergraduate student), Mathieu Paillé (linguistics PhD student), and John Sylliboy (education PhD student) also helped out. Margaret Noodin's daughter Fionnan Noori (Nitaaniimikwesens) attended, and wound up helping out at the conference desk. A special thanks to Ian Puppe for driving the boxes of books from the University of Western Ontario for the book sale.

All of the attendees gathered for breakfast and coffee on the first day, and several people brought greetings from their institutions, territories, and nations. The group acknowledged the current First Nations of Quebec, including the Cree, Mi'qmaq, Naskapi, Algonquin, Montagnais, Abenaki, Mohawk, Attikamekw, Huron, and Malecite.

In addition to the papers published in this volume, the following papers were presented at the conference:

Irene Appelbaum (University of Montana): Obviative NPs and Discourse Participants in Ktunaxa.

Amy Dianne Bergseth (University of Oklahoma): Relationality and Other Indigenous Technologies for Rebuilding in the Era of Forced Removal.

Sidney Bittman (University of Colorado Boulder): Semantic Categorization and Its Effects on Co-Occurrence of Arapaho Lexical Preverbs.

Robert Brightman (Reed College, emeritus): Boreal Algonquian Animism(s) and Ecology(ies).

Julie Brittain and Yvan Rose (Memorial University): Acquiring Preverbs in Cree: A Longitudinal Case Study.

Amy Dahlstrom (University of Chicago): Antitopics and Episode Structure in Meskwaki.

Rose-Marie Déchaine (University of British Columbia), Monique Dufresne (Queen's University), and Charlotte Reinholtz (Queen's University): The DP Syntax Continuum in the Cree Continuum.

Leighton Delgado (Montaukett Indian Nation), Irene Navas (Center Moriches Schools), Conor Quinn (University of Southern Maine), Tina Tarrant (Shinnecock Indian Nation), Wunetu Tarrant (Shinnecock Indian Nation and University of Arizona), and Harry Wallace (Unkechaug Nation): Digital Documentation Training for Long Island Algonquian Community Language Researchers: A New Paradigm for Community Linguistics.

Lynn Drapeau (Université du Québec à Montréal): Gradability and the Derived Verbal Diminutive in Innu-aimun.

Émile Duchesne (Université de Montréal): Transformation of Gifts in Commodities among the Innus of Unamen Shipu.

Ryan E. Henke (University of Hawai'i at Mānoa): Number Marking for Animate Obviatives: Evidence from Relational Constructions.

Dianne Friesen (University of Victoria) and Barbara Sylliboy (Eskasoni School Board): Mapping Argument Structure to Grammatical Roles with Mi'kmaw.

Maria Patricia Farfán (McGill University): The Nasa Yuwe: Cultural Preservation and Recognition through Nasa-Paéz Traditional Language and Architecture.

Atticus G. Harrigan and Antti Arppe (University of Alberta): Automatic Semantic Classification of Plains Cree Verbs.

Marie-Odile Junker (Carleton University), with Jérémie Ambroise, Antti Arppe, Chantale Cenerini, Inge Genee, Bill Jancewicz, Mimie Neacappo, Jean Okimasis, Claire Owen, Delasie Torkornoo, and Arok Wolvengrey: A Digital Infrastructure to Sustain Algonquian Languages: Dictionaries and Linguistic Atlas: Progress Report 3 / Une infrastructure numérique commune pour que vivent les langues Algonquiennes: dictionnaires et atlas linguistique: Rapport 3.

Marie-Odile Junker, Véronique Chachai, Nicole Petiquay, and Cécile Planchon (Carleton University): Dictionnaire et ressources en ligne pour la langue Atikamekw.

Philip S. LeSourd (Indiana University Bloomington): An Unusual Agreement Pattern in Maliseet-Passamaquoddy Explained.

Monty McGahey II (Chippewas of the Thames First Nation): Re-viewing Nishnaabemwin of Bkejwanong.

Paul J. Meighan (McGill University): Addressing Colonial Threats to Linguistic Heritage: A Framework for Indigenous Language Revitalization Using *TEK-Nology*.

Aandeg Muldrew (University of Winnipeg): Word Order in Short Anishinaabemowin Texts.

Margaret Noodin (University of Wisconsin–Milwaukee): Ohkwa:li – Makwa: Tales of Bear's Tails in the Oneida and Ojibwe Classroom.

Tiffany Prieh (University of Manitoba): Transitivity of Objectless TIs.

Ian Puppe (University of Western Ontario): "We've been here forever!": Assertions of Algonquin Presence in Algonquin Provincial Park.

Conor Quinn (University of Southern Maine): Keeping It Simple: The Minimal Course Model for Helping English Speakers Learn Core Conversation Patterns in Algonquian Languages.

Charlotte Reinholtz (Queen's University): The Syntax of the REALIS/IRREALIS Contrast in Swampy Cree.

Carl Schaefer (National Museum of Natural History, Smithsonian Institution): Conjunct and Subjunctive in the Shawnee Law.

Katherine Schmirler (University of Alberta): Negation in a Plains Cree Corpus.

Katherine Schmirler and Antti Arppe (University of Alberta): Plains Cree Actors and Goals: Across Time Periods and Genres.

Morgan Siewert (University of Texas at Austin): Storywork, Performance, and Analytic Authority in an Anishinaabe Community.

Lucy Thomason (National Museum of Natural History, Smithsonian Institution): Meskwaki Double-Headed Participles.

Susan Wade (University of Wisconsin–Milwaukee): Writing Methodologies and Indigenous Perspectives of Anishinaabewakiing.

Fiona Wilson (University of Toronto): Negative Particles in Muskeg Cree: A Variationist Approach.

Arok Wolvengrey (First Nations University of Canada): *tānispīhk wīhkāc ōma kē-āpatahk!?: wīhkāc* as a Polarity Item in Plains Cree.

Lexical Relationships in Central Algonquian

Jerome Biedny, Andrea Cudworth, Sarah Holmstrom, Monica Macaulay, Gabrielle Mistretta, Joseph Salmons, Charlotte Vanhecke, and Bo Zhan

This paper examines lexical data from a set of Algonquian languages spoken in the center of the family's geographical range in search of patterns of relatedness (see Map 1).[1] The family has been recognized since the 18th century (Campbell and Poser 2008:6–7), but internal relationships within the family are less clear. In fact, to date, the only widely accepted subgroup has been Eastern Algonquian (Goddard 1978, 1980, and elsewhere).[2]

Understanding the non-Eastern languages in purely diffusionist terms, Goddard (1994) surveys phonological, morphological, and lexical evidence of relatedness between Algonquian languages and concludes that the oldest layer is found among the western languages, "with a series of successively shallower time-depths further east" (1994:187). He identifies what he calls "dialectal subgroupings," while arguing that the only genetic subgroup is Eastern Algonquian. Oxford (2015:319) represents this 'west-to-east cline' as shown in Figure 1.

As Figure 1 shows, Goddard treats one subset of the central languages—Ojibwe-Potawatomi, Fox-Kickapoo, Shawnee, and Illinois—as forming a dialect group that he calls "Core Central" (1994:194), #4 in the diagram. Rhodes (1989, 2011), in contrast, has argued explicitly for a genetic subgroup within the Central languages,

MAP 1. Algonquian languages

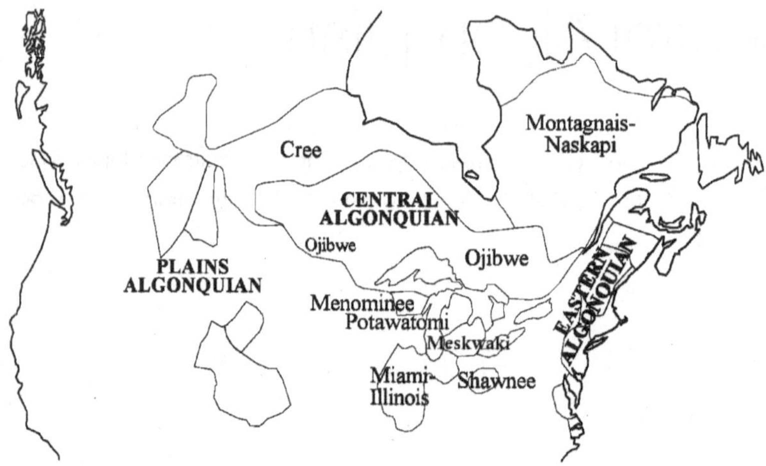

(based on map from Oxford 2015:318, used with permission)

based on shared phonological innovations. His “Eastern Great Lakes” consists of the same languages or groups as Goddard’s Core Central: Proto-Potawatomi-Ojibwe, Proto-Sauk-Fox-Kickapoo, Shawnee, and Miami-Illinois. While Rhodes includes selected lexical data, to our knowledge, no one has published a systematic lexicostatistical study of Algonquian.[3]

Both major proposals thus posit some kind of central group (be it genetic or areal) and both treat Menominee and Cree as falling outside this group. Table 1 compares the proposals of Goddard and Rhodes to the languages examined here, also highlighting differences in language or dialect names. Crucial throughout will be the distinction between geographically central languages (the seven listed

FIGURE 1. Goddard’s west-to-east cline. 1: All languages other than Blackfoot, the most divergent member of the family. 2: Languages that merge */θ, l/. 3: Languages that merge */ʔC/ and */hC/ clusters. 4: Languages that shift */ʔl, hl/ to /hs/. 5: Languages that merge */i:/ with /i/ and */o:/ with /o/. (Oxford 2015:319)

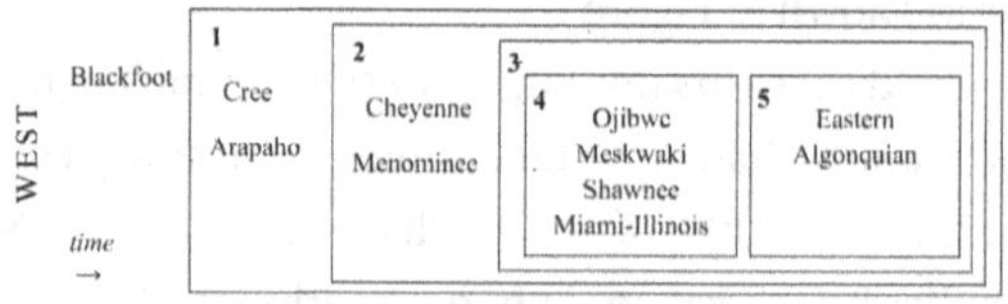

TABLE 1. 'Central' languages: Goddard, Rhodes, the present study

GEOGRAPHICAL OR GENETIC GROUP	THIS PAPER	GODDARD 1994: CORE CENTRAL DIALECT GROUP	RHODES 1989: EASTERN GREAT LAKES SUBGROUP
Central	Potawatomi	Ojibwe-Potawatomi	Proto-Potawatomi-Ojibwa
	SW Ojibwe		
	Meskwaki	Fox-Kickapoo	Proto-Sauk-Fox-Kickapoo
	Shawnee	Shawnee	Shawnee
	Miami-Illinois	Illinois	Miami-Illinois
	Menominee		
	Plains Cree		

in Table 1) and proposed groupings, areal (Goddard) or genetic (Rhodes). That is, we use 'central' merely as a regional designation when not otherwise specified.[4]

Comparative linguistics and evolutionary biology recognize character-based and distance-based approaches. Here, we adopt a distance-based approach, taking a set of words to build a measure of similarity or difference and calculating distance between pairs of languages. We look at proportions of vocabulary shared by languages in the central region broadly construed: Potawatomi, Meskwaki, Shawnee, Miami-Illinois, and Menominee, plus Plains Cree as a representative of the Cree dialect continuum and Southwestern Ojibwe as a representative of the Ojibwe languages and dialects. In addition, we include Cheyenne (from the Plains region) and Passamaquoddy-Maliseet (from the Eastern branch) as a form of control from other parts of the family. In other work, we are undertaking character-based analysis, searching for shared innovations of the kind used in historical reconstruction. Both approaches, of course, will ultimately need to be supplemented with deeper understanding of historical demographics and community histories.

In the next section we discuss lexical lists, which focus on words that are unlikely to be borrowed, and after that we describe our methods, including issues that arise in using such lists with polysynthetic languages. The results yield a novel picture of relationships among this set of Algonquian languages, corresponding to neither Goddard's Core Central area nor to Rhodes's Eastern Great Lakes branch. Instead, they reflect the modern geographical distribution of the languages, supporting relatively recent contact as a source of shared vocabulary.

Lexical Lists and Algonquian Languages

Lexical lists focusing on a set of "core" vocabulary are used for a variety of purposes across a range of subfields of linguistics. Here we discuss two: the Swadesh list, and the one that we used, the Leipzig-Jakarta list.

The Swadesh List(s)

The best known lexical list in comparative-historical linguistics is the Swadesh list (or more precisely, lists), developed by Morris Swadesh for glottochronology, one kind of lexicostatistics. The premise of glottochronology was that core vocabulary changes at a constant rate, parallel to how carbon is used in radiocarbon dating, and that once that rate is known, the linguist can determine the time depth at which some set of related languages diverged: "the percentage of retained elements in a suitable test vocabulary therefore indicates the elapsed time" (1952:452). Like most other modern researchers, we regard dating as wildly unreliable; instead, the matter of "suitable test vocabulary" interests us here. Because he wanted to run tests using retained elements, Swadesh wanted the list to minimize the chance that words were borrowed rather than original to a language. Appealing to common knowledge, he claimed that "though words are readily borrowed, it has long been known that the borrowings take place primarily in the 'cultural' part of the vocabulary and that the 'intimate' vocabulary resists change" (1952:455).

Swadesh did give criteria for inclusion of lexical items, for example that words "must refer to things found anywhere in the world and familiar to every member of a society, not merely to specialists or learned people" and that "they must be easily identifiable broad concepts" (1952:457; also 1955). However, he did not provide evidence or justification for the "basicness" of particular words, nor their likelihood of being borrowed in practice.

Various other lists have been proposed since Swadesh, and next we describe a relatively recent one of those, the Leipzig-Jakarta list (Tadmor et al. 2010), focusing on unique challenges that polysynthetic languages pose for lexical lists generally.

The Leipzig-Jakarta List

While Swadesh's purpose in developing his list was to apply it to studies in glottochronology, the goal of the Loanword Typology Project (https://wold.clld.org)

was to advance research on borrowing more generally. The Leipzig-Jakarta list (L-J henceforth) is one of the results of that work, an empirically based 100-word list of terms least likely to be borrowed.

L-J was drawn from a database compiled by specialists in 41 languages who assembled, for each language, a list of 1,460 words including information on any known borrowings. Tadmor et al. acknowledge (2010:229) that the set of languages represented is not a random sample, but it is a large sample, far broader than Swadesh's and others'.[5]

In using the L-J list, we found a set of principles from Swadesh useful for identifying words in the target languages:

> (a) Try to find one simple equivalent for each item by disregarding specialized and bound forms and the less common of two equivalents. (b) Use a single word or element rather than a phrase, even though the meaning may be broader than that of the test item. (c) Where it is impossible to find a single equivalent, omit the form (Swadesh 1952:457).

Despite L-J's improvements over the Swadesh list, it nonetheless proved difficult to use, and following principle (c) above, we omitted many items. This was due in part to lexical category issues and in part because of the generally complex structure of words in Algonquian languages, especially verbs.

Traditionally, Algonquian languages are described as having three major word classes: verbs, nouns, and particles, plus minor classes like pronouns and negators (e.g., Bloomfield 1962:25 for Menominee). Particles make up a large, heterogeneous set distinguished from verbs and nouns by the fact that they carry no inflection. Other Algonquianists' inventories of lexical categories have over the years remained fairly consistent with Bloomfield's, although refinements have been proposed (e.g. Oxford 2014, who convincingly argues for the existence of prepositions in Innu-aimun). But there is no distinct class of adjectives or adverbs, for example.

L-J contains words that are, in English, nouns (*fire, ear, child*), pronouns (first, second, and third singular), verbs (*to go, to say, to know*), adjectives (*bitter, big, red*), an adverb (*far*), a demonstrative (*this*), a preposition (*in*), and a few WH-question words (*who, what*). To understand the problems this posed for our project, consider first adjectives: words expressed by adjectives in a language like English are distributed in the Algonquian languages primarily across verbs and prenouns (a small, closed class of bound words that are compounded with nouns). Examples (1a–e), from Plains Cree, illustrate for the adjective 'big'.[6]

(1) Plains Cree (PCOD)
  a. kihci- 'great, big' (prenoun)
  b. mahki- 'big, large' (prenoun)
  c. misi- 'big, large, great' (prenoun)
  d. misâw 'it (inanimate) is big' (verb)
  e. misikitiw 's/he/it (animate) is big, s/he/it (animate) is large (in height or girth), s/he is a big person; she is large with child, she is pregnant' (verb)

The first problem here is choosing which word from this language should be compared with which words from the other languages. We could decide to hold category constant, and compare, e.g. prenouns with prenouns, but then which prenoun should be used?

In some situations, the thicket of lexical variants is too dense for us to establish rigorous form-meaning pairings for verbs. For instance, the entries in the list presume that simple verbs exist in the language in question. But verbs (and most content words, in fact) are invariably morphologically complex in Algonquian languages. Furthermore, the verbs often specify more information than the simple entries in the list represent. In (2), for example, we show just some of the results of a search for 'to carry' in the *Ojibwe People's Dictionary*. Note that each entry represents at least two verbs, often four or more.

(2) Ojibwe verbs meaning 'carry' (OPD)
able to take, carry; able to carry or lift on the back; arrive carrying; arrive carrying on the back; carry, take ashore; carry, take ashore on the back; take, carry about; carry about on the back; carry across; carry along; carry along on the back; carry away; carry away on the back; take, carry down to the shore; take, carry downhill; take, carry from a certain place; carry from a certain place on the back; take, carry home; carry in the mouth; carry inland; carry off on the back; take, carry outside; carry over a portage; take, carry to a certain place; carry to a certain place on the back; carry uphill; take, carry upstairs; carry using something; lift and carry; carry a load along

As (2) shows, there is no neutral verb meaning simply 'to carry'. Ultimately, parallel sets for other "basic" verbs led us to omit that category from our lexical comparison entirely. And since most English adjectives are expressed with verbs in Algonquian languages, we omitted those as well.

With nouns and members of minor categories it was generally possible to make clearer decisions. Still, in a few cases, languages lacked a single general term for some concept, opting instead for a larger number of specific terms. This happened with 'skin, hide', as shown in (3), mostly derived from an animal name plus a suffix meaning 'skin, hide, covering, garment':

(3) Menominee (MITW)

a. 'hide'

apāēhsosokom 'deerskin, deer hide'
pāēsekokasiwakom 'horsehide'
pesāēhkiwakom 'cowhide'

b. 'skin'

akuahkōhsewakom 'gopher skin'
anāēmwakom 'dog skin'
awāēhsaehsakom 'bearskin'
āēhsepanakom 'raccoon skin'
ketāēmīwakom 'porcupine skin'
maeqnakwahkakom 'badger pelt, skin'
mānestānehsewakom 'sheepskin'
mekīkwakom 'otter skin'
menūkuaposwakom 'goatskin'
namāēhkwakom 'beaver pelt, skin'
nenōk 'my skin'
ocīkwakom 'fisher skin'
onāwanīkwakom 'squirrel skin'
sāhkīhsewakom 'mink skin'
sekōhsewakom 'weasel skin'
uqsāskwakom 'muskrat skin'
wāposokom 'rabbit skin'

Although the word *nenōk* 'my skin' might appear generic, in fact it specifically refers to human skin. We decided to omit this item entirely from our comparison.

Due to considerations like the above, we ultimately wound up with 52 words from L-J that we felt reasonably confident in using.

Methods

As described earlier, we looked at a set of Algonquian languages centered around the Great Lakes, namely, Plains Cree, Menominee, Southwestern Ojibwe, Potawatomi, Miami-Illinois, Meskwaki, and Shawnee. Much past scholarship has pointed to this geographic area as one of intense contact between different Algonquian-speaking groups, and this contact is often cited as a source of borrowing and shared areal features (e.g. Costa 2013). This picture of diffusion has blurred the determination of genetic subgrouping in the Algonquian family, and as already noted, there is no current agreement about subgrouping involving the languages of this region.

The 52 words were compared in the seven languages (plus our two controls), but not every language had a form for all 52 words. Reconstructed forms are available for these items, from Hewson 2019, Aubin 1975, and specialized studies especially by Goddard. The foundation of this kind of work is, again, secure and rigorous alignment of form and meaning. When there was doubt as to cognacy of forms, we were conservative and treated them as non-cognate.

To illustrate our data, the first word of our modified L-J list was 'fire', for which Hewson (2019) provides Proto-Algonquian (PA) *eškwete·wi. Table 2 lists the forms for this word in the seven central languages we looked at. For this word, the forms in all languages were judged cognate after accounting for regular sound changes.

Often, forms had relationships that separated into two or more sets of cognate forms. A good example is 'knee', provided in Table 3, where a long line of work posits PA *meketekw- (apparently first posited by Michelson 1935:144 and adopted by others, e.g. Berman 2006). The bolded forms were judged to be a separate set of cognates.

Once the individual forms were coded for cognacy, we calculated the proportion of cognates, dividing by the total forms available for the languages being compared. For example, Southwestern Ojibwe had 37 forms that were judged to be cognate with Plains Cree. Both languages had entries for all 52 possible words. The ratio of 37 cognates from 52 comparisons yields a proximity of 0.712, or 71.2 percent. When comparing Meskwaki and Miami-Illinois, forms for only 49 of 52 possible

TABLE 2. Words for 'Fire'

PA	PC	MEN	SWO	POT	MIA	MESK	SHAW
*eškwete·wi	iskotêw	eskōtāēw	ishkode	shkodé	koteewi	ashkotêwi	škote

TABLE 3. 'Knee', including reflexes of PA *meketekw-

PC	MEN	SWO	POT	MIA	MESK	SHAW
mihcikwan	**nekāētek**	**nigidig**	njigwen	**nihkitikwia**	nechîkwani	*hočiikwani

entries were present. Thus, the 38 cognates found were divided by 49, resulting in a proximity of 0.76. The smallest set of words available for comparison was 41, between Cheyenne and Passamaquoddy-Maliseet.

Results and Discussion

The cognacy rates for each pair of languages are provided in Table 4. These numbers encode lexical proximity for the 52-word set for each pair. The numbers start from an unsurprising low of 0.27 between Cheyenne and Passamaquoddy-Maliseet, the two most geographically distant languages, one from the Plains and the other Eastern. The closest relationship, or least distance, was unexpectedly between Menominee and Potawatomi. These languages have been immediate neighbors in recent times, but the latter is reckoned as part of "Core Central" or "Eastern Great Lakes" while the former is not.

Comparative linguists of course often, though by no means universally, use trees or dendrograms to visually represent such relationships. One simple and very traditional method for creating a tree is by a hierarchical clustering algorithm, such as the unweighted pair group method with arithmetic mean, or UGPMA. This is shown in Figure 2. The tree was produced in R drawing on the code and discussion in Johnson (2008: chapter 6).

In Figure 2 we can more easily see broader relationships. Consider our first two examples from the discussion of Table 4. To the first, Passamaquoddy-Maliseet is the most distant from the rest of the family, to the extent that it forms its own branch, while Cheyenne, the next farthest from Central, clusters with the central languages. To the second, Menominee and Potawatomi cluster before linking next to Ojibwe. Rhodes and more recently Lockwood (2019) posit an Ojibwe-Potawatomi branch, making this structure perplexing. The other geographically central language not regarded as part of a central genetic or areal group previously is Cree, which appears next, closest to Ojibwe. From there, Meskwaki and Miami-Illinois form a node farther out, and Shawnee is the most distant.

In short, the relationships revealed by this test do not comport with other

TABLE 4. Cognacy across selected Algonquian languages, pruned L-J list

	CHEY	PC	SWO	MEN	POT	MESK	SHAW	MIA	PM
CHEY	0	0.53	0.56	0.67	0.6	0.62	0.56	0.52	0.27
PC	0.53	0	0.71	0.67	0.71	0.65	0.54	0.55	0.38
SWO	0.56	0.71	0	0.73	0.76	0.63	0.56	0.57	0.33
MEN	0.67	0.67	0.73	0	0.78	0.71	0.63	0.69	0.43
POT	0.6	0.71	0.76	0.78	0	0.74	0.65	0.68	0.38
MESK	0.62	0.65	0.63	0.71	0.74	0	0.63	0.76	0.38
SHAW	0.56	0.54	0.56	0.63	0.65	0.63	0	0.57	0.35
MIA	0.52	0.55	0.57	0.69	0.68	0.76	0.57	0	0.33
PM	0.27	0.38	0.33	0.43	0.38	0.38	0.35	0.33	0

FIGURE 2. Cluster dendrogram based on pruned L-J

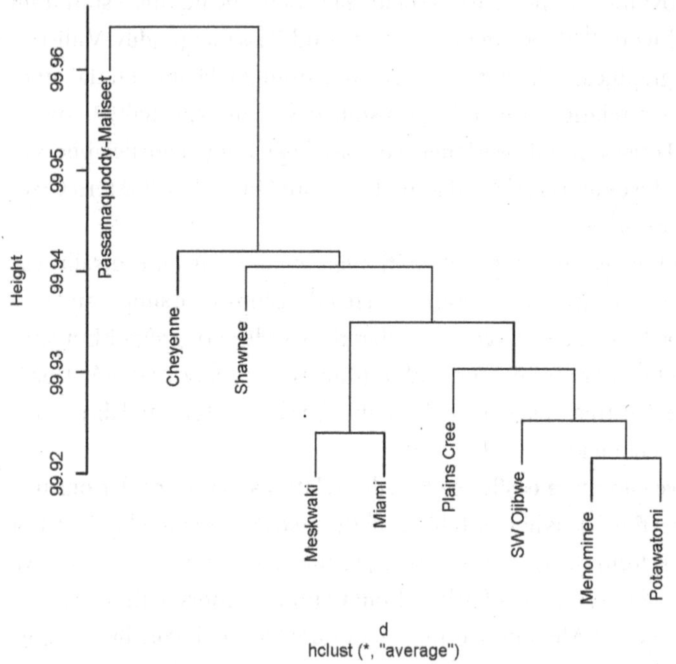

proposed views of central Algonquian in any sense—areal or genetic. But the distribution does show an obvious correlate: High sharing of cognates is found in languages that are immediate geographical neighbors, as shown in Map 1. (Recall from note 1 that that map represents time of European contact, and so does not encompass more recent contact among the various groups.)

Figure 1, with the areal view it represents, is shown again as Figure 3. The mismatches from our dendrogram are striking. We illustrate this with two examples, Cree and Menominee, which are placed by Goddard in distinct layers outside of Core Central.

Map 2 displays the central region with Menominee highlighted. From this perspective, the Menominee connection to Potawatomi becomes less surprising, as does the further link to (Southwestern) Ojibwe.[7]

Map 3 presents the same material from the vantage point of Cree. Here too, patterns of relatively recent and intense contact seem clear. As Goddard writes (1994:195–196):

> It is pretty well known that innovations have diffused between Cree and Ojibwa in both directions (Rhodes 1989). These reflect secondary contact between these languages after considerable divergent history had taken place.

Our lexical data seem to reflect such patterns of "secondary contact." We see other promising patterns as well. For example, Shawnee appears to have been geographically most marginal compared to other central languages, with Shawnee

FIGURE 3. West-to-east cline highlighting non-central/central languages

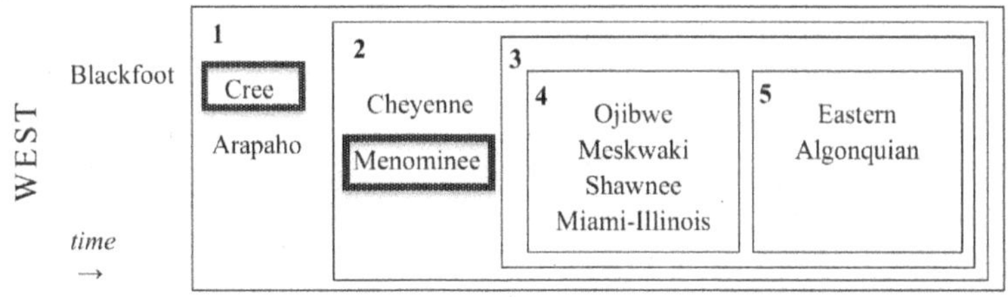

communities apparently mobile in the times since we have records and with close contacts to Delaware (see Pentland 1979: chapter 3). That is, the position of Shawnee in our tree fits the broader pattern.

The language that may fit this scenario least comfortably is Meskwaki. The dendrogram could be capturing its proximity to Miami-Illinois, but Meskwaki is otherwise less tied to languages shown here as its closest neighbors.

MAP 2. Menominee and its neighbors

MAP 3. Cree and its neighbors

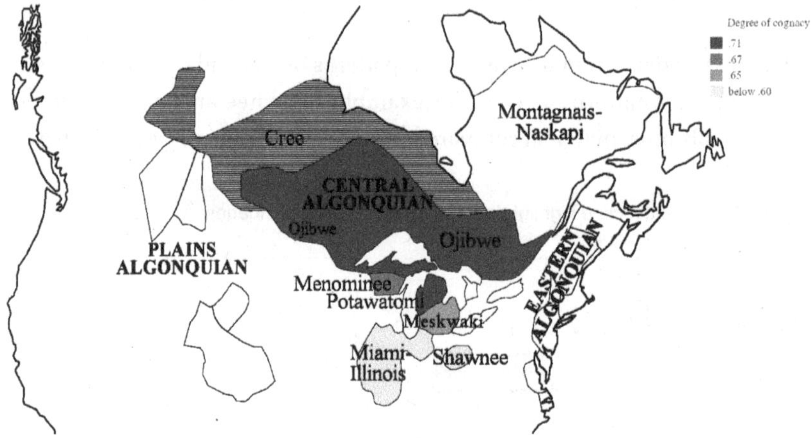

Still, the base map, whatever its shortcomings due to our incomplete knowledge, comes far closer to correlating with the lexical relationships we have found than either the familiar areal-diffusion or genetic subgroup views.

A Parallel Case

Extensive borrowing of basic vocabulary is unexpected in most views, but it is not unattested. An earlier and far more developed account that aligns with our findings comes from Mazatec, an Otomanguean language spoken in Oaxaca, Mexico. Gudschinsky published a set of lexicostatistical studies on Mazatec, including a study of neighboring and closely related dialects. Among other things, she concludes about two dialects that

> the dialect of San Miguel separated from the dialect of Huautla early, and . . . the lexical closeness of the San Miguel dialect to the Huautla dialect is due to recent lexical reborrowing. I postulate this on the basis of documented cases of recent reborrowing, the geographical proximity of the villages, the economic and political dependence of San Miguel on Huautla, and the cultural dominance of Huautla. (Gudschinsky 1955:148)

Léonard et al. (2019) use a set of approaches from complexity science to build on Gudschinsky's findings, which they describe this way:

(4) Gudschinsky's 1955 dialect dynamics model (Léonard et al. 2019:8)

1. Homogeneity, followed by the rise of Huautla and Jalapa.
2. Emergence of a transitional buffer zone between Huautla and Jalapa.
3. (a) The lowland zone splits in two, with the emerging variety of San Pedro Ixcatlán.
   (b) Both Huautla and San Pedro Ixcatlán areas diversify: San Mateo Yoloxochitlán emerges in the highlands, whereas San Miguel Soyaltepec splits from San Pedro Ixcatlán. In the buffer zone, San Miguel Huautla also emerges. Flows of lexicon and variables still pass from the lowlands to the highlands.
4. Further and more clear-cut differentiation between San Pedro Ixcatlán and San Miguel Soyaltepec, in the lowlands.
5. Consolidation of the six dialects: sharper frontiers.

Starting from a distance matrix very similar to ours, they apply further measures to capture relationships, including Levenshtein Distance and mapping in geographical space to lexical data.[8] They conclude that their analyses confirm Gudschinsky's model and they are in fact able to go far beyond it.

Conclusion

We set out to test two views of linguistic relationships among a geographically central group of Algonquian languages, one a diffusionist position and the other positing a genetic subgroup. Though they differ in what they see as the source of similarities, both views propose similar organization of the languages, namely, a central group including Ojibwe-Potawatomi, Meskwaki, Shawnee, and Miami-Illinois, but excluding Cree and Menominee from the same region.

We compiled data using the Leipzig-Jakarta list with considerable adjustments to accommodate the Algonquian data, and used probably the simplest and most traditional way of clustering the data, UGPMA. To our real surprise, the lexical data support neither of the traditional accounts but instead correlate better with modern geographical proximity and known patterns of contact. That is, the lexical connections look like relatively recent patterns overlaid on top of whatever earlier relationships existed. Borrowing of most basic vocabulary runs against traditional lexicostatistical expectations but has been found in some instances of intimate contact between very closely related languages, including Mazatec internal contacts.

We stress that these results are not in fundamental conflict with previous findings. We have simply employed different methods, of a type not used in the family previously. Indeed, these findings differ dramatically from our own findings in a character-based study of Algonquian subgrouping (Biedny et al. 2019). We suggest that these different measures are capturing different aspects of the family's history. Parallel to Gudschinsky (1955) and Léonard et al. (2019), phonological innovations likely represent an earlier layer, while shared lexical material in a part of the lexicon thought to be highly resistant to borrowing likely comes from far more recent contact among closely related languages.

Our next steps are already clear. We are first continuing to check data and refine the data set. Second, with refinement, we are now ready to apply more sophisticated mathematical methods to the data, including cladistics and perhaps the complexity models employed by Léonard et al. (2019). Third, we have barely begun to explore what current understanding of social history, historical demographics, and related research can tell us. Finally, we are working to integrate these findings with our character-based subgrouping proposal.

APPENDIX 1. Sources of Data

LANGUAGE	SOURCE ABBREV.	SOURCE
Cheyenne	CDO	Cheyenne dictionary (online): http://www.cdkc.edu/cheyennedictionary/index.html
Menominee	LB75 MITW	Bloomfield 1975 Menominee Indian Tribe of Wisconsin 2012
Meskwaki	GT	Goddard and Thomason 2014
Miami-Illinois	BC	Baldwin and Costa 2005
Passamaquoddy-Maliseet	PMLP	Passamaquoddy-Maliseet Language Portal: https://pmportal.org/browse-dictionary
Plains Cree	PCOD	Plains Cree Dictionary (online): https://dictionary.plainscree.atlas-ling.ca/#/help
Potawatomi	FC HL	Forest County Potawatomi Community 2014 Lockwood 2017
Proto-Algonquian	PAD	Proto-Algonquian Dictionary (Hewson): https://protoalgonquian.atlas-ling.ca/
Shawnee	BP CS	Pearson 1995 Schaefer 2019
SW Ojibwe	OPD	Ojibwe People's Dictionary: https://ojibwe.lib.umn.edu

NOTES

1. This paper grew initially from a seminar at the University of Wisconsin–Madison in Spring 2019 and is one part of a bigger project on Algonquian historical and comparative linguistics. The authors' names are in alphabetical order. An early version of this paper was presented to Linguistics Fridays at the University of Wisconsin–Madison, October 2019. In addition to that audience, the audience at the Algonquian Conference, and two anonymous reviewers, we thank the following for valuable comments and suggestions: jessie little doe baird, David Costa, Hunter Lockwood, Eric Raimy, and Savana Stauss. Map 1 is based on Oxford (2015:318), which in turn is based on Goddard (1996), and represents the locations of the languages at the time of European contact, rather than at a given point in time overall. For maps and discussion of the Great Lakes region, see Tanner 1987.
2. See Biedny et al. 2019 for a more structured tree, i.e. one with more subgrouping.
3. Pentland (1979:329) reports that Hewson did some preliminary lexical work, and Bakker (n.d.) uses lexical data in discussing possible relationships of Algic with Salish.
4. In the figures and tables that follow, we use the following abbreviations for language

names: Cheyenne = Chey, Menominee = Men, Meskwaki = Mesk, Miami-Illinois = Mia, Passamaquoddy-Maliseet = PM, Plains Cree = PC, Potawatomi = Pot, Proto-Algonquian = PA, Shawnee = Shaw, Southwestern Ojibwe = SWO (or SW Ojibwe in Table 1).

5. The sample, however, contains only one North American language, Yaqui, a Uto-Aztecan language spoken in Arizona (United States) and Sonora (Mexico).
6. We list the data sources we consulted (and their abbreviations) in Appendix 1.
7. Recall that we use Southwestern Ojibwe and Plains Cree as examples of the much larger Ojibwe and Cree language groups, respectively. Our data and maps would be considerably more nuanced with inclusion of other Ojibwe and Cree languages/dialects.
8. Levenshtein Distance is widely used in comparative linguistics and dialectometry. Léonard et al. define it as: "The LD L(a;b) is a basic measure of the level of difference between two strings a and b, defined as the minimum number of operations (represented by insertions, deletions, or editions) needed to turn a into b or vice versa" (2019:9).

REFERENCES

Aubin, George. 1975. *A Proto-Algonquian Dictionary*. Canadian Ethnology Service, Mercury Series Paper, 29. Ottawa: National Museums of Canada.

Bakker, Peter. [n.d]. Salish and Algonquian. Unpublished manuscript.

Baldwin, Daryl, and David J. Costa. 2005. *myaamia neehi peewaalia kaloosioni mahsinaakani: A Miami-Peoria Dictionary*. Miami, OK: Miami Nation.

Berman, Howard. 2006. Studies in Blackfoot Prehistory. *International Journal of American Linguistics* 72(2):264–284.

Biedny, Jerome, Andrea Cudworth, Sarah Holmstrom, Monica Macaulay, Gabrielle Mistretta, Joe Salmons, Charlotte Vanhecke, and Bo Zhan. 2019. A More Structured Family Tree: Algonquian Subgrouping. Unpublished manuscript. University of Wisconsin–Madison.

Bloomfield, Leonard. 1962. *The Menomini Language*, ed. by Charles F. Hockett. New Haven: Yale University Press.

Bloomfield, Leonard. 1975. *Menominee Lexicon*, ed. by Charles F. Hockett. Milwaukee: Milwaukee Public Museum Publications in Anthropology and History 3.

Campbell, Lyle, and William J. Poser. 2008. *Language Classification: History and Method*. Cambridge: Cambridge University Press.

Costa, David J. 2013. Borrowing in Southern Great Lakes Algonquian and the History of Potawatomi. *Anthropological Linguistics* 55(3):195–233.

Forest County Potawatomi Community. 2014. *Ézhe-bmadzimgek gdebodwéwadmi-zheshmomenan: Potawatomi Dictionary*. Self-published.

Goddard, Ives. 1978. Eastern Algonquian Languages. *Handbook of North American Indians*, vol. 15: *Northeast*, ed. by Bruce G. Trigger and William C. Sturtevant, pp. 70–77. Washington: Smithsonian Institution.

Goddard, Ives. 1980. Eastern Algonquian as a Genetic Subgroup. *Papers of the Eleventh Algonquian Conference*, ed. by William Cowan, pp. 143–158. Ottawa: Carleton University.

Goddard, Ives. 1994. The West-to-East Cline in Algonquian Dialectology. *Actes du vingt-cinquième Congrès des algonquinistes*, ed. by William Cowan, pp. 187–211. Ottawa: Carleton University.

Goddard, Ives (ed.). 1996. *Handbook of North American Indian Languages*, vol. 17: *Languages*. Washington: Smithsonian Institution.

Goddard, Ives, and Lucy Thomason. 2014. *A Meskwaki-English and English-Meskwaki Dictionary*. Petoskey, MI: Mundart Press.

Gudschinsky, Sarah C. 1955. Lexico-Statistical Skewing from Dialect Borrowing. *International Journal of American Linguistics* 21:138–149.

Hewson, John. 2019 [1993]. *A Computer-Generated Dictionary of Proto-Algonquian*. Canadian Ethnology Service, Mercury Series Paper 25. Hull: Canadian Museum of Civilization. https://protoalgonquian.atlas-ling.ca.

Johnson, Keith. 2008. *Quantitative Methods in Linguistics*. Malden, MA: Blackwell.

Léonard, Jean Léo, Els Heinsalu, Marco Patriarca, Kiran Sharma, and Anirban Chakrabo. 2019. Patterns of Linguistic Diffusion in Space and Time: The Case of Mazatec. *Complexity Applications in Language and Communication Science*, ed. by Àngels Massip-Bonet, Gemma Bel-Enguix, and Albert Bastardas-Boada, pp. 139–170. Cham, Switzerland: Springer.

Lockwood, Hunter Thompson. 2017. How the Potawatomi Language Lives: A Grammar of Potawatomi. PhD thesis, University of Wisconsin–Madison.

Lockwood, Hunter Thompson. 2019. Revisiting the Position of Potawatomi in (Central) Algonquian. *Papers of the 48th Algonquian Conference*, ed. by Monica Macaulay and Margaret Noodin, pp. 143–158. Lansing: Michigan State University Press.

Menominee Indian Tribe of Wisconsin. 2012. *Omāēqnomenēweqnaesen Wēhcekanan: Menominee Dictionary*. Self-published.

Michelson, Truman. 1935. Phonetic Shifts in Algonquian Languages. *International Journal of American Linguistics* 78:131–171.

Oxford, Will. 2014. A Survey of Locative Expressions in Innu-aimun. *Papers of the 42nd Algonquian Conference*, ed. by J. Randolph Valentine and Monica Macaulay, pp. 181–201. Albany: SUNY Press.

Oxford, Will. 2015. Patterns of Contrast in Phonological Change: Evidence from Algonquian

Vowel Systems. *Language* 91:308–358.

Pearson, Bruce L. (ed.). 1995. *Shawnee Language Dictionary: Preliminary Edition.* Absentee Shawnee Tribe of Oklahoma. Columbia, SC: Yorkshire Press.

Pentland, David. 1979. Algonquian Historical Phonology. PhD thesis, University of Toronto.

Rhodes, Richard. 1989. The Cree Connection. Paper read at the 28th Conference on American Indian Languages, Washington, DC.

Rhodes, Richard. 2011. Cree-Ojibwe Language Contact. Paper read at the annual meeting of the Society for the Study of the Indigenous Languages of the Americas, Pittsburgh, PA.

Schaefer, Carl. 2019. Alford Gospels. Unpublished manuscript.

Swadesh, Morris. 1952. Lexico-Statistic Dating of Prehistoric Ethnic Contacts with Special Reference to North American Indians and Eskimos. *Proceedings of the American Philosophical Society* 96(4):452–463.

Swadesh, Morris. 1955. Towards Greater Accuracy in Lexicostatistical Dating. *International Journal of American Linguistics* 21(2):121–137.

Tadmor, Uri, Martin Haspelmath, and Bradley Taylor. 2010. Borrowability and the Notion of Basic Vocabulary. *Diachronica* 27(2):226–246.

Tanner, Helen Hornbeck (ed.). 1987. *Atlas of Great Lakes Indian History.* Norman: University of Oklahoma Press.

Prenouns and Noun Compounding in Miami-Illinois

David J. Costa

Algonquian languages have a seldom-discussed category of morpheme conventionally called PRENOUNS. Prenouns are morphemes usually secondarily derived from initials, verb stems, and noun stems, which, as the name would imply, immediately precede and modify their following nouns. In most Algonquian languages, prenouns have roughly adjectival meanings, but they are also used when a noun modifies another noun. In Miami-Illinois, a few dozen prenouns have been identified, the great majority of them having adjectival semantics. While a few prenouns derived from nouns have been identified in Miami-Illinois, the language diverges from other Algonquian languages in freely allowing simple noun + noun compounds, even as far back as the old Illinois records of the early eighteenth century. In this paper I will discuss prenouns and noun compounding in Miami-Illinois, describing the derivation and semantics of prenouns, and demonstrating the formation of noun compounds.

Prenouns

The most frequently encountered Miami-Illinois prenouns have meanings associated with stative adjectives in English, with prenouns deriving from basic color terms being especially common.[1] Some of the most commonly seen Miami-Illinois prenouns are given in Table 1.

Miami-Illinois prenouns all underlyingly end in vowels. Many of the most common prenouns straightforwardly derive from initials; if the initial ends in a consonant, the prenoun formative *-i* is added (Table 2).[2] Several common prenouns, however, do not end in *-i*, but rather in long vowels (Table 3). Many prenouns ending in long vowels are derived directly from AI or II stems (Table 4). Several month names, especially in Illinois, contain prenouns derived directly from AI, II, or TI stems (Table 5). If the following noun begins with a vowel, the final *-i* of the prenoun is usually deleted (Table 6). Occasionally, perhaps in deliberate speech, prenouns ending in vowels retain their final *-i* before vowel-initial nouns (Table 7). If the final vowel of the prenoun is long *ee*, *ii*, or *aa*, but the following noun begins with a short vowel, the initial vowel of the noun is deleted (Table 8).[3]

'Black Raccoon' in Table 8 shows that when a prenoun ending in *ee* precedes a noun beginning in *ee*, the *ee* + *ee* sequence is resolved as simple *ee*. At present no examples have been found where a prenoun ending in a long vowel precedes a noun beginning with a different long vowel, but presumably in such a case both vowels would be retained.

While examples are not numerous, there are a handful of cases of prenouns ending in *-i* deriving from animate noun stems, the usual way many Algonquian languages do noun compounding (Table 9).

In several cases (especially in the modern language), nouns ending in *-e·wa* and *-iwa* reduce this ending to *-ia* when preceded by a prenoun (Table 10); this is because the addition of the prenoun increases the syllable count of the word, and thus triggers the reduction of final *-Vwa* to *-ia* seen in long words (see Costa 2003:162–163).[4]

Most prenoun + noun combinations are semantically transparent in that their meanings are basically predictable. However, prenouns are often used to coin new names for things, and so some prenoun + noun constructions are semantically unpredictable and thus lexicalized (Table 11). Especially in the modern language, some prenouns undergo initial change, either optionally or obligatorily, when compared to the initials from which they are derived (Table 12).[5] A few prenouns are of unknown meaning, found on only one noun, and show initials attested nowhere else (Table 13; the phonemicizations of all these prenouns are very tentative).

As a result of the deletion of word-initial short vowels in modern Miami-Illinois, there are several nouns that have been reanalyzed as consonant-initial in the later records in regards to the allomorphy of prenouns (Table 14). That is, there are nouns with initial short vowels that trigger the deletion of the final *i* of preceding prenouns in old Illinois and the early modern records, yet which by the late 19th century and early 20th century had deleted their word-initial short vowels and been reanalyzed as consonant-initial, then restoring final *-i* to preceding prenouns.

Noun + Noun Compounding

A notable feature of Miami-Illinois distinguishing it from its sister languages is that the language freely allows simple noun + noun compounds, with no prenoun marker on the the first noun. While noun + noun compounds are very common among all speakers in the modern language from the 19th century onward, they are also attested in the old Illinois records (especially LeBoullenger), confirming that these constructions are not a result of English influence. Table 15 contains examples of noun + noun compounds consisting of two animate nouns.

Many month names, especially in the modern language, consist of a plain animate noun plus the noun *kiilihswa* 'sun, moon, month'. Typical is the set of month names obtained by Jacob Dunn from Peoria speaker George Finley (Table 16), most of which are also found in calendars obtained from other speakers (though not always with the same translation). Although this strategy for forming month names is not as common in old Illinois, it is still attested in all three missionary dictionaries (Table 17).

There are also documented examples of noun + noun compounds with two inanimate nouns (Table 18). Furthermore, in noun compounds the two nouns need not be the same gender; Table 19 provides examples of noun + noun compounds with an animate noun modifying an inanimate head noun. There are a few attested examples of the reverse as well; i.e. noun + noun compounds with an inanimate noun modifying an animate noun (Table 20).

The question arises, when a noun + noun compound is pluralized, how is this plurality marked? There are unfortunately few examples of this, but two different strategies are seen; the first example in Table 21 contains an example of a noun + noun compound with an animate singular noun modifying an animate plural noun, while the second example consists of two animate plural nouns. LeBoullenger's dictionary contains several examples of noun + noun compounds where a plural noun modifies a singular noun; these constructions are all translated by LeBoullenger as singulars (Table 22).

At this point it should be noted with noun + noun compounds where the first noun is inanimate, as in Tables 18 and 20, it is technically impossible to tell whether the first noun is simply that, an ordinary inanimate noun, or whether these might in fact be examples of the first noun taking the prenoun formative *-i*. This is the reason why the only verifiable examples of prenouns being derived directly from nouns are ones where the modifying noun is animate, as in the examples seen in Table 9. The rarity of such examples seems to indicate that in the Miami-Illinois language, even in the earliest period, simple noun + noun compounding has largely replaced the use of prenouns derived from noun stems. Since not all the Illinois sources may pattern the same way in this regard, a key goal of future research at this point is to see whether the heavy use of simple noun compounds characteristic of the LeBoullenger manuscript is corroborated by the earlier Pinet and Gravier/Largillier dictionaries.

TABLE 1. Common Miami-Illinois prenouns

PRENOUN	GLOSS
ahkipaki-, iihkipaki-	'blue'
alaaminaa-, eelaaminee-	'holy, Christian'
ileni-, (a)leni-	'particular kind, special'*
kataki-, kitaki-	'spotted'
kihci-	'big'
maci-	'bad, evil, wicked'
mahkatee-	'black'
mihši-, mihsi-	'big'
nakaani-	'old'
nalaawahki-	'wild'
neehpiki-	'red'
oonsaawi-, oonsaa-	'yellow'
peehki-	'pretty, good'
waapi-	'white'

* I thank Hunter Lockwood for his suggestions on how to translate this Algonquian prenoun.

TABLE 2. Prenouns ending in *-i**

PRENOUN	GLOSS	BASE NOUN	FORM WITH PRENOUN	ORIGINAL FORMS
(a)skipaki-	'blue'	*mootayi* 'holder, pouch, pocket, chest, cloth'	*skipaki-motayi* 'blue blanket'	Gr ‹skipakim8taï› 'couverture bleüe'
ašaahsi-	'painted'		*ašaahsi-motayi* 'painted bag'	LB ‹achassem8taie› 'sac matache'
(i)leni-	'particular kind, special'	*miteewa* 'Medicine Rite practicioner'	*ileni-miteewa* 'great Medicine Rite practicioner'†	Gr ‹irenimite8a› 'grand jongleur'
kataki-, kitaki-	'spotted'	*maankwa* 'loon'	*kataki-maankwa, kitaki-maankwa* 'Spotted Loon' (personal name)	Gt ‹kitáki=mángwa›, Mc ‹katákimʌñgwa'›
kihci-	'big'	*papikwani* 'gun'	*kihci-papikwani* 'cannon'	Gt ‹kítchi papíkwani›, D ‹kitcipapikwani›
		minooteeni 'town'	*kihci-minooteeni* 'big town'	LB ‹kitchi min8tene› 'beau grand village'
		mooswa 'deer'†	*kihci-mooswa* 'big deer'	LB ‹kitchi m8ns8o› 'grand [chevreuil]'
maci-	'bad, wicked, evil'	*mootayi* 'holder, pouch, pocket, chest, cloth'	*maci-motaya* 'towels, rags'	Gr ‹matchim8taïa› 'torchones, haillons'
		manetoowa 'manitou'	*maci-manetoowa* 'bad manitou'	LB ‹matchimanet8a›, Tr ‹mōtshee monaātwau›, Gt ‹matchi-manätowa›
mihsi	'big, great'	*siipiiwi* 'river'	*mihsi-siipiiwi* 'Mississipi River'	Gr/P/LB ‹missisipi8i›, Gt ‹missisipíwi›
mihši-	'big, great'	*kineepikwa* 'snake'	*mihši-kineepikwa* 'grand serpent, manitou'	Gr ‹michikinebic8a› 'grand serpante, grand manit8'
		maalhsi 'knife'	*mihši-maalhsa* 'American, white person'	Tr ‹shemōlsee›, Gt ‹mshímalsa›, Mc ‹cimā́l^{ε}sa^{n}›, Mi/H ‹mš·imâ·lsa›
		pakaani 'nut'	*mihši-pakaana* 'beech nuts, large nuts'	Gr ‹michipacana› 'fruit de hestre'
nakaani-	'old'	*wiiyoohsi* 'meat'	*nakaani-wiiyoohsi* 'old dried meat'	LB ‹nacane 8i8sse›, P ‹nakane 8hia8si›
		maalhsi 'knife'	*nakaani-maalhsi* 'old knife'	D ‹nakánĭ malsĭ›
		wiikiaami 'house'	*nakaani-wiikiaami* 'old house'	Gt ‹nakáni wikiámi›
		mitemohsa 'woman'	*nakaani-mitemohsa* 'an oldish woman'	LB ‹nacani mitem8ssa› 'une femme agée', D ‹nakani mitämsa›

PRENOUN	GLOSS	BASE NOUN	FORM WITH PRENOUN	ORIGINAL FORMS
nalaawahki-	'wild'	*peehkiihsa* 'goose'	*nalaawahki-peehkiihsa* 'wild goose'	D ‹nalaúkkĭ pắkĭssa›
		pinšiwa 'bobcat, cat'	*nalaawahki-pinšiwa* 'wildcat'	D ‹nälaúĭkĭ pĭ^{n}jiwa›, Mc ‹nʌlauwʌ'ki pi^{n}jĭ́wa'›
		pileewa 'turkey, chicken'	*nalaawahki-pileewa* 'wild turkey'	Gt ‹nalauxki pilắwa›, D ‹nälaukkĭ pilắwa›
oonsaawi-	'yellow'	*kaakatakilenkwia* 'butterfly'[§]	*oonsaawi-kaakatakilenkwia* 'yellow butterfly'	D ‹onzawĭ kakatắkĭlängwĭa›
		šooli 'money'	*oonsaawi-šooli* 'gold'	V ‹honzaouéchoulé›, Gt ‹u^{n}zawíshōli›, D ‹o^{n}záwĭcólĭ› (cf. Po *wzaw žonya*)
peehki-	'good, pretty'	*nipi* 'water'	*peehki-nipi* 'good water'	Gt ‹pắ'ki nípi›
		nakamooni 'song'	*peehki-nakamooni* 'pretty song'	Gt ‹pắ'ki nakámuni›
tipehki-	'night'	*kiilihswa* 'sun, moon, month'	*tipehki-kiilihswa* 'moon'	LB ‹tepeki kiriss8o›, Th ‹tipahke kelissua›, Tr ‹tepāāhkee kēēlswau›
waapi-	'white'	*mihtohseenia* 'person'	*waapi-mihtohseenia* 'white person'	Gt ‹wápi mitussäniáki› (pl.)
		waawiinaakani 'bread'	*waapi-waawiinaakani* 'white bread'	P ‹8abi8a8inagane›
		maankwa 'loon'	*waapi-maankwa* 'White Loon' (personal name)	Gt ‹wapimángwa›, D ‹wápĭmángwa›, Mc ‹wâpimÁñgwa›
wiski-, weehki-	'new'	*papikwani* 'gun'	*wiski-papikwani* 'new gun'	LB ‹8skipapic8ane›
		kiilihswa 'sun, moon, month'	*weehki-kiilihswa* 'new moon'	Tr ‹wāāhkee kēēlswau›
wiihkapi-	'sweet'	*miincipi* 'corn'	*wiihkapi-miincipi* 'sweet corn'	LB ‹8iscape mintchipi›, Gt ‹wikápi mínžipi›

* The following abbreviations are used in this paper: D = Jacob Dunn's fieldnotes on Miami-Illinois, Gr = the Largillier/Gravier Illinois-French dictionary, Gt = Albert Gatschet's fieldnotes on Miami-Illinois, Hk = John Heckewelder's Miami vocabulary, Hn = Charles Handy's Miami vocabulary, Ki = Kickapoo, LB = LeBoullenger's French-Illinois dictionary, Mc = Truman Michelson's Peoria fieldnotes, Mi-H = Charles Hockett's Miami fieldnotes, Mn = Menominee, P = Pinet's French-Illinois dictionary, P/D = Jacob Dunn's Peoria fieldnotes, P/H = Charles Hockett's Peoria fieldnotes, pl. = plural, Po = Potawatomi, Pr = William Preston's Miami vocabulary; Sh = Shawnee, Th = William Thornton's Miami vocabulary, Tr = Charles Trowbridge's Miami fieldnotes, V = Volney's Miami wordlist, WP = the anonymous (1837) Wea Primer. For a discussion of the various data sources on Miami-Illinois, see Costa (2003).

† In the present work, Illinois *r* is phonemicized as *l* for uniformity.

‡ From the 1790s on this noun appears as Miami-Illinois *moohswa*.

§ The literal meaning of this term is 'spotted-winged one'.

TABLE 3. Prenouns ending in long vowels

PRENOUN	GLOSS	BASE NOUN	FORM WITH PRENOUN	ORIGINAL FORM
ihpetee-	'daytime'	*kiilihswa* 'sun, moon, month'	*ihpetee-kiilihswa* 'the sun'	P ‹ippete kiriss8a›, LB ‹ehpete kiriss8o›, V ‹ifpêté-kílixsoua›, Th ‹ifpete-kilissua›; cf. Mn *espɛ·t-ke·soʔ* 'the sun'
kiintee-	'new, young'	*mihtohseenia* 'person, Indian'	*kiintee-mihtohseeniaki* 'young Indians'	Gt ‹kîndä mitusseniáki›, D ‹kĭndä m'tosänĭakĭ›
mahkatee-	'black'	*mihkwa* 'swallow'	*mahkatee-mihkwa* 'black swallow, swift'	Gr ‹macatemisc8a›, LB ‹macatemic8o›
		mahweewa 'wolf'	*mahkatee-mahwia* 'black wolf'	D ‹mäkatämawhia›
		ciinkwia 'thunder'	*mahkatee-ciinkwia* 'Black Thunder' (personal name)	Gt ‹ma'katätcingwia›
		maankwa 'loon'	*mahkatee-maankwa* 'Black Loon' (personal name)	Gt ‹makatemángwa›, Mc ‹ma'katämÁñgwa'›
napalee-	'half'	*šooli* 'money'	*napalee-šooli* 'half dollar'	Gt ‹napálä shúli›, D ‹napálä cólĭ›
		kiilihswa 'sun, moon, month'	*napalee-kiilihswa* 'half moon'	LB ‹naparekissi8o› [sic], D ‹näpálä kĭ́lswa›
		neekatikašia 'horse'	*napalee-neekatikašia* 'mule'	D ‹näpalä näkátĭkáca›
pihkontee-	'night'	*kiilihswa* 'sun, moon, month'	*pihkontee-kiilihswa* 'moon'	Hk ‹pichguntigilswa›, Hn ‹pe kōn da keel swaw›, Gt ‹pikûnde kilswa›

TABLE 4. Prenouns derived from AI and II stems

PRENOUN	GLOSS	FORM WITH PRENOUN	UNDERLYING STEM	ORIGINAL FORMS
alaaminaa-, *ęelaaminee-*	'Christian, holy'	*alaaminaa-wiikiaami* 'church'	*alaaminaa-* 'pray, worship' (AI)	LB ‹aramina 8ikiami›
		alaaminaa-nipi 'holy water'		LB ‹aramina nipi›
		eelaaminee-kiišikwe 'Sunday'		Gt ‹elamenäkishíkwe›
alantee-	'red'	*alantee-ahpwaakani* 'red pipe'	*alantee-* 'be red' (II)	P/LB ‹aranteap8agane›
saakiiwee-	'emerging'	*saakiiwee-siipiiwi* 'coming-out-river'; (name of St. Joseph's river)	*saakiiwee-* (AI/II) 'emerge, be a confluence'	D ‹sakĭwäsĭpíwĭ›
waahsee-	'daytime, daylight'	*waahsee-kiilihswa* 'the sun'	*waahsee-* 'be dawn, daytime, light' (II)	LB ‹8assekiriss8o›, Gt ‹wasse=kílswa›; cf. Ki *waaθeikiiseθwa* 'the sun'

TABLE 5. Month names derived from AI and II stems

PRENOUN	GLOSS	FORM WITH PRENOUN	DERIVED FROM	ORIGINAL FORMS
aamalee-	'rutting'	*aamalee-kiilihswa* 'November/ October'	*aamalee-* 'be in heat, rutting' (AI)	LB ‹amâre kiriss8o›, P ‹emare kiriss8a›; cf. Ki *aamanwiiha* 'November'
aciihciikata-	'hilling corn'	*aciihciikata-kiilihswa* 'June/July'	*aciikatam-* 'hill it up (e.g. the corn)' (TI)	Gr ‹atchicata kiris.› 'Juin', LB ‹achicata [kiriss8o]› 'L epi paroist juin'
kiišiinkwee-	'roasting ear'	*kiišiinkwee-kiilihswa* 'August'	*kiišiinkwee-* 'it (the corn) is ripe, finished growing; roasting ear' (II)	Tr ‹kēēshingwaa kēēlswa›, Gt ‹kishîngwe kílswa›)
moonaha-	'plowing'	*moonaha-kiilihswa* 'May/June'	*moonaham-* 'dig it, cultivate it' (TI)	LB ‹m8naha kiriss8o›, P ‹m8naha kiriss8a›
pinawee-	'shedding (as of antlers)'	*pinawee-kiilihswa* 'December/ November'	*pinayowa, peenawita* 'he drops his horns, sheds his antlers' (AI)	Gr ‹pina8e kiris.›, P/LB ‹pina8e kir[iss8a]›; cf. Sh *penawe* 'he is shedding'
takwaaki-	'autumn'	*takwaaki-kiilihswa* 'July / August'	*takwaakiwi* 'it is autumn, fall'	Gr ‹tac8aki kiris8a›, LB ‹tac8aki kiriss8o›

TABLE 6. Final *-i* of prenouns deleted before vowels

PRENOUN	GLOSS	BASE NOUN	FORM WITH PRENOUN	ORIGINAL FORM
ahkipaki-, *iihkipaki-*	'blue'	*alamoni* 'ocher, vermillion'	*ahkipak-alamoni* 'blue ocher'	LB ‹kipacaramoni›
		aalahkwatwi 'cloud'	*iihkipak-aalahkwatwi* 'blue cloud'	Gt ‹íkipakalkwatwi›, D ‹ĭkĭpak alkwatwĭ›
(i)leni-	'particular kind, special'	*akoohsi(w)a* 'mouse'	*(i)len-akoohsi(w)a* 'rat'	LB pl. ‹rênac8ssi8oki›, Gr ‹irenac8ssia›, Gt ‹länakú'hsia›
		ahkihkwa 'kettle'	*ilen-ahkihkwa* 'earthen pot made by the Indians'	Gr ‹irenakic8a›[*]
		ahseemaawa 'tobacco'	*ilen-ahseemaawa* 'native wild tobacco'	Gr ‹irenacema8a›[†]
kataki-	'spotted'	*akooka* 'frog'	*katak-akooka* 'spotted frog'	Gr ‹catakac8ca›
maci-	'bad, wicked, evil'	*ileniwa, ilenia* 'man'	*mac-ileniwa* 'bad man, wicked man'	LB ‹matchireni8o›, ‹matchirenia›
mihši-	'big, great'	*apiloohsa* 'child'	*mihš-apiloohsa* 'big child'	Gr ‹mechaber8ssa›
niihpiki-	'red'	*uulahkwahki* 'cloud'	*niihpik-aalahkwahki* 'red cloud'	Gr ‹nipicarac8i› 'ciel rouge'
oonsaawi-	'yellow'	*ahkihkwi* 'kettle'	*oonsaaw-ahkihkwi* 'brass kettle'	Tr ‹oañn̄gzaoa kēēhkwaa›, Gt ‹u^{n}sauxkíxkwi›, D ‹onzawĭkikwĭ›
		aalahkwahki 'cloud'	*oonsaaw-aalahkwahki* 'yellow cloud'	D ‹onzawalkwaki›
		eemihkwaani 'pumpkin'	*oonsaaw-eemihkwaani* 'yellow pumpkin'	P/LB pl. ‹8nsa8emic8ena›
waapi-	'white'	*ahseenihsa* 'buckskin'	*waap-ahseenihsa* 'white buckskin'	Gr ‹8abassenissaki› 'peaux de petits chevreuils passees'
		anikwa 'squirrel'	*waap-anikwa* 'white squirrel'	Gr ‹8abanic8a›
		eehsipana 'raccoon'	*waap-eehsipana* 'white raccoon'	D ‹wah-pă-sáy-pon›
wiilinwi-	'fat'	*ahsena, ahseni* 'stone'	*wiilinw-ahsena*, *wiilinw-ahseni* 'quartzite'	LB ‹8irin8sen8i›, Gt ‹wilinwáxséna›, D ‹wilinwasäni›
wiipinkwi-, *weepinkwi-*	'gray'	*anikwa* 'squirrel'	*wiipink-anikwa*, *weepinkw-anikwa*[‡] 'gray squirrel'	P ‹8iping8anic8a›, Gt ‹wepíngwanikwa› (cf. Sh *wiipekwanikwa*)

* This form is glossed 'pot de terre fait par les sauvages'; cf. Potawatomi *nən-kək* 'brass pail, brass kettle'.

† This form is glossed 'fenesque, tabac sauvage plus petit et plus dous que le franç[ais]'; cf. Potawatomi *nənsema* 'Indian tobacco' and Shawnee *(hi)lenilahθeema*, glossed by Voegelin (1938–40:348–349) as 'man tobacco (the pre-white N. rustica)'.

‡ Also attested is the apparent dialectal variant *weepinkweenikwa* (Gr ‹8eping8enic8a›, D ‹wäpíngwäníkwa›), which would seem to represent an initial *weepinkwee-* plus the final *-anikw*, and not the prenoun *weepinkwi-* plus the noun *anikwa*; see Table 12.

TABLE 7. Final *-i* preserved before vowels

PRENOUN	GLOSS	BASE NOUN	FORM WITH PRENOUN	ORIGINAL FORMS
maci-	'bad, evil, wicked'	*alemwa* 'dog'	*maci-alemwa* 'bad dog'	Tr ‹mōtshee ulāāmoa›
nalaawahki-	'wild'	*alenaswa* 'buffalo, cow'	*nalaawahki-alenaswa* '(wild) buffalo'	Tr ‹naalāuoakee ulaanāuzwaa›
neehpiki-	'red'	*aalahkwahki* 'cloud'	*neehpiki-aalahkwahki* 'red cloud'[*]	D ‹näpíkialkwákĭ›
oonsaawi-	'yellow'	*aamaahwia* 'bee'	*oonsaawi-aamaahwia* 'hornet'	V ‹honzâoué amohouia›
wiihkapi-	'sweet'	*eemihkwaani* 'pumpkin'	*wiihkapi-eemihkwaani* 'sweet melon'	Gr ‹8iscapi emic8ane› (cf. LB ‹8icapemic8en›)[†]
wiihsaki-	'bitter'	*eemihkwaani* 'pumpkin'	*wiihsaki-eemihkwaani* 'bitter melon'	Gr ‹8issakiemic8ane›

* Note also the unchanged Illinois form *niihpik-aalahkwahki* in Table 6.

† The Largillier form is glossed 'melon'; the LB form is glossed 'melon' and 'citrouilles sucrées'.

TABLE 8. Initial vowels of nouns deleted after long vowels

PRENOUN	GLOSS	BASE NOUN	FORM WITH PRENOUN	ORIGINAL FORMS
kiintee-	'new, young'	*alenia* 'man'	*kiintee-lenia* 'a new man'	Gt ‹kîndé länia›, D ‹kíndälänĭa›
mahkatee-	'black'	*anikwa* 'squirrel'	*mahkatee-nikwa* 'black squirrel'	P ‹makatenic8a›, Gt ‹maxkatäníkwa›
		eehsipana 'raccoon'	*mahkateehsipana* 'Black Raccoon' (personal name)	Gt ‹mkátäsípana›, D ‹m'katäsĭpana›
		alenia 'man'	*mahkatee-lenia* 'black man'	Gt ‹mkátelänia›, Mc ‹ma'kátelä$^{\varepsilon}$nya›
oonsaa-	'yellow'	*amehkwa* 'beaver'	*oonsaa-mehkwa* 'Yellow Beaver' (personal name)	Gt ‹u^{n}zamä́'hkwa›, D ‹onzamäkwa›
		alamoni 'vermillion, ocher'	*oonsaa-lamoni* 'bloodroot (*sanguinaria canadensis*)'	D ‹ó^{n}zalamóni›; cf. Meskwaki *asa·wanamona* 'yellow ocher'
		anikwa 'squirrel'	*oonsaa-nikwa* 'fox squirrel'	Gr/P ‹8nsanic8a›, Gt ‹û́nzaníkwa›; D ‹ó^{n}zaaníkwa›
waawiyii-	'round'	*ahpena* 'potato'	*waawiyii-hpina* 'turnip'	Hk pl. ‹wawiechpeniegi›, Gt ‹wáwiyipínā›, D ‹wawĭ́ĭpĭ́na›

TABLE 9. Prenouns from animate noun stems

PRENOUN	GLOSS	FORM WITH PRENOUN	BASE NOUN	ORIGINAL FORMS
akaansi-	'Kaw, Ohio river'	*akaansi-pakaani* 'pecan'	*akaansa* 'Kaw, Kansa'*	LB ‹acansipacane›, P pl. ‹acansepacana›
kiteepihkwanwi-	'buffalo fish'	*kiteepihkwanwi-siipiiwi* 'Tippecanoe River'	*kiteepihkwanwa* 'buffalo fish'	Gr ‹kitepic8n8a› espece de grosse carpe', Gt ‹kitäp'kwánwa›
mihtohseeni	'human'	*mihtohseeni-wiiyoohsime* 'human body, human flesh'	*mihtohseenia* 'human, person'	Gt ‹mitʊhsäni wiuhsimä›
mooswi-	'deer'	*mooswi-kiilihswa* 'October' (deer month)	*mooswa* 'deer'	P ‹m8ns8i kiriss8a›
myaalameekwi-	'catfish'	*myaalameekwi-siipiiwi* 'Meramec River' (?)	*myaalameekwa* 'catfish, channel cat'	LB ‹miaramec8i›†
myaami-	'Miami'	*myaami-miincipi* 'blue corn, squaw corn'	*myaamia* 'Miami'	Gt ‹miámi mínžipi›, D ‹miami mĭndjĭpĭ›

* See Costa (2000:31) for a discussion of this term.

† In LeBoullenger's dictionary under 'barbue', he first gives ‹miaramec8o›, followed by ‹miaramec8i› glossed as 'riv. de maramec', without ‹sipi8i› (*siipiiwi*); presumably *‹miaramec8i sipi8i› is intended. This almost certainly denotes the Meramec River in Missouri.

TABLE 10. Noun-final *-e·wa* and *-iwa* reduced to *-ia* after prenouns

BASE NOUN	PRENOUN	GLOSS	FORM WITH PRENOUN	ORIGINAL FORMS
mahweewa 'wolf'	(*i*)*leni-*	'particular kind, special'	(*i*)*leni-mahwia* 'coyote'	Gr ‹irenima8eïa›, LB pl. ‹irenima8e8aki›, Gt ‹lắnimá'wia›, D ‹länĭmáwhĭa› (cf. Po *nəni-mʔwe*)[*]
	mahkatee-	'black'	*mahkatee-mahwia* 'Black Wolf' (personal name)	D ‹mäkatämawhia›
pileewa 'chicken, turkey'	*waapi-*	'white'	*waapi-pilia* 'turkey'	Gt ‹wapipilía›, D ‹wapĭpilĭa›, P/H ‹wapipíʔilyɑ›
pinšiwa 'bobcat'	*alaami-*	'under'	*alaami-pinšia* 'underwater panther'	Gr ‹aramipichia› (cf. Meskwaki *na·mi-pešiwa*)
	(*i*)*leni-*	'particular kind, special'	*léni-pinšia* 'underwater panther'	Gt ‹lenipí^{n}zha›, D ‹lĕnĭpĭ́nja›, Mc ‹länipī^{n}ja^{n}›
	waapi-	'white'	*waapi-pinšia* 'white-cat'; a mythic aquatic monster	Gt ‹wapipí^{n}zhia›, D ‹wah pi pin zhia›
	wiihkwee-	?	*wiihkwee-pinšia* 'Canada lynx'	Gr ‹8ic8epichia›, D ‹wíkwĭpinzhĭa›, Gt ‹wäkwäpī́zha›

* The Gravier forms are glossed 'loup d'un basse taille' and 'loup'; LeBoullenger's plural form is erroneously glossed 'renards'. Potawatomi *nəni-mʔwe* is given by Hockett (1948:224) as 'some special kind of wolf', but the Forest County Potawatomi Community (2014) dictionary has the (probably newer) alternate *nani-mʔəwe* correctly glossed as 'coyote'. It is mysterious why the prenoun is *nəni* and *nani* rather than the etymologically expected *nən*, but all Potawatomi sources agree in transcribing it thus. Menominee also has a form *nani·maʔawe·w* that Bloomfield (1975:142) glosses 'wolverine'; this species identification is probably incorrect, not only given its resemblance to the Potawatomi and Miami-Illinois forms, but also due to the fact that several modern Menominee learners have this word as 'coyote' (Macaulay 2012; Macaulay 2019, personal communication). This Menominee word is very likely a Potawatomi loan. Additionally, some speakers Macaulay has interviewed pronounce the Menominee word as *nani·maʔwew*, which is more similar to the older Potawatomi and Miami-Illinois forms. Further complicating matters, Albert Gatschet's (1884) fieldnotes on Oklahoma Ottawa have a form ‹nenímwe nínuak› glossed as 'wolf clan', apparently literally 'coyote men'.

TABLE 11. Prenoun + noun combinations with unpredictable semantics

PRENOUN	GLOSS	BASE NOUN	FORM WITH PRENOUN	ORIGINAL FORMS
(i)leni-	'particular kind, special'	*mahweewa* 'wolf'	*ileni-mahweewa, léni mahwia* 'coyote'	Gr ‹irenima8e8a›, LB pl. ‹irenima8e8aki›, Gt ‹lănimá'wia›, D ‹länĭmáwhĭa›
		wiihkwaya 'glue made from deer horn'	*ileni-wiihkwaya* 'glue made of sturgeon or fish'	Gr ‹ireni8ic8eïa› 'colle d'eturgeon, de poisson'
mahkatee-	'black'	*mihšiiweewa, mihšiiwia* 'elk'	*mahkatee-mihšiiwia* 'moose'*	Gr ‹macatemichi8e8a›, LB ‹macatemichi8ia›, Th ‹muhkata misheeuiah›
neehpiki-	'red'	*pihcita* 'small bird, sparrow'	*neehpiki-pihcita* 'cardinal'	Th ‹nahpeeki petshiatoh›, Gt ‹nepíki=pitchíta›, D ‹näpíkĭpitcĭta›
oonsaa-	'yellow'	*peehkateeki* 'flower'	*oonsaa-peehkateeki* 'Jerusalem artichoke'	D ‹onzapäkatäkĭ›
oonsaawi-	'yellow'	*aamaahwia* 'bee'	*oonsaawi-aamaahwia* 'hornet'	V ‹honzâoué amohouia›
waapi-	'white'	*ahsena* 'stone'	*waap-ahsena* 'limestone'	Gt ‹wapsená›
		siipiiwi 'river'	*waapi-siipiiwi* 'Milky Way'	LB ‹8apisipi8i› 'via lactea'
		kwaahkwa 'Pileated woodpecker'	*waapi-kwaahkwa* 'Ivory-billed woodpecker'†	Gr pl. ‹8abic8ac8aki›, D ‹wapĭkwakwa›
		mootayi 'holder, pouch, pocket, chest, cloth'	*waapi-motayi* 'blanket'‡	Gr/P/LB ‹8abim8taï›, Hk ‹wapimotey›, Tr ‹wāūpee mootīīyaa›, Gt ‹wápimutáyi›, D ‹wápĭmotáĭ›§
		moohswa 'deer'	*waapi-moohswa* 'sheep'	Gt ‹wápimúxswa›, D ‹wápĭmóswa›, Mi/H ‹wapimos·wα›
		pakaani 'nut'	*waapi-pakaani* 'hickory nut'	Gr ‹8abipacani›, Gt ‹wapípakáni›, D ‹wápipakánĭ›
waapihki-‖	'white'	*moohsia* 'bug, worm'	*waapihki-moohsia* 'grub worm'	Gr ‹8abiskim8sse8a›#, D ‹wápkĭmósĭa›
waapiki-	'white'	*šooli* 'money'	*waapiki-šooli* 'silver'	Gt ‹wapíki shúli›, D ‹wapíkĭcólĭ›
waawiyii-	'round'	*ahpena* 'potato'	*waawiyii-hpina* 'turnip'	Hk pl. ‹wawiechpeniegi›, Gt ‹wáwiyipínā›, D ‹wawĭĭpĭna›

PRENOUN	GLOSS	BASE NOUN	FORM WITH PRENOUN	ORIGINAL FORMS
wiihsaki-	'bitter'	*miimia* 'passenger pigeon'	*wiihsaki-miimia* 'mourning dove'	Th ‹uisakimemiah›, Gt ‹wíssaki mímia›, D ‹wisákĭ mímĭa›
wiilenwi-	'fat'	*ahsena, ahseni* 'stone'	*wiilinw-ahsena, wiilinw-ahseni* 'quartzite'	LB ‹8irin8sen8i›, Gt ‹wilinwáxséna›, D ‹wilinwasäni›

* The ancestors of the Miami-Illinois moved into an area where moose were not found (Indiana, Illinois, and Ohio), and so the older PA 'moose' word **mo·swa* shifted to designate the white-tailed deer. The use of a construction basically meaning 'black elk' to mean 'moose' in Miami-Illinois also has a parallel in Delaware: *mó·s* is the general Delaware word for 'elk' and *nsə́ki-mó·s* (literally 'black elk') is the Munsee term for 'moose', as recorded by J.N.B. Hewitt in his fieldwork at Cattaraugus (Ives Goddard, personal communication 2019).

† Cf. Shawnee *kwahkwahθi* 'Pileated woodpecker' and *waapimeeme* 'Ivory billed woodpecker'.

‡ Cf. Shawnee *waapimotaawali* 'linen wrappings' (Alford 1929:John 20:5, ‹wrpi mudrwvli›).

§ The Gravier form is glossed 'chemise, habit d'etoffe blanche'; the Pinet and LeBoullenger forms are glossed 'linge'; the Trowbridge form is glossed 'white blanket', but all other attestations from the 1790s on are merely glossed 'blanket'.

|| It is not certain what the semantic difference is in Miami-Illinois between *waapi-*, *waapihki-*, and *waapiki-*, though *waapi-* is by far the most common of these three alternates. An anonymous reviewer has helpfully informed me that the Meskwaki initial *wa·p-* means 'pale' or 'white', whereas the initial *wa·pešk-* (cognate with Miami-Illinois *waapihki-*) can only mean 'white'.

\# Gravier's ‹8abiskim8sse8a› is unglossed, but he also gives a diminutive plural ‹8abikim8sensaki› glossed 'espece de vers dans le bois'.

TABLE 12. Prenouns undergoing initial change

UNCHANGED INITIAL	CHANGED PRENOUN	GLOSS	FORM WITH PRENOUN	ORIGINAL FORMS
alaaminaa-	*eelaaminee-*	'Christian, holy'	*eelaaminee-kiišikwe* 'Sunday'	Gt ‹elamenäkishíkwe›
ahkipak-	*iihkipaki-*	'blue'	*iihkipak-aalahkwatwi* 'blue cloud'	Gt ‹íkipakalkwatwi›, D ‹ĭkĭpak alkwatwĭ›
mihš-	*meehši-*	'big, great'	*meehši-siipiiwi* 'Mississipi River'	W/Gt ‹mäshi sipíwi›
niihpik-	*neehpiki-*	'red'	*neehpiki-aalahkwahki* 'red cloud'	D ‹näpíkialkwákĭ›
			neehpiki-pihcita 'cardinal'	Th ‹nahpeeki petshiatoh›, Gt ‹nepíki=pitchíta›, D ‹näpíkĭpitcĭta›
wiipinkw-	*weepinkwi-*	'gray'	*weepinkw-anikwa** 'gray squirrel'	Gt ‹wepíngwanikwa›
wihk-	*weehki-*	'new'	*weehki-kiilihswa* 'new moon'	Tr ‹wāāhkee kēēlswau›

* See also *wiipinkwanikwa* in Table 6.

TABLE 13. Prenouns of unknown meaning

PRENOUN	GLOSS	BASE NOUN	EXAMPLE	ORIGINAL FORMS
mawahki-	?	(*a*)*lenia* 'man'	*mawahki-lénia* 'headman, leading man'	Gt ‹mawaxkí länia› 'headman', D ‹mawákĭ länĭa›
mitehki-	?	*mootayi* 'holder, pouch, pocket, chest'	*mitehki-motayi* 'side pocket, dress pocket'	Gt ‹mitä́xki mutáyi›
paa(*h*)*saki-*	?	*miimia* 'passenger pigeon'	*paa*(*h*)*saki-miimia* 'wild pigeon'	Gt ‹pássaki mimia›
peeši-	?	*kintiwa* 'Golden eagle'	*peeši-kintiwa* 'spotted eagle'	Gt ‹päshikíndiwa›
wiihkwee-[*]	?	*pinšiwa* 'bobcat'	*wiihkwee-pinšia* 'Canada lynx'	Gr ‹8ic8epichia›, D ‹wíkwĭpinzhĭa›, Gt ‹wäkwäpī́zha›

[*] Lucy Thomason and Ives Goddard (personal communication, 2019) have suggested that the *wiihkwee-* prenoun in this word is cognate with the Meskwaki initial *wi·hkwe·-* 'bulging out', as seen in verbs like Meskwaki *wi·hkwe·wi* 'it sags out'. If so, this would presumably be a reference to the facial fur of lynxes, giving a literal meaning something along the lines of "puffed-out bobcat" (Lucy Thomason, personal communication, 2019).

TABLE 14. Nouns reanalyzed as consonant-initial after prenouns

PRENOUN	GLOSS	BASE NOUN	LATER FORM	ORIGINAL FORMS
iihkipihsi-	'straight'	(*a*)*htawaani* 'tree, wood, stick'	*iihkipihsi-htawaani* 'straight stick'	Gt ‹ikipí^{n}ssi tawáni›
nalaawahki-	'wild'	(*a*)*lenaswa* 'buffalo, cow'	*nalaawahki-lénaswa* 'buffalo'	Th ‹nalaohkeh lanansuoh›, D ‹nalaúxki léna^{n}swa›
		(*a*)*lenia* 'man'	*nalaawahki-lénia* 'wild man'	Gt ‹nalaúxki länia›
		(*a*)*hpena* 'potato'	*nalaawahki-hpéniiki* 'wild potatoes'	Gt pl. ‹nalaúxkipänīki›
oonsaawi-	'yellow'	(*a*)*hkihkwi* 'kettle'	*oonsaawi-hkihkwi* 'brass kettle'	Gt ‹u^{n}sauxkíxkwi›, D ‹onzawĭkikwĭ›
peehki-	'good, pretty, very'	(*a*)*hkiyošia* 'old man'	*peehki-hkíyošia* 'very old man'	Tr ‹pāāhkee kēēoosh›

TABLE 15. Compounds of two animate nouns

FIRST NOUN	SECOND NOUN	NOUN COMPOUND	GLOSS OF COMPOUND	ORIGINAL FORMS
aamaa(h)wia 'bee'	*waapiihkicia* 'bumble bee, white-rumped one'	*aamaawia waapiihkicia*	'bumble bee'	D ‹amáwĭa wápĭkĭtc›
	keekaanwikania 'wasp'	*aamaawia keekaanwikania*	'wasp'	D ‹amáwĭa kakánwĭkánĭa›
	šinkwa 'pitch, resin'	*aamaahwia šinkwa*	'bee's wax'	Gt ‹amá'wia shíngwa›
mahkwa 'bear'	*wiilinwa* 'fat'	*mahkwa wiilinwa*	'bear fat'	LB ‹mac8o 8irin8o› 'lard d'ours'
mihšiiwia 'elk'	*akoowa* 'doe, young female animal'	*mihšiiwia akoowa*	'female elk'	LB ‹michi8ia ac8o› 'fem. [cerf]'

TABLE 16. Noun + noun compounds in Peoria month names

FIRST NOUN	MONTH NAME	GLOSS OF MONTH NAME	ORIGINAL DUNN FORMS
mahkwa 'bear'	*mahkwa kiilihswa*	'January'	‹makwá kilswa›
mahkoonsa 'bear cub'	*mahkoonsa kiilihswa*	'February'	‹makónsa kilswa›
cécaahkwa 'Sandhill crane'	*cécaahkwa kiilihswa*	'March'	‹tcätcakwa kilswa›
aanteekwa 'crow'	*aanteekwa kiilihswa*	'April'	‹andäkwa kilswa›
oohkoowia 'whippoorwill'	*oohkoowia kiilihswa*	'May'	‹okowia kilswa›
kiišiinkwia 'roasting ear'	*kiišiinkwia kiilihswa*	'August'	‹kicingwia kilswa›
ayaapia 'buck'	*ayaapia kiilihswa*	'November'	‹iapia kilswa›
ayaapeenihsa 'buck (diminutive)'	*ayaapeenihsa kiilihswa*	'December'	‹iapänsa kilswa›

TABLE 17. Noun + noun compounds in Illinois month names

FIRST NOUN	NOUN COMPOUND	GLOSS OF COMPOUND	ORIGINAL FORMS
cécaahkwa 'Sandhill crane'	*cécaahkwa kiilihswa*	'March' (LB), 'February' (P)	LB ‹chatchac8o kir.›, P ‹tchetchak8a kiriss8a›
eehsipana 'raccoon'	*eehsipana kiilihswa*	'February' (LB), 'January' (P)	LB ‹assepana kiriss8o›, P ‹essibana kiriss8a›
mihšiiwia 'elk'	*mihšiiwia kiilihswa*	'September' (LB/P), 'August' (Gr)	Gr ‹michi8eïa kiris›, P ‹michi8eïa›, LB ‹michi8ia kiriss8o›
mooswa 'deer'	*mooswa kiilihswa*	'December' (LB), 'October' (P)	LB ‹m8ns8o kiriss8o›

TABLE 18. Compounds with two inanimate nouns

FIRST NOUN	SECOND NOUN	NOUN COMPOUND	GLOSS	ORIGINAL FORMS
ahseni 'stone, rock'	*siipiiwi* 'river'	*ahseni siipiiwi*	'Great Miami River'	Pr ‹osanesepewe›, Tr ‹usāānee seepēēwe›
aweentioni 'peace, alliance'	(*ah*)*tawaani* 'tree'	*aweentioni ahtawaani*	'peace tree'	Tr ‹awaandeeōānee tauwāūnee›
miišaakani 'leather'	*ahkolayi* 'cape, robe'	*miišaakani ahkolayi*	'leather robe, leather hood'	LB ‹minchagane acorai› 'capot de cuir'
sakinteewi 'glass, bottle'	(*a*)*laakani* 'dish, plate'	*sakinteewi laakani*	'glass dish'	P/D ‹sakindäwi lakani›

TABLE 19. Compounds with an animate noun + an inanimate noun

FIRST NOUN	SECOND NOUN	NOUN COMPOUND	GLOSS	ORIGINAL FORMS
aamaawia 'bee'	*pankosaakani* 'sugar'	*aamaawia pankosaakani*	'honey'	Gt ‹amá'wia pangósakan›, Mc ‹'ʌmā́wiya' pʌñgṓ'sʌkʌni›
ahkihkwa 'drum'	*pakantaakani* 'hammer, pestle'	*ahkihkwa pakantaakani*	'drumstick'	Gt ‹kíxkwa pakándakan'›
kaansa 'Kaw, Kansa'	*pakaani* 'nut'	*kaansa pakaani*	'pecan'	Gt ‹ká^{n}za pakani›
kiihkoneehsa 'fish'	*alahakayi* 'shell, scale'	*kiihkoneehsa alahakayi*	'fish scale'	LB ‹kiconessa araacai›
maamistakošia 'Frenchman'	*wiipici* 'flint'	*maamistakošia wiipica*	'gun flints'	LB ‹mamistag8chia 8apitcha›
mahkwa 'bear'	*wiilaamišaahkwi* 'food tree'	*mahkwa wiilaamišaahkwi*	'wild cherry tree'	Gt ‹maxkwa wílamisháxkwi›
pileewa 'turkey, chicken'	*siipiiwi* 'river'	*pileewa siipiiwi*	'Ohio River'	Gt ‹pilǟwa sipíwi› (cf. Sh *peleewaaθiipi*)
šaawanwa 'Shawnee'	*nakamooni* 'song'	*šaawanwa nakamooni*	'Shawnee song'	Gr ‹cha8an8a nagam8ni›*
waapanswa 'rabbit'	*wiiloomiši* 'food tree'	*waapanswa wiiloomiši*	'rabbit willow'	Gt ‹wapánswa wilomínzhi›

* Glossed by Gravier as 'chançon impure venüe des Chauanons'.

TABLE 20. Compounds with an inanimate noun + an animate noun

FIRST NOUN	SECOND NOUN	NOUN COMPOUND	GLOSS	ORIGINAL FORMS
nipi 'water'	*teentia* 'plover'	*nipi teentia*	'snipe'	Gt ‹nipi tắndia›
waapamooni 'mirror, glass'	*(a)laakana* 'dish, plate'	*waapamooni laakana*	'glass dish'	D ‹wápamónĭ lakána›

TABLE 21. Animate singular nouns modifying animate plural nouns

FIRST NOUN	SECOND NOUN	NOUN COMPOUND	GLOSS	ORIGINAL FORMS
aamaawia 'bee'	*waawaapiihkiciaki* 'hornets'	*aamaawia waawaapiihkiciaki*	'hornets'	D ‹amáwĭa wawapĭkĭcákĭ›
ciinkweensaki 'young thunder beings'	*manetoowaki* 'manitous'	*ciinkweensaki manetoowaki*	'young thunder spirits'	Tr ‹tschingwiizāūkee monaatewāūkee›

TABLE 22. Plural nouns modifying singular nouns

FIRST NOUN	SECOND NOUN	NOUN COMPOUND	GLOSS	ORIGINAL FORMS
kóciihsaki 'beans'	*alahakayi* 'shell, scale'	*kóciihsaki alahakayi*	'bean shell, bean pod'	LB ‹c8tchissaki araacaï› 'cosse de feve'
mahkiskiwa 'marshes'	*miincipi* 'corn'	*mahkiskiwa miincipi*	'wild rice or French wheat'	LB ‹makiski8o mintchipi› 'fole avoine ou bled franc.'
pakaana 'nuts'	*alahakayi* 'shell, scale'	*pakaana alahakayi*	'nut shell'	LB ‹pacana araacaï› 'coquille de noix'
	pimi 'grease, oil'	*pakaana pimi*	'nut oil'	LB ‹pacanapimi› '(huisle) de noix'
waawa 'eggs'	*alahakayi* 'shell, scale'	*waawa alakayi*	'egg shell'	LB ‹8a8o araacai›, ‹8a8o araacaie› 'coque d oeuf'

NOTES

1. An interesting fact about prenouns, in Miami-Illinois at least, is that they virtually never occur in elicitation as the Miami-Illinois equivalent of English adjectives. For example, when asked to translate 'white', speakers always give verbal forms such as *waapiki* 'it is white' or *waapisita* 'he is white'. The sole exception to this is 'wild', for which speakers regularly give the prenoun *nalaawahki*. This may be due to the fact that there appears to be no basic Miami-Illinois verb meaning 'he is wild' or 'it is wild'.
2. Throughout this paper I write hyphens between prenouns and their following nouns simply for clarity, though prenoun + noun compounds constitute single words grammatically and phonologically (for example, see Table 10).
3. One apparent exception to this is *alantee-ahpwaakani* 'red pipe' (P/LB ‹aranteap8agane›); see Table 4.
4. A consistent exception to this is the prenoun *nalaawahki-* 'wild', after which noun-final -Vwa sequences never reduce: see *nalaawahki-pileewa* 'wild turkey' and *nalaawahki-pinšiwa* 'wildcat' in Table 2. Another apparent exception to this rule is *peeši-kintiwa* 'spotted eagle', with the semantically mysterious prenoun *peeši-* (see Table 13).
5. Of the prenouns in this table, all but *mihši-/meehši-* are obligatorily changed in the modern language.

REFERENCES

Alford, Thomas Wildcat. 1929. *The Four Gospels of Our Lord Jesus Christ in Shawnee Indian Language*. Xenia, OH: Dr. W. A. Galloway.

Anonymous. 1837. *The Wea Primer, Wev Mvs Nv Kv Ne, to Teach the Wea Language*. Cherokee Nation: Mission Press.

Bloomfield, Leonard. 1975. *Menomini Lexicon*, ed. by Charles F. Hockett. Milwaukee Public Museum Publications in Anthropology and History 3. Milwaukee: Milwaukee Public Museum Press.

Costa, David J. 2000. Miami-Illinois Tribe Names. *Papers of the 31st Algonquian Conference*, ed. by John Nichols, pp. 30–53. Winnipeg: University of Manitoba.

Costa, David J. 2003. *The Miami-Illinois Language*. Lincoln: University of Nebraska Press.

Dunn, Jacob P. [n.d.](a). Miami filecard dictionary. Manuscript, Indiana State Library, Indianapolis.

Dunn, Jacob P. [n.d.](b). Various notes on Miami. Manuscript, Indiana State Library, Indianapolis.

Forest County Potawatomi Community. 2014. *Ézhe-bmadzimgek gdebodwéwadmi-zheshmomenan: Potawatomi Dictionary*. Crandon, WI: Forest County Potawatomi.

Gatschet, Albert. [n.d.] Vocabulary and Text (three original Miami and Peoria field notebooks). Manuscript 236, National Anthropological Archives, Smithsonian Museum Support Center, Suitland, MD.

Gatschet, Albert. 1884. Fieldnotes on Oklahoma Ottawa. Manuscript 228, National Anthropological Archives, Smithsonian Museum Support Center, Suitland, MD.

Gatschet, Albert. 1895a. Peoria- and Miami-English Dictionary. Manuscript 2481, National Anthropological Archives, Smithsonian Museum Support Center, Suitland, MD.

Gatschet, Albert. 1895b. Peoria- and Miami-English Dictionary. Manuscript 2483, National Anthropological Archives, Smithsonian Museum Support Center, Suitland, MD.

Heckewelder, John. [n.d.] Vocabulary of the Shawanese Language. Manuscript, American Philosophical Society, Philadelphia.

Hockett, Charles F. 1948. Potawatomi IV: Particles and Sample Texts. *International Journal of American Linguistics* 14:213–225.

Hockett, Charles F. 1985. Notes on Peoria and Miami. *Algonquian & Iroquoian Linguistics* 10(4):29–41.

Largillier, Jacques. [ca. 1700]. Illinois-French Dictionary. Manuscript, Watkinson Library, Trinity College, Hartford, CT. (Manuscript previously attributed to Jacques Gravier.)

LeBoullenger, Antoine-Robert, SJ. [ca. 1725]. French and Miami-Illinois Dictionary. Manuscript at the John Carter Brown Library, Brown University, Providence, RI.

Menominee Indian Tribe of Wisconsin. 2012. *Omāēqnomenēweqnaesen Wēhcekanan: Menominee Dictionary*. Keshena, WI: Menominee Language and Culture Code Commission of the Menominee Indian Tribe.

Michelson, Truman. 1916. Notes on Peoria. Manuscript 2721, National Anthropological Archives, Smithsonian Museum Support Center, Suitland, MD.

Pinet, Pierre-François. [ca. 1702]. French-Miami-Illinois dictionary. Manuscript, Archives des jésuites au Canada, Montréal, Québec.

Preston, William. 1796. Miami Vocabulary. Manuscript #21, National Anthropological Archives, Smithsonian Museum Support Center, Suitland, Maryland.

Schoolcraft, Henry R. 1852. *Historical and Statistical Information Respecting the History, Condition, and Prospects of the Indian Tribes of the United States*. Vol. 2. Philadelphia: Lippincott, Grambo. (Contains Charles Handy's Miami vocabulary.)

Thornton, William. 1802. Vocabulary of the Miami Language taken at the City of Washington. Manuscript, American Philosophical Society, Philadelphia.

Trowbridge, Charles C. 1824–1825. Unpublished fieldnotes on the Miami. Manuscript, Bentley

Historical Library, University of Michigan, Ann Arbor.

Voegelin, Carl F. 1938–1940. *Shawnee Stems and the Jacob P. Dunn Miami Dictionary.* Indiana Historical Society Prehistory Research Series 1, pp. 63–108, 135–167, 289–323, 345–406, 409–478. Indianapolis: Indiana Historical Society.

Volney, Constantin F. C. de. 1857. *Œuvres Completes de Volney.* Paris: Chez Firmin Didot Frères, Fils et Cie.

How Many Classifiers in Arapaho?

Andrew Cowell

As is well known, medial classifiers in Algonquian languages are of the verbal classifier type as commonly defined (Aikhenvald 2000; Grinevald 2000, 2002). Cross-linguistically, verbal classification involves a nominal-type element that occurs within the verb, and that "classifies" some independent nominal form that is overtly present in the sentence, or that is not overtly present but is clear from context. It is often further specified that the independent noun in question is a core argument of the verb (Grinevald 2000:67; Aikhenvald 2000:149), but I will take a broader approach in the paper and also consider peripheral nominals, for reasons that will be discussed more fully at the end of the paper.

Defining Classifiers in Arapaho

It is apparent from previous work (Sanders and Cowell 2020, Drapeau 2014, Drapeau and Lambert-Brétière 2011) that classifiers in Algonquian languages have a number of features in common with noun incorporation. This is not surprising, since Mithun (1986) suggests that the origins of verbal classifiers can be found in noun incorporation processes, wherein the incorporated noun becomes partially grammaticalized and bleached of more specific referential meaning. This paper provides further evidence for this pathway. This means, however, that it may be difficult to tell whether a verbal medial involves noun incorporation or classification. The most obvious way to distinguish the two situations is to assume that if a medial is an example of incorporation, then no related or equivalent noun can occur independently in the sentence. Thus in Arapaho one can say either of the following (medials are underlined in all examples):[1]

(1)	Heesowowutii-noo	no'oo3
	hurt-1s	1s.leg
	'My leg is hurting me.'	

(2)	Toow-oon-ee-noo
	IC.broken-leg-VAI-1s
	'I have a broken leg.'

One cannot, however, say:

(3)	*toow-oon-ee-noo	no'oo3
	IC.broken-leg-VAI-1s	1s.leg

In contrast, it is perfectly acceptable to say:

(4)	Heey-oocei-[ei]hi-t	nehe'	seenook
	IC.long-rope.like-VAI-3s	this	rope
	'This rope is long.'		

This is because *-oocei-*, as a classifier, has a broad semantic range, and can be used in correlation not only to ropes, but to strings, pipes, water hoses, fish guts, worms, snakes, audio cassette tape, and many other items (Sanders and Cowell 2020), whereas *-oon-* is limited specifically to legs (or in some other uses, to 'body' or 'meat'), and never co-occurs with an overt noun. The most basic way to distinguish classificatory behavior from noun incorporation in Algonquian languages is therefore to see if a given medial can co-occur with an independent, semantically similar nominal form—and in particular, with more than one such form. This definition is a key criterion given for verbal classifiers (Aikhenvald 2000; Mithun 1986, 1999; Grinevald 2000, 2002; Senft 2000). A further argument for the classificatory status of a medial is the criterion that it *must* be used when certain nouns are referred to. In other words, Arapaho speakers reject the sentence **heeneihit nehe' seenook* 'this rope is long' using the basic verb *heneihi-* 'be long.' The verb with the classifier (*heyooceihi-* 'be a long string-like object') *must* be used, whether or not an overt nominal occurs in the sentence.

Some scholars have argued for formal mechanisms within the verb itself, specifically in the shape of the medial, that would distinguish classifiers from incorporated nouns (see Biedny et al. 2021). Nothing of the sort is evident in Arapaho. Since the incorporation/classifier boundary is inherently a continuum (see similar findings in Biedny et al. 2021:2), due to the nature of the grammatical trajectory from incorporation to classifiers, we would not expect formal morphological features to exist that would unambiguously distinguish the two.

We should also recognize that verbal classifiers are notable cross-linguistically in that they can have anaphoric functions as well (Aikhenvald 2000:149–150). In actual Arapaho natural discourse, most classifiers rarely occur with an overt noun, even in the types of very clear-cut classifier verbs with Proto-Algonquian analogs. This makes it difficult to distinguish lexical extensions of an incorporated noun (or a new lexicalization) from a classificatory function in natural discourse. Thus one must turn to elicitation and noun co-occurrence (with multiple nouns) to make this distinction—though of course there are many examples of noun co-occurrence in a large enough sample of discourse. More generally—but beyond the scope of this paper—the NP dropping and anaphoric behavior raises the question of whether "classifier" is really the best label for "verbal classifier" systems used in at least some polysynthetic languages.

The semantics of co-occurrence is complicated by the fact that Algonquian languages show a complex variety of roles for a classificatory medial. Two key functions are reference to an object acted on, and a topic about which something is predicated, but another is to specific instruments by means of which action is done. This instrumental type of medial function meets the same test as for object/topic classification:

(5) Honoow-oocei-in-o' hi'iihi' nuhu' seenook-uu
IC.down-string.like-VTI-3S INSTR.PART this rope-OBV
'He is lowering it with this rope.'

(6)	Honoow-oocei-in-o'	hi'iihi'	nuhu'	bei'ci3eiseenook-uu
	IC.down-string.like-VTI-3S	INSTR.PART	this	chain-OBV
	'He is lowering it with this chain.'			

(7)	Noot-oo'-oh-owoo	hi'iihi'	bes
	IC.seek-stick.like-VTI-1S	INSTR.PART	stick
	'I am poking around for it with a stick.'		

(8)	Noot-oo'-oh-owoo	hi'iihi'	hookoto
	IC.seek-stick.like-VTI-1S	INSTR.PART	cane
	'I am poking around for it with a cane.'		

In all these instrumental cases, it is uncommon to use an independent nominal, since the nominal element is normally clear from context, and instrumental constituents are typically less important pragmatically than the grammatical subject and object. However, speakers optionally can specify the nature of the instrument in question, should it not be clear. Secondarily, the use of the medial to refer to clearly different instruments, even if the instrument itself is not named explicitly, is a strong indication of classificatory status. In Arapaho, for example, one can use the medial *-oo'-* 'stick.like' in reference to wagons, horse trailers, wheelchairs, and many other instruments:

(9) no'-oo'-usee-
arrive-stick.like-walk.VAI-
'arrive by wagon'

(10) no'-oo'-ukoohu-
arrive-stick.like-run/drive.VAI
'arrive by/in horse trailer'

(11) no'-oo'-uxoh-
arrive-stick.like-bring.VTA-
'bring by wagon, bring by horse trailer'

(12) heenein-oo'-uxoh-eti-

aimless.REDUP-stick.like-bring.VTA-REFL.VAI
'roll oneself around in a wheelchair'

Finally, there are a fourth and fifth role fulfilled by classificatory medials: to indicate the medium of action as well as action by something having the nature of the classifier. The fourth role most commonly involves water or some other liquid:

(13) Nih-'it-en-owoo
PAST-get-VTI-1s
'I got it, I took it.'

(14) Nih-'it-ou-n-owoo
PAST-get-in.water-VTI-1s
'I got it out of liquid, I took it out of liquid.'

(15) Noot-ou-n-owoo ho'oeetiin-e'
IC.seek-in.liquid-VTI-1s paint-LOC
'I am looking for it in the paint.' (referring to an item dropped into a can of paint)

Note that here, when the medium of action is overtly specified, a locative inflection is normally used on the noun.

The fifth role involves objects such as snakes or worms, which move in a rope-like way, and must be described in this way:

(16) honoow-oocei-[o]'oo-t
IC.down-string.like-VAI.go-3s
'It is crawling down (a slope).'

Note also that Arapaho has two different incorporation/classification constructions. The first involves a root plus a medial (17a), while the second involves a complex initial (based on an independent verb stem) plus a medial (17b):

(17) a. bo'-oow-u-
red-liquid-VII
'be/flow as a red liquid'

b. benoh- > benoh-ooxeb-ei-
offer.water.VTA offer.water.VTA-domestic.animal-VAI.O
give water to s.o.' 'water a domestic animal'

How Many Classifiers in Arapaho?

For this paper, work was done with three male native speakers of Arapaho, all over the age of 70, and all from the eastern (Arapahoe/St. Stephens) side of the reservation. A common verb was selected that would typically be used with each classifier, based on personal knowledge of the language plus investigation of corpus data (over 90,000 sentences). For 'string-like' for example, the verb *heyooceihi-* 'be a long, string-like object' was selected. Then speakers were given simple sentences of the verb plus some overt noun ('it is a long, string-like rope,' 'it is a long, string-like chain,' 'it is a long, string-like snake,' etc.) and asked if this would be an acceptable sentence in Arapaho. If this was the case, then additional nouns were supplied, to check the range of classificatory use. Using this approach, it turns out that there are more classifiers in Arapaho than I had realized. A second finding, of which I was generally aware but had never formalized, is that the classifiers used in Arapaho sometimes vary according to the function of the classifier. In particular, for liquids, we find the situation illustrated in Table 1. The element *-ec-* most commonly occurs medially as *-ecei-*.

Another way of saying this is that a single liquid, such as water, may be referred to by several different classifiers according to the nuance that one wants to express in relation to the liquid. Biedny et al. (2021:7) note that this is common in Algonquian languages, but the semantics of the different classifiers are often not clarified, so the lists below will contribute to that clarification. Examples of verbs with the liquid medials are:

TABLE 1. Classifiers used with liquids

CONCEPT	CLASSIFIER
liquid as subject/topic (talking about color, temperature, etc.)	-oow-
liquid as instrument of action	-ookoon-
liquid as medium in which another action occurs	-ou-
liquid as object of action ('useful' liquids)	-ook-
liquid as engaged in action (leaking, for ex.)	-ec-ei-

(18)	a. hoxesiin-oow-u-	VII	muddy liquid
	b. woti'-ookoon-ee-	VII	removed by liquid (as a house in a flood)
	c. not-ou-n-	VTI/TA	search for s.t. in liquid
	d. hit-ook-ohei-	VAI.O	get a useful/already-processed liquid (such as in a bucket or bottle)
	e. bis-ecei-[o]'oo-	VII	a liquid appears out of s.t., as in leaking

In contrast, for rope-like objects, the single classifier *-oocei-* fulfills all four of the possible functions (there is no rope-like medium of action):

(19)	a. heey-oocei-[ei]hi-	VAI	long rope-like object
	b. hoow-oocei-in-	VTA/VTI	lower s.o. or s.t. using a rope-like object
	c. het-oocei-in-	VTI	remove a rope-like object from inside s.t.
	d. cow-oocei-[o]'oo-	VAI	move along in a rope-like way (a snake)

The total number of classificatory medials I have so far found, along with the functions they can fulfill, are listed in Table 2, based on the elicitation test described above. In most cases, the medial status is clear, as the elements listed are followed by common and well-understood TA/TI action finals such as -(*e*)*n* 'by hand' or *-oh* 'by tool', VAI/VII stative finals *-ehi/-yoo* or*-ee*, or VAI.O unspecified object final *-yei*. Forms with asterisks could be treated as complex finals, in that they never occur with these types of abstract finals.

This is a larger number of classifiers than are normally reported for Algonquian languages. Note that there is no classifier for metal, rocks, or hard rock-like objects, unlike for many other Algonquian languages. As with other Algonquian languages, there is also no default classifier for otherwise unclassified objects. Many of these classifiers are cognate with forms in other Algonquian languages (see Valentine 2001 for a very detailed study of Ojibwe) and with Proto-Algonquian (see Bloomfield 1946).

It will be useful to give an illustration of a form that turned out not to be a classifier. The VAI verb *ciit-o'ohn-ii-* means 'put on shoes.' Speakers said this must refer specifically to shoes or moccasins. When some other footwear such as boots or galoshes was introduced, speakers rejected the use of *ciito'ohnii-* and instead used VTI *ciito'-* 'put on an item of clothing': *ciito'-oo heyo'oono'ohno* 'put on your boots!' Thus *-o'ohn-* is an incorporated noun. The VTI verb *ciit-o'-* itself includes the classifier *-o'-* for clothing items, on the other hand.[2]

TABLE 2. Arapaho classifier medials

CLASSIFIER	MEANING
-oocei-	rope-like (topic, tool, object, actor)
*-oot-i- (VII)	cloth-like (topic)
-oo'-	stick-like (topic, tool, object)
-oow-	liquid (topic)
-ou-	liquid (medium)
-ookon-	liquid (tool)
-ook-	'useful' liquid (object)
-ecei-	liquid (actor [involuntary])
-ibin-, -uwun-	berry, fruit (topic, object)
-es-	grass-like (topic, object)
-oobe'ei-	dirt, earth, etc. as object (moved, carried, reshaped)
-o'ow-	dirt, earth, etc. as topic
-o'owuu-	dirt, earth, etc. as object in place (plowed, etc.)
-o'oow-	buildings (topic, object)
-oxesinou-	sticky substances (topic, tool, object, medium)
-ooxew-	domestic animals (object, topic)
-e3ee-	fire, heat, etc. (object, topic)
-ou(')-	commonly counted or numbered objects (topic, object)
-oxoe-	woven items (topic, object, tool)
-ex-/-ox-	'useful' wood (topic, object)
-o'-	clothing (object)

(20) Ceniit-o'-owoo hookou-biixuut
IC.enter-item.of.clothing.VTI-1s thick-shirt
'I am putting on a jacket'

(21) Ceniit-o'on-o' koyootee
IC.enter-item.of.clothing.VTA-1s/3s belt
'I am putting on a belt'

Similar verbs are VTI *neet-o'-* 'take off item of clothing', VTI *hokoot-o'-* 'change item of clothing', VTI *teek-o'-* 'fit item of clothing'.[3]

Another non-classificatory example is the verb *se'esoonee-* 'slice meat flat, to dry', which includes the medial *-oon-* ('leg, body, meat'). Speakers rejected sentences such as **see'esoonee-noo hiwoxuuhuunoseino'* 'I am slicing elk meat flat' or any sentence where I supplied an overt noun that would further specify the type of meat in question. Instead, they said that one would have to say *see'ex-owoo* *hiwoxuuhuunoseino'* 'I am slicing it flat elk meat' with the VTI verb *se'ex-* 'slice s.t. in flat pieces.' They also rejected **see'esoonee-noo hoseino'*, with *hoseino'* 'meat' added as an independent noun. They did however accept the form *see'esoonee-noo* as potentially referring to any type of meat. We must therefore analyze *-oon-* as an incorporated noun, but this noun is more general in meaning than the specific independent nouns that it replaces, as it refers to either meat generically, or any specific type of meat. Thus even noun incorporation can involve a "pseudo-classificatory" semantic component in Arapaho, further illustrating the scalar nature of incorporating/classifying functions.

One issue that arose in the fieldwork is that the youngest speaker sometimes accepted fewer nouns with the classifiers than the two other older speakers. While normally this did not affect the determination that an item was a classifier, in one case it did; the younger speaker accepted *-ooxew-* as a medial only for horses, with some additional but hesitating willingness to accept it for cows. Thus for him this would be effectively an incorporation form. The other two speakers accepted the term for a wider variety of domestic animals, and thus for them it was a classifier.

There is no space in this brief publication to provide examples of all the classifiers in full sentences. A natural discourse example of the first classifier is (Arapaho Text Database, EAG.254):

(22)	he'ih'etoocein	nuhu'	hitiine'	nuhu'	hoote.
	he'ih- 'etoocein	nuhu'	hi-tiin-e'	nuhu'	hoote
	NARRPAST- pull.rope.like.thing.out	this	3s-mouth-LOC	this	sinew
	'He took the sinew out of his mouth.'				

Examples of the kinds of nominals that can occur with the various medials based on elicitation sessions are given in Table 3. Sanders 2015 contains additional details on *-oow-*, *-oot-*, and *-ex-/-ox-*.

Extensions and Development of New Classifiers

One finding of research in this area, at least for Arapaho, is that some classifiers are much more widely used than others. The 'cloth-like' classifier for example is actually not used in many cases where one would imagine it could be used (dresses, sheets, curtains, tepee liners, carpets). In contrast, the 'rope-like', 'liquid-like', and

TABLE 3. Co-occurring nominal referents for Arapaho classifiers

CLASSIFIER	RANGE OF REFERENTS
-oocei-	ropes, string, yarn, thread, vines, water hoses, water pipes, netting, fish guts, arteries, veins, suspenders, fishing line, cassette tape, electric cords, lines of cars or trains, snakes, worms, caterpillars (see Sanders and Cowell 2020)
*-oot-i- (VII)	shirts, flags, sheets of rubber, canvas, tarps, silk
-oo'-	guns, sticks, bows, travois, wagons, trailers, wheelchairs, fire pokers, brakes, screwdrivers, bats, horns (as tools), keys, corkscrews, digging, sticks, forked sticks for carrying or supporting items, tent poles, and frames
-oow-	water, paint, condiments, beverages, ice cream, popsicles, soup, stew, chili, milk, cream, olive oil, ponds, lakes, puddles, rivers
-ou-	water, paint, condiments, liquor
-ookon-	water, bleach, detergent, liquor
-ook-	water, liquor
-ecei-	water, sweat, blood, gasoline, oil, coolant, antifreeze
-ibin-, -uwun-	all types of berries, some fruits with 'berry' included in the name
-es-	grass, hay, oats, barley, wheat, flowers, corn(?)
-oobe'ei-	dirt, sand, clay, gravel, similar construction materials
-o'ow-	dirt, earth, land
-o'owuu-	dirt, sand, clay, gravel, similar construction materials
-o'oow-	any building, building complexes, forts, campuses, towns
-oxesinou-	mud, glue, plaster, dough, wet concrete
-ooxew-	horses, cows, donkeys, and mules (pig, goats, sheep)
-e3ee-	heat, fire, stoves, lights
-ou(')-	money, time/hours, dates of the month, grades in school, uniform numbers
-oxoe-	willow lodges or shelters, fences, boxing rings
-ex-/-ox-	trees, shrubs, firewood, fishing poles, pencils, switches, tepee poles, bats, wood used in houses, and by extension the house
-o'-	any clothing item except hats, pants, socks, shoes (gloves)

'stick-like' classifiers have a very broad range of uses. The reason for the restricted usage of 'cloth-like' *-oot-* remains unclear to me.

In other cases, the classifier, by its very nature, simply has a limited range of corollary nouns. For example *-ooxew-* 'domestic animals' is actually limited to larger hooved animals that are raised for food or work purposes. It is most commonly used for horses, cows, donkeys, and mules. The oldest speaker accepted it for the widest range of animals, including pigs, goats, and sheep as well. This pretty much exhausts its range—it is not used with dogs and cats. The *-es-* 'grass-like' classifier is limited to grass, weeds, flowers, hay, and grain crops. The *-ook-* 'action on liquid' classifier is actually more specifically used in relation to drinkable liquids. In reality, it is used almost entirely for water or various types of alcohol—curiously, speakers do not use it with home-prepared drinks such as tea or coffee, nor is it used in relation to soft drinks. This usage parallels the semantic extension of the independent nominal *nec* 'water', which is also commonly used secondarily to refer to alcohol.

Not only is semantic extension important in relation to water, but this process is in fact a key issue for understanding all Arapaho classifiers. All of the "traditional" Arapaho classifiers as documented in early sources such as Kroeber's texts from 1899 (Cowell, C'Hair, and Moss 2016) have continued in use up to the present, and indeed, have expanded the range of corollary nouns that they accept, as part of a more general process of semantic and lexical extension. The extension is clear, since many of the nouns with which classifiers are now used did not even exist until well into the twentieth century. Sanders and Cowell (2020) cover this extensively for *-oocei-*, which is used with items such as cassette tape, or veins and arteries as part of heart bypass surgery. To take another example, *-oo'-* 'stick-like', which originally was likely prototypically used with bows (as objects of action), was extended to refer to rifles and then all guns. It was also extended from usage related to the travois (as means of action) to cover wagons, then horse trailers, and even wheelchairs. Thus both classificatory verbs and the broader classificatory process have remained vigorously productive up to the present in Arapaho. (The one interesting exception is in counting. My oldest early consultants said that counting numbers once included classifiers: *nees-ooceihi-* 'to be three string-like items.' This usage is reported to have disappeared by around 1950 however.)

A number of the classifiers are in fact likely new (as classifiers), and the result of the process of semantic extension. One example is the narrow classifier *-oxoe-*, perhaps originally used only for willow shelters (or at least this is the only pre-contact item with which it is used today), then extended by analogy to fences, corrals, and so forth (none of which would have been known until the 19th century, excluding things like rock game-drive walls), and on from there to boxing rings. The most obvious example is the *-ooxew-* 'domestic animal' classifier. Prior to European contact, the Arapaho had only one domestic animal, the dog, and use of this medial would have thus necessarily been noun incorporation, referring specifically to dogs. With the advent of the horse, the medial was extended to horses (known as 'elk dogs'), and then eventually came to be seen as prototypically referring to horses and similar animals. It was then extended to cows and other animals encountered in the 19th and 20th centuries. Thus an incorporated medial would have shifted referents, then expanded its range to other similar referents to become today's classifier. Note also that the possessive verb *hitonih'i-* in Arapaho (< it-onih'-i- POSSESS-domestic. animal-VAI-) underwent the same process, and also has classificatory functions. The verb must originally have meant 'possess a dog,' but is now glossed by speakers as 'possess a pet/domestic animal' and can be used with any domestic or tamed animal, so that one can say *hiitonih'i-noo tekoonineihii* 'I have a pet raccoon.' Possessed nouns in this type of possession-verb construction are not normally treated the same as things like body-part medials or verbal-medial classifiers in analyses of Algonquian languages, but clearly they could be treated as a type of classificatory medial. Another such verb in Arapaho is *hi-wo3onohoen-i-* 'possess paper', which can be used in reference to all types of specific things such as driver's licenses, ID cards, diplomas, homework, enrollment documents, checks, and so forth (with these specifiable by overt nouns where necessary).

Returning to the medials we have already been discussing, one wonders if the medial *-es-* 'grass-like' underwent an expansion similar to *-ooxew-*. Aboriginally, it was most likely an incorporated medial referring specifically to grass (it is difficult to imagine what else it could even have referred to). Note however this sentence in a text collected by Kroeber in 1899 (Arapaho Text Database, K142.358):

(23)	Nihbii'ineihok	heetoh'eyesooni'i	woxu'uno.
	nih-bii'ineihi-hok	heetoh-'eyesoo-ni'i	woxu'uno
	past-found-SUBJ	where-grass.is.high-0.OBV.PL	grass/hay
	He was found where the grass was high.		

This sentence shows a classificatory function already at this point. In the reservation era, this classifier was extended to hay, alfalfa, oats, wheat, barley, rye, and so forth. Perhaps under that process of extension it was then extended to wildflowers as well: Arapaho ethnobotany distinguishes grasses and roots from flowers as two separate categories, culturally and linguistically (see Cowell 2018:208–211), so covering both of them with the same incorporated medial would have been unlikely in earlier times. The classifier *-oxesin-ou-*, clearly related to *hoxes* 'mud', may have evolved in a similar way, as more and more sticky substances came into Arapaho life in the process of acculturation to aspects of Euro-American society. The important point here is that just because *-es-* can now refer to two different pre-contact items, grass and wildflowers, does not mean it was necessarily a classifier in pre-contact times. Rather, acculturation could have driven extension, turning incorporation into classification, and then once this happened other older items could be "back-filled" into the new, broader classifier's range of referents.

We can imagine that in the initial stages of extension, where a noun had only two or three potential meanings, either independently or in its incorporated form, it would have been clear from context what particular meaning was intended the vast majority of the time. But as a noun and/or nominal medial became extended further, the chances for confusion of exact meaning would have grown, and this would have then required speakers to begin adding an overt nominal in many cases to clarify the exact noun referent in question, perhaps initially in apposition, then eventually as part of the main verb phrase. Consider the following code-switching example (Arapaho Text Database, 56c.196):

(24) beebe'e3eenoo'ou'u, those lights
bee-be'e3eenoo'ou-'u those lights
REDUP-red.lights.flashing-0.PL those lights
His red lights were turned on, those lights [on the police car].

The verb is more specifically *be'-e3ee-noo'oo-* = red-heat/fire-INCHOAT(VII)-. Here the English addition clarifies the nature of the fire, heat (or in this case, by metaphorical extension, light) source. Given that nominal constituents are more loosely bound to verbs in Algonquian languages than in a language such as English, it is difficult to tell whether 'those lights' should be really treated as in apposition, or rather as a main constituent of a single clause (the pause here is quite short).

More generally I would postulate that during the process of gradual lexical extension, when an incorporated noun was used with its prototypical referent, it would continue to be used without any added overt nominal, but when newer, lesser prototypical referents occurred, overt nominals would be much more likely to be used. Eventually, lexical extension would have crossed over into a classificatory function (for some incorporated nouns). This process would account for the ambiguous distinction between classifiers and incorporated nominals noted by several Algonquian scholars (Valentine 2001:332; Drapeau and Lambert-Brétière 2011:299; Biedny et al. 2021:45). As Aikhenvald notes, verbal classifiers and noun incorporation can co-exist, "reflecting different stages of grammaticalization" (2000:149). I am proposing here that lexical extension can lead to an intermediate stage, between noun incorporation and grammaticalized classification.

Formal Ambiguities

A formal ambiguity arises in attempts to identify classificatory medials, in that it can be difficult to distinguish medial+abstract final combinations from complex finals—a problem widely noted for Algonquian languages (Slavin 2012; Goddard 1990). If we take the perspective that all classificatory functions in Algonquian languages are expressed via verbs that show noun incorporation-type morphosyntax, and that all noun incorporation in Algonquian languages involves medials, then this distinction is very important. Functionally however, this question is not equivalent to whether a verb that includes nominal-like semantic elements meets the test for being a classificatory verb as described earlier. There is no cross-linguistic restriction that classifiers in verbal classifier languages be medials—they must simply "appear on the verb" (Aikhenvald 2000:149). As already seen above, Arapaho VAI possession verbs of the form *hi-* + NOUN + *i-* do not include medials in the classic Algonquian sense (since full independent nominal forms are incorporated, and the initial element is entirely abstract), yet they can in some cases have classificatory functions. More generally, I want to argue here that attempts to appeal to Proto-Algonquian, or to the status of semantically nominal constituents of verbs in other Algonquian languages, or to ambiguous (and often diachronically driven) distinctions between medials and finals are not adequate for conclusively deciding which nominal elements are or are not classifiers in a given Algonquian language, from a synchronic perspective.

Verbs with instrumental finals are an especially interesting and problematic case. Semi-lexical/semi-abstract verb finals such as Arapaho *-en-* VTI/VTA 'by hand' or *-oh-* VTI/VTA 'by tool' could be considered to include nominal-like, potentially classificatory elements in a verb, though in reality, a specific instrument is rarely if ever specified when these verbs are used, suggesting that the finals are bleached of almost any real nominal sense, and are abstract. Conversely, the VTI/VTA finals *-ex-/-es-* 'by blade' are so narrowly lexically specified in Arapaho that speakers reject even the use of axe or hatchet with these forms (one uses a verb with the *-oh-* final instead).

Consider however the VII final *-etee-* 'by fire/heat'. Functionally, it resembles a medial such as *-oocei-* 'string-like': it is used not only for instrumental meanings, but also for topical uses such as *nühoonetee'* 'it has a yellow flame' or *bee'etee'* 'it is a red fire'. Formally it resembles medials of the form *-oon-ee-* (see (2)), so Arapaho speakers could easily analyze *-etee-* as *-et-ee-*. And in instrumental uses, it can occur with overt nominals, as in the following natural discourse example (Arapaho Text Database 18b.185):

(25)

Ne'iini,	nuhu'	ne'nih'iisiini.	huut
ne'iini	nuhu'	ne'nih'iisiini	huut
then	this	that.was.how/what	here

koo'oekuu3etee'			nuhu'	hocoo3eihii
koo'oekuu3-	etee-	'	nuhu'	hocoo3eihii
slow.intense.action-	by.heat.VII-	0s	this	griddle/fryer

'Then this one [my wife], that's how she [prepared them]. {Gestures, indicates frying.} They were fried up nice and slow on the fryer.'

The analysis of this sentence is ambiguous. The speaker does not use a locative marker with the noun, so the intended focus does not appear to be merely on/at the location of the griddle or fryer (as opposed to some other potential location). Rather, the griddle is both location and means of cooking. The noun can thus potentially be understood as an overt nominal that serves to clarify the instrument or form of heat, which thus makes *-etee-* a kind of "classificatory (instrumental) final." This final also shows recent lexical extension in Arapaho, as it can be used not only in reference to heat, fire, or sunlight, but also stoves and ovens, engines, heaters, gunshots, fireworks and firecrackers, and beer (due to the popping sound it makes when opened), both in instrumental/non-volitional actor and topical uses, as well as occasional volitional instrumental uses as in the example above. Thus what is formally a concrete final shows some evidence of becoming functionally, via (perhaps) reanalysis and (definitely) lexical extension, a nominal classifier.

On the other hand, this final can occur with another classifier as well, as in this natural discourse example:

(26) beneet-ecei-[e]tee-'
IC.finish.off-liquid-by.heat.VII-0s
'All the coolant was used up [in the car]' (lit. 'burned up')

This example uses *-ecei-* as a classifier for any liquid that is an actor or product of an action (such as sweating). The final *-etee-* seems to have its basic meaning of 'by heat' or 'burn up'. In this case, the fact that the car's engine is the source of that heat seems fairly incidental to the overall statement, which focuses on the fact that the coolant is gone, and only secondarily on the means by which this happened, whereas in (25) the focus is much more on the source of the heat—and that sentence also has no medial element.

A similar process to example (25) can be seen with the concrete finals *-ote-* (VII) and *-o3i(ne)-* (VAI) 'by cold'. These finals can refer to either topics (ice, cold weather, refrigerators, freezers), or instrumental uses of these same topics. Likewise the VTA/VTI final *-exoh'-* is used to refer to volitional action using a heat source. This can include fire, lightning (considered volitional), electricity, engines, heaters, ovens, stoves, dryers, guns and gunshots, and even dyes (especially black or brown, and especially hair dyes). Clearly these instrumental finals have undergone significant lexical extension in modern Arapaho. It is quite rare in natural discourse to add an overt specifying noun, but this can occur, and in elicitation speakers were quite willing to accept such overt nominals. A natural discourse example is (Arapaho Text Database 106b.217):

(27)	ne'nihi'ii'wo3onoxoh'oo3i',	nuhu'	heesiteeni'
	ne'-nih-i'-ii'-wo3onoxoh'-oo3i'	nuhu'	heesitee -ni'
	that-PAST-INSTR-when-brand.s.o.-3PL/4	this	IC.hot-0.OBV
	'Then ('that was when') they branded them with this branding iron ('hot thing').'		

If one accepts instrumental uses of *-oocei-* as in examples (5)–(8) as being classificatory in nature, it is then extremely difficult to see why one would not accept the use of *-exoh'-* (surface *-oxoh'-* in this case) as an equivalent example of a classificatory function.

Conclusions

The results shown in this paper indicate that in a language where classification is already done with verbal classifiers (themselves the long-term product of noun incorporation processes), acculturation and semantic extension may result in a greatly extended range of corollary referents for a given classificatory element. The results at least suggest that we can also see a shift of noun incorporation elements towards classificatory elements (see Aikhenvald 2000:352–361). Language-external reasons for the extension or even development of classification systems have been discussed (see Aikhenvald 2000:382–389), but language contact and areal diffusion have received much more attention than the processes of lexical acculturation.

It is already known cross-linguistically that the exact usage and function of a specific classificatory element can be quite broad in some cases, but highly specific in others (Aikhenvald 2000:307). More generally, the findings here suggest that one should not assume that all individual classificatory elements are exactly parallel in usage in a language—some may be developing classifiers, while others are full-fledged classifiers. Thus there may not always be a way to neatly say exactly how many classifiers there are in a language, especially in polysynthetic verbal classifier languages where overt nouns are often not present and classifiers often have subsidiary anaphoric uses.

I have also shown that a strict limitation of verbal classifiers to verbs with prototypical medial elements is insufficient to capture the full range of classificatory verb behavior in Arapaho, and perhaps in other Algonquian languages as well.

Finally, we have seen that instrumental constructions, at least in Arapaho, are particularly interesting when we examine classificatory elements. These are less prototypical examples of classificatory function, and indeed if we accept the limitation that classified nouns must be arguments of the verb (Grinevald 2000:69), they would not be classifiers at all (nor would the "medium of action" medials given above). Yet the same form (*-etee-* for example) can serve as both an instrumental and a more prototypical topic concrete-final classifier. Likewise the form *-oocei-* is clearly a medial, and clearly classificatory in its topic, object, and actor-mode-of-action uses, so it is unclear why instrumental uses of this medial should be excluded from classificatory consideration. One could also argue that examples such as (9)–(12) are ambiguous as to whether they should be considered instrumental or mode-of-action usages, since all of the examples are parallel to (16). The subject literally "walks in a rope-like way" in (16), and literally "walks in a stick-like way" (traveling by wagon) in (9). Thus mode-of-action and instrumental uses converge in some cases. It is beyond the scope of this paper to resolve the issue of instrumental classification, but the relevance of the question is hopefully apparent.

NOTES

1. See Cowell and Moss (2008) for a general grammar. Abbreviations: 0 = inanimate person, 1 = first person, 2 = second person, 3 = third person, IC = initial change, INCHOAT = inchoative, INSTR = instrumental, LOC = locative, OBV = obviative, NARRPAST = narrative

past tense, PART = particle, PAST = past tense, PL = plural, POSSESS = possession, REDUP = reduplication, REFL = reflexive, S = singular, s.o. = someone/something (animate), s.t. = something, SUBJ = subjunctive mode, VAI = verb, animate subject, intransitive, VAI.O = verb, animate subject, intransitive, unspecified object, VII = verb, inanimate subject, intransitive, VTA = verb, transitive, animate subject, VTI = verb, transitive, inanimate subject.

2. Here if we treat the verb in (23) as *ciit-o'-ow-* = enter-item.of.clothing-VTI-, with the inflection being only the final element *-oo* (the analysis dictated by Proto-Algonquian), then *-o'* is a medial; the VTA form is *ciit-o'-on-*.
3. Note the medial is used only with clothing items that cannot be directly incorporated into the verb (socks, shoes, pants, and hats are normally incorporated: VAI *ciit-osouh'un-ii-* 'put on socks,' VAI *ciit-otooh-oe-* 'put on pants', etc.).

REFERENCES

Aikhenvald, Alexandra. 2000. *Classifiers*. Oxford: Oxford University Press.

Biedny, Jerome, Matthew Burner, Andrea Cudworth, and Monica Macaulay. 2021. Classifier Medials across Algonquian: A First Look. *International Journal of American Linguistics* 87(1):1–47.

Bloomfield, Leonard. 1946. Algonquian. *Linguistic Structures of Native America*, ed. by Cornelius Osgood, pp. 85–129. New York: Viking Fund.

Cowell, Andrew. 2018. *Naming the World: Language and Power among the Northern Arapaho*. Tucson: University of Arizona Press.

Cowell, Andrew. 2020. *Arapaho Text Database: An Interlinearized Corpus of Arapaho Natural Discourse*. Boulder: University Press of Colorado.

Cowell, Andrew, and Alonzo Moss Sr. 2008. *The Arapaho Language*. Boulder: University Press of Colorado.

Cowell, Andrew, William C'Hair, and Alonzo Moss Sr. 2016. *Arapaho Stories, Songs and Prayers: A Bilingual Anthology*. Norman: University of Oklahoma Press.

Drapeau, Lynn. 2014. *Grammaire de la langue Innue*. Québec: Presses de l'Université du Québec.

Drapeau, Lynn, and Renée Lambert-Brétière. 2011. Verbal Classifiers in Innu. *Anthropological Linguistics* 53(4):293–322.

Goddard, Ives. 1990. Primary and Secondary Stem Derivation in Algonquian. *International Journal of American Linguistics* 56:449–483.

Grinevald, Colette. 2000. A Morphosyntactic Typology of Classifiers. *Systems of Nominal*

Classification, ed. by Gunter Senft, pp. 50–92. Cambridge: Cambridge University Press.

Grinevald, Colette. 2002. Making Sense of Nominal Classification Systems: Noun Classifiers and the Grammaticalization Variable. *New Reflections on Grammaticalization*, ed. by Ilse Wischer and Gabriele Diewald, pp. 259–276. Philadelphia: John Benjamins Publishing Company.

Mithun, Marianne. 1986. The Convergence of Noun Classification Systems. *Noun Classes and Categorization*, ed. by Collette Craig, pp. 379–393. Amsterdam: Benjamins.

Mithun, Marianne. 1999. *The Languages of Native North America*. Cambridge: Cambridge University Press.

Sanders, Allison. 2015. *Nominal Classification in Arapaho*. MA thesis, University of Colorado, Boulder.

Sanders, Allison, and Andrew Cowell. 2020. Exploring an Arapaho Classifier: Prototypes, Markedness, and Double Lexical Selection. *Papers of the 49th Algonquian Conference*, ed. by Monica Macaulay and Margaret Noodin, pp. 223–238. East Lansing: Michigan State University Press.

Senft, Gunter. 2000. *Systems of Nominal Classification*. Cambridge: Cambridge University Press.

Slavin, Tanya. 2012. Phonological and Syntactic Evidence for Sem Structure in Oji-Cree. *International Journal of American Linguistics* 78:497–532.

Valentine, Randolph. 2001. *Nishnaabemwin Reference Grammar*. Toronto: University of Toronto Press.

The Deployment of Ojibwe Discourse Markers

R.-M. Déchaine, M. Dufresne, and S. Frazier

[Discourse markers are] akin to salt, sprinkled
through the language to give it spice and flavor.
—Randolph Valentine, *Nishnaabemwin Reference Grammar*

Though the functions of Ojibwe discourse markers (DMs) are beginning to be better understood, there currently exists no satisfactory account of their syntactic properties. Drawing on examples from a counseling speech by Nancy Jones (2013), we address the question of how DMs are syntactically integrated into the utterance they appear in. After introducing the text from which our dataset is drawn, we give representative examples of DMs, introduce the tools we use to analyze them, and discuss how these tools account for their syntactic distribution.

The Text We Are Looking At: Jones (2013)

Our analysis is based on the bilingual Ojibwe-English publication of a counseling speech by Nancy Jones, titled *Gakina Dibaajimowinan Gwayakwaawan* (All Teachings Are Correct), pp. 9–10. It was published in *Dibaajimowinan* by the Great Lakes Indian Fish and Wildlife Commission in 2013. The speech contains 19 paragraphs, and we discuss the first four, which comprise the introductory section. The book is accompanied by a CD with an audio recording, so it is possible to examine the prosody of DMs.[1]

Where Discourse Markers Are Found

Fairbanks (2016) recognizes two position classes for DMs:

> Ojibwe Position 1 (P1) Discourse Markers:
>
> They [. . .] occur in initial position, may have tonic stress, show syntactic detachability from their containing clauses, [. . .] and have both primary functions in the ideational plane of discourse (in sentence grammars) and secondary functions in other planes of discourse (above the sentence-level). (Fairbanks 2016:45)
>
> Ojibwe Position 2 (P2) Discourse Markers:
>
> Ojibwe [. . .] makes heavy use of second-position particles—particles that typically occur only in the second position of an utterance. . . . [A] significant number of [. . .] discourse markers [. . .] find a home in second position. . . . [They]

TABLE 1. Discourse markers attested in section 1 (§§1–4) of Jones (2013)

F2016	J2013	FUNCTION
P1	*(i)nashke*	'look!', attention-getter (F46); *nashke* ~ *shke* ~ *ke* ~ *inake*
	mii	marks deixis of physical reference or time frame (F67)
	aaniish	'well, after all'; marks rationale for action/behavior (F99)
	ahaw	'come on, ok' interjectional particle (V149)
P2	*go*	emphatic (F117)
	(i)sa	marks end of event/utterance/narrative (F103)
	(i)naa	increases attitudinal force of speaker to utterance (F137)
	(i)dash	marks contrast, discourse sequences (F70, F73)
P1+P2	*mii dash*	advances narrative (F67)
	aaniish-inaa	aligns interlocutor expectations with speaker's (F103)

> have [a] function in sentence grammar as well as within discourse above the sentence level. (Fairbanks 2016:72f)

Table 1 lists the DMs attested in the stretch of narrative that we discuss; relative to Fairbanks's (2016) classification, we observe P1 DMs, P2 DMs, and stacked DMs.[2]

Examples of a P1 DM are given (1) and (2) with *nashke*, which functions as an attention-getter. Examples of P2 DMs include *go* (3), *sa* (4), and *dash* (5).

(1)	**Nashke**	ingoji	gii-okwabiyang	omaa	ingoji P1
	nɪʃˈkʰe	ɪngoˈje	ˈgi oˈkʰwəˌbiyaŋ	oma	ɪngoje
	nashke	[ingoj-i	gii-okw-ab-i-yang	o-maa	ingoj-i
	PC.ISC.INTER	somewhere-PC	PFV.IC-√group-sit-ai-2l.cj	PXL-LOC	somewhere-PC
	DM.INTER	√loc.npi-PC	PFV-√RT-√RT-INTR3-21.CJ	PXL-√LOC	√LOC.NPI-PC

'So—anywhere, whenever you and me gather there'

gakina,	gakina	bebakaan,	gidayaamin
ˌgakʰɪˈnaː	ˈgakʰɪ.na	ˈbebaˌkʰan	gɪˌdaˈyaːmɪn
gakina	gakina	bebakaan]	gid-ayaa-min
all	all	MNR.all.different	2-√have.intr-21.idp
√QNT.V3	√QNT.V3	√RT.RED	2-√RT.INTR-21.IDP

dibaajmowinan.
diˈbaʒˌmowɪnn̩
dib-aajim-o-win-an
√measure-mouth.TA-AI-NFF-NI.PL
√RT|mouth.TR3|DETR3-NMLZ-0PL
'All (of us), each (one of us) different—you and I have teachings.' (J§2.2)

(2)	Minik	gego	gaa-izhi-dibaajimot	awe,
	ˈmɪnɪˌkʰe	go	gaĩʒɪdɪˈbagɪmətʰ	əwə
	minik	gego	gaa-izhi-dib-aajim-o-t	a-we
	so.much	NEG	PV.PRF.IC-thus-√measure-mouth.TA-AI-3SG.CJ	NA.SG-DEM
	ADV.QNT	NEG	PRF-thus-√rt-mouth.TR3-DETR3-3SG.CJ	DXS3-√D

'There are not many things that this one doesn't thus speak about.' (J§3.3a)

nashke	omaa	geniin
naʃkʰeˈ	mɪn	ˌgeˈnɪn
nashke	o-ma	ge-n-iin

<table>
<tr><td>PC.DISC.INTER</td><td>PXL-LOC</td><td>FOC.ADD-PRN-1</td></tr>
<tr><td>DM.INTER</td><td>PXL-√LOC</td><td>and-PRN-1</td></tr>
</table>

gaa-izhi-gikinoo'amaagowaan. **P1**
gaɪʒɪgikinoˌmʌgoˈwaːn
gaa-izhi-gikinoo-'-amaa-go-waan
PV.PRF.IC|PV.REL|teach-TA-APL-INV-3'>3PL.CJ
PRF.IC|thus|√RT-TR3-APL-VCE3:1-3'>3PL.CJ
'such as I was also taught here.' (J§3.3b)

<table>
<tr><td>(3)</td><td>. . . aapiji</td><td>go</td><td>awe.</td><td>P2</td></tr>
<tr><td></td><td>|| apˈjɪ</td><td>ˈgo</td><td>oˈwe</td><td></td></tr>
<tr><td></td><td>aapiji</td><td>go</td><td>a-we</td><td></td></tr>
<tr><td></td><td>√very</td><td>PC.EMPH_ASSERT</td><td>NA_SG-DEM</td><td></td></tr>
<tr><td></td><td>√DEG</td><td>√DM2.EMPH</td><td>3.DXS-√D</td><td></td></tr>
</table>

'It is especially this.' (J§2.1d)

<table>
<tr><td>(4)</td><td>Jibwaa</td><td>maajitaayan</td><td>gegoo</td><td>owe</td></tr>
<tr><td></td><td>jɪbwo</td><td>mɑʧˈdɑ͡iɪn</td><td>gego</td><td>owe</td></tr>
<tr><td></td><td>ji-bwaa</td><td>maaj-itaa-yan</td><td>gegoo</td><td>o-we</td></tr>
<tr><td></td><td>FUT2-before</td><td>√start-DO.AI-2SG.CJ</td><td>PRN_INDF_NI</td><td>PRON_NI_SG</td></tr>
<tr><td></td><td>IRR-before</td><td>√RT|INTR3-2SG.CJ</td><td>√QNT.$0</td><td>DXS0-√D</td></tr>
</table>

wii-izhichigeyan,
wiː-ɪʧage
wii-izhi-t-ige-yan
FUT.VOL-√thus-TI-AI.GNR-2SG.CJ
ASP.PROSP-√RT-TR0-DETR3.GNR-2SG.CJ
'Before you start doing anything, this is what you're going to do,'

<table>
<tr><td>akawe</td><td>sa</td><td>gidasemaa</td><td>gidoodaapinaa.</td><td>P2</td></tr>
<tr><td>ak^{h}awe</td><td>se</td><td>dɪdaˈsema</td><td>gadoˈdap^{h}ɪna</td><td></td></tr>
<tr><td>akawe</td><td>sa</td><td>gid-asemaa</td><td>gid-oodaap-in-aa</td><td></td></tr>
<tr><td>first</td><td>PC.EMPH.NVL</td><td>2-√tobacco.NA</td><td>2-√pick.up-hand.TA|DIR_IDP</td><td></td></tr>
<tr><td>ADV.TMP</td><td>DM.EMPH.NVL</td><td>2-√RT.3</td><td>2-√RT-hand.TR3|VCE3_IDP</td><td></td></tr>
</table>

'first, you pick up your tobacco.' (J§4.1)

(5)

Gaawiin	**dash** win	awiya	wiikaa
‖ gan	ˈdɪʃ wɪn	əwyə	ˈwikʰa
gaa-wiin	dash=win	awiya	wiikaa
NEG-PC.DISC.CNTR	PC.SEQ=FOC	PRN.INDF.NA	ever.ADV.TMP
√NEG-FOC	√DM.SEQ=FOC	√QNT.∃	√ADV.NPI

indaa-aanwetawaasii **P2**
ɪndaən̩wettʰˈwasi
in-daa-aanwet-aw-aa-sii
1-FUT.IDP-√disbelieve-TA-1>3.NEG.IDP
1-IRR.IDP-√RT-TR3-1>3.IDP.NEG
'And so then, it's not that anyone, never would I disbelieve.' (J§2.3)

In addition, it is possible for DMs to stack, as shown in (6) and (7), where a P1 DM (*mii*) combines with a P2 DM (*dash*).

(6) **P1+P2**

mii	**dash**	iye	gaa-onji-ikidowaan
mɪ	dəʃ	i	geongiɪdoˈgaaî
mii	dash	i-ye	gaa-onji-iN-gido-waan
PC.FOC	PC.SEQ	NI-DEM	FUT_CJ_IC|from|thus|√SPEAK.AI-1SG.CJ
DM.FOC	DM.SEQ	DXS0-√D	IRR_CJ_IC|DIR|MNR|√RT3-1SG.CJ

'And so, that is why I will speak in this way.' (J§3.1b*)

(7)

Mii-dash	awe,	ge-wiiji'ik	awe
mi dɪʃ	awe	ˈgewi jekʰ	owe
mii-dash	a-we	ge-wiij-i'-ik	a-we
PC.FOC-PC.SEQ	NA.SG-DEM	FUT2.CJ.IC-√with-TA-INV-3>2.cj	NA.SG-DEM
DM.FOC-DM.SEQ	DXS-√D	IRR.CJ-√RT-TR3-VCE3:2-3>2.CJ	DXS3-

weweni **P1+P2**
wewenɪ
weweni
properly
√D√ADV.MNR.RED
'And it is this one(tobacco), this one(tobacco) that will properly help you . . . ' (J§4.2)

Though the P1/P2 contrast is confirmed in the data from Jones (2013), there are cases that resist this classification. In (8), *anishaa*, classified as a P1 DM by Fairbanks (2016), appears in non-initial position. Even more problematic is the occurrence of the complex DM *aaniish-naa* (with the P1 DM *aaniish* and the P2 DM *naa*) in final position, in (9).

(8) gawiin, gaawiin awiiya **anishaa**
gāĩwɪn gāĩwɪn wia anɪsh^{h}ə
gaa-wiin gaa-wiin awiiya aanish-aa
NEG NEG PRN.INDF.NA PC.SEQ-PC.INTER
NEG NEG √QNT.∃3 DM.SEQ-DM.INTER

indaa-inendanzii. **P1**
ɪndaɪndənsi
in-daa-in-end-an-zii-n
1-FUT.IDP-√thus-thought.TI-TH-NEG-0.IDP
1-IRR.IDP-√RT-thought.TR0-VCE3:0-NEG-0.IDP
'No, look, of nobody, would I think of them in this way.' (J§3.1b)

(9) gaawiin dash win awiya wiikaa
gan ˈdɪʃ wɪn əwyə ˈwik^{h}a
gaawiin dash win awiya wiikaa
NEG PC.SEQ FOC PRN.INDF.NA ever
NEG.IDP NEG DM_SEQ-FOC √QNT.∃3 √ADV.NPI

indaa-aanwetawaasii **aaniish-naa.** **P1+P2**
ɪndaənˌwett^{h}ˈwasi ˈaːnɪʃˌna
in-daa-aanwet-aw-aa-sii aaniish-naa
1-PV.PRF-√disbelieve-TA-TH-1>3 PC.SEQ-PC.INTER
1-PRF-√RT|TR|VCE3.1>3.NEG.IDP DM.SEQ-DM.INTER
'So let's see, so then, it's not that I would ever disbelieve anyone.' (J§2.3)

DMs also appear in contexts where they associate with non-verbal predicates, as in (10), where the DM$_{1}$ *ahaw* 'okay' co-occurs with the predicative particle *miigwech* 'thanks' (derived from DM_1 *mii-* in combination with *gwech*), and the complex DM *aaniishinaa* 'so let's see' occurs with the DP *awe aya'aa* 'this thing'.

(10)

Ahaw	**miigwech.**	||
ˌaˈhaw	ˈmiːˌgweʧ	
a-haw	mii-gwe-ch	
PC.ITJ-PC.ITJ	PC.PRED|√enough-PC	
√DM.ITJ-√DM.ITJ	√DM.PRED~√RT-PC	

'Okay; thanks.' (J§1.1)

Aaniishinaa	awe	aya'aaaa.
ˈaːˌnɪʃɪnaːˌ	oˈw	aː
aaniish-inaa	a-we	aya-'aa-aa
PC.SEQ-PC.INTER	NA.SG-DEM	√entity-NA.SG-EXP
DM.SEQ-DM.INTER	DXS3-√D	√RT-3-EXP

'So let's see this thing.' (J§1.2)

Analyzing Discourse Markers

Before proceeding to what Ojibwe DMs reveal about syntax-prosody integration, we introduce our background assumptions about syntax and prosody respectively.

Syntactic Analysis of Discourse Structure

The most obvious fact about Ojibwe DMs is that they are located outside the verbal complex; syntactically the latter is generally agreed to be a CP (Lochbihler and Mathieu 2016), so this means that DMs attach outside CP, as in (11a). And while P1 DMs are at the left periphery of the utterance (11b), P2 DMs must be preceded by another constituent (XP), (11c). Distinguishing DM_1 from DM_2 captures the fact that they can combine, yielding stacked DMs, as in (11d). We might expect an equivalence relation between the XP position in (11c) and the DM_1 position in (11d), as both can host DM_2.[3] In a related vein, prosodically, we might expect DM_1 to be heavier, consistent with its ability to attract tonic stress; syntactically, we might expect it to show phrasal characteristics, consistent with its detachability.[4]

(11) a. [DM [$_{CP}$ . . .]]
b. [**DM$_1$ [$_{CP}$ . . .]]
c. [XP [DM$_2$ [$_{CP}$ . . .]]]
d. [**DM$_1$ [DM$_2$ [$_{CP}$ . . .]]]

There are several confounds in adjudicating the syntax of DMs. One is the fact that Ojibwe is a discourse-configurational language (see Baker 1996; Jelinek 1984; Russell and Reinholtz 1996); consequently, in addition to DMs, a large set of phrasal expressions attach to CP (via adjunction), including DPs, adverbials, locatives, and other CPs. Also, Ojibwe makes extensive use of nominal predication in the form of equative structures that introduce relative clauses (which adjoin to their DP host). We see both of these options at play in (12). The analysis that we adopt for such a sentence is based on the syntactic principles in (13), which represent a specific implementation discourse-configurationality.

(12)

minik	ge	niin	gegoo	gaapi-izhi-waawiindamaagowaan
ˈmɪˌnʌk^{h}	ge	ˈnɪn	ˈgeˌgo	ˈgaː pi ˈeɪʒiˌwawɪndˌmagowən
minik	ge	n-iin	gegoo	gaa-pi-izhi-√waawii-nd-amaa-go-waan
much	also	1-PRN	PRN.INDF.NI	FUT.IC-HITHER-PV.REL-name|hear.TI|
√QNT	√FOC.ADD	1-√PRN	√QNT.∃0	IRR.IC-path-MNR.CJ|√RT.RED|hear.TR0|

gii-pi-ombigiyaan,
gip^{h}omˈbɪgiˌyʌn
gii-pi-omb-igi-yaan
APL.TA|INV|X>1SG.CJ
APL3|VCE3|X>1SG.CJ
'As for me also, there is much that someone would come to explain to me as I was growing up.' (§2.1b)

(13) Principles for syntactic analysis of complex sentences
a. verbal complexes are CPs;
b. complement/modifying clauses are CPs adjoined to CP (and not extraposed);
c. relative clauses are CPs adjoined to DP;
d. equative structures involve two DPs in an identity relation; mediated by a (null) predicative identity operator ([$_{PRED}$ =]);
e. all other expressions left- or right-adjoin to the CP/PredP they scope over.

Applying these parsing principles to (12) yields the analysis in (12'): (i) the first conjunct mode clause is a relative clause (a CP adjoined to DP); (ii) the DP host of the relative clause is in an equative structure headed by [$_{\text{PRED}}$ =]; (iii) the second conjunct mode clause is a modifying clause (CP$_{§2.1b(I)}$ right-adjoined to CP$_{§2.1b}$); (iv) the modifying elements that occur at the beginning of the sentence—*minik* 'much' and *ge niin* 'and me'—are adjoined to the clause they scope over, here PredP.

(14') Syntactic Parse of (14)

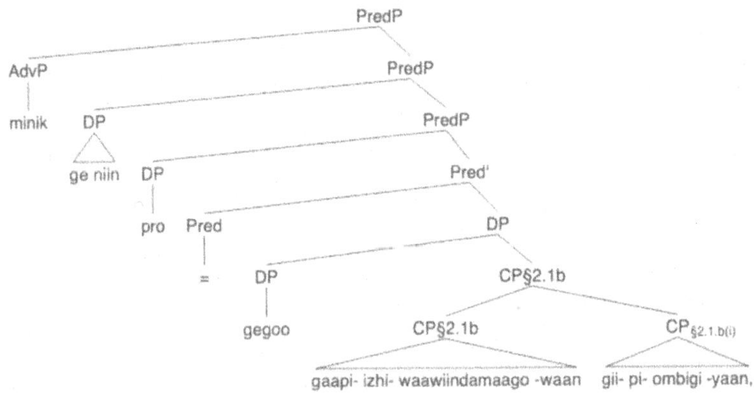

We have deliberately illustrated the parsing principles with an utterance that does not contain DMs; §5 examines how DMs are integrated into such syntactic structures.

Software Used to Analyze Prosody

Our prosodic analysis used two types of software: Audacity was used in the pre-analysis phase; PRAAT was used to conduct the prosodic analysis. Audacity is a free editing and recording software that can be used to mix, splice, and cut audio, as well as many other editing processes. We used it to clean the audio recording by running the audio through the Audacity Noise Reduction filter twice to eliminate as much background noise as possible, without distorting the audio. The filters used for both run-throughs were: Noise Reduction: 8 dB, Sensitivity: 4, and Frequency Smoothing (bands): 1. These settings were chosen because they are the standard noise-reduction settings. The cleaned audio was then used for the PRAAT analysis.

The prosodic analysis was performed on selected discourse spans with PRAAT, a freeware program used to analyze acoustic data and which offers a variety of procedures including neural networks, spectrographic analysis, and articulatory synthesis (Lieshout 2003). Because the beginning of the narrative contains important scene-setting information, to preserve textual coherence we did not omit the first 30 seconds of audio (something that is otherwise standard when doing acoustic analysis).

Our use of PRAAT focused on identifying salient phonetic markers in speech, including pauses, pitch prominence, and changes in amplitude. Phrases were determined by pauses in speech. To make sure PRAAT did not misidentify background noise as having the highest pitch (a well-known weakness of PRAAT), the PRAAT analysis was double-checked with listening by a human. The PRAAT pitch settings used were the default settings of 100 to 500 Hz; pitch line was set to automatic. Thus, for each phrase, we identified the GREATEST CHANGE IN PITCH using two measures: (i) PRAAT's built-in pitch settings; (ii) listening for large pitch changes. To find the HIGHEST PITCH OF EACH PHRASE, again two measures were used: (i) the PRAAT-generated pitch line; (ii) listening for the highest pitch.

Syntactic Integration of Ojibwe Discourse Markers

Our dataset of Ojibwe DMs allows us to enrich previous descriptions and analyses in two ways. First, we show that, for DMs that seem to depart from Fairbanks's (2016) P1/P2 distinction, if ordering restrictions are stated relative to CP, these anomalies disappear. Second, the PRAAT analysis allows us to examine prosody-syntax mapping: not only does this contribute to our understanding of the prosody-syntax interface, it allows us to use DMs as a diagnostic for syntactic structure. We introduce the notion of "minimal utterance" (MU), and propose that DMs anchor to MUs. We next consider in turn DMs in canonical and non-canonical positions. We then show that once the syntax of DMs is properly understood, we can detect abstract syntactic structure; this is relevant for the analysis of relative clauses and stranded DMs.

Discourse Markers Attach to the Minimal Utterance (MU)

Figure 1 shows the prosodic coding of Paragraph 1, which has two sentences both of which contain DMs: while §1.1 contains one DM (*ahaw*), §1.2 contains two DMs (P1 *aaniish* and P2 *inaa*).

FIGURE 1. Prosodic Coding of Paragraph 1 (see (10))

	OJIBWE	ENGLISH
§1.1	[$_{\text{DM}_1}$ A**haw] ***miigwech** ||	'Okay; thanks.'
§1.2	[$_{\text{DM}_1}$ Aanii-sh] [$_{\text{DM}_2}$ **inaa] awe ***aya'aaaa** ||	'So let's see this thing.'

As shown by the pitch lines in Figures 2 and 3, DMs attract max pitch and both occur at the beginning of their respective utterances. For §1.1, *ahaw miigwech*, the difference in pitch between *haw* and *mii* is relatively large; moreover, *gwech* has an undefined pitch and is reduced by the speaker. This, supplemented by careful listening, led us to assign max pitch to *haw*. For §1.2, *aaniishinaa awe aya'aaaa*, max pitch is on *inaa*, with another pitch prominence on *aya*. The max pitch on *inaa* is interesting because it is a P2 DM, which Fairbanks (2016:103) describes as increasing the speaker's attitudinal force toward the utterance; the fact that it attracts max pitch suggests the speaker is drawing attention to their attitudinal force. Syntactically, this first paragraph uses nominal predication to anchor discourse-initial scene-setting DMs; this is shown in (10'), which is the syntactic representation of (10).[5] Paragraphs §1.1 and §1.2 each exemplify a "minimal utterance" (MU), the smallest unit that a DM combines with. This means that nominal predicates—which we analyze as PredP—constitute an MU in Ojibwe: §1.1 has a [DM_1+PredP] combination; §1.2

FIGURE 2. Pitch and waveform of §1.1: *ahaw miigwech*

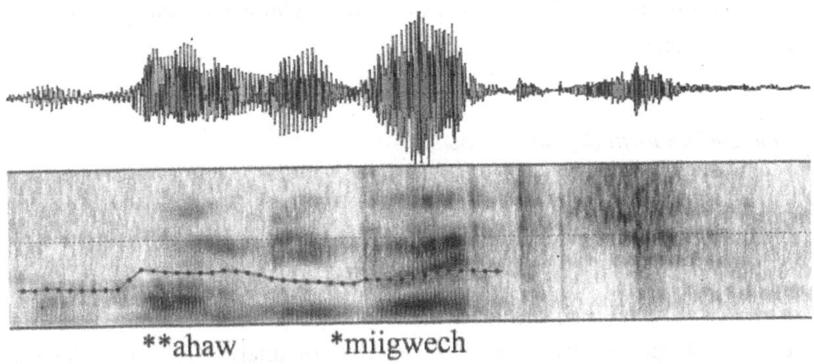

FIGURE 3. Pitch and waveform of §1.2: *aaniishinaa awe aya'aaaa*

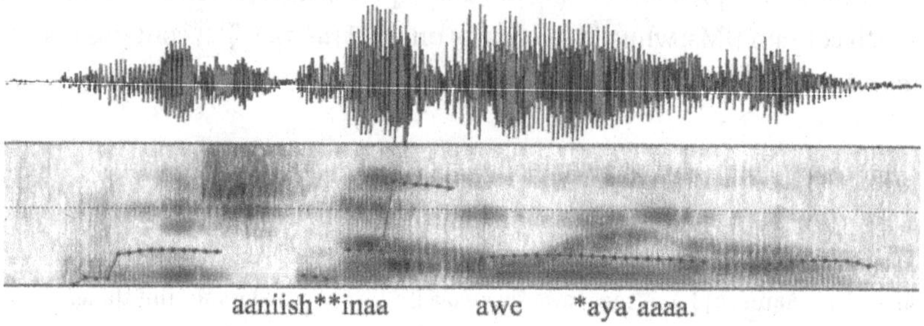

(10') Syntactic parse of §1.1, §1.2 (see (10))

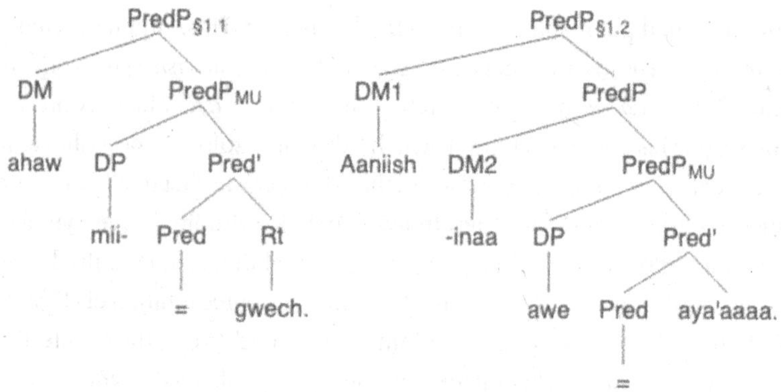

has a stacked DM, namely [DM_1+DM_2+PredP]. The PredP analysis, together with the recognition that PredP constitutes an MU, explains why DMs can be hosted by non-verbal clauses.

Discourse Markers in Canonical Position

DMs in canonical position are readily found in Jones's (2013) counseling speech; we illustrate this with one example each of DM_1 and DM_2, and then an example of DM stacking (i.e. DM_1 in combination with DM_2).

Consider first the DM_1 *nashke*, an attention-grabbing element akin to English 'look!', which is attested twice in the section we are analyzing; here we look at its

FIGURE 4. Pitch and waveform of §2.2(i): ***nashke*** *ingoji gii-okwabiyang omaa ingoji gakina*; (see (1))

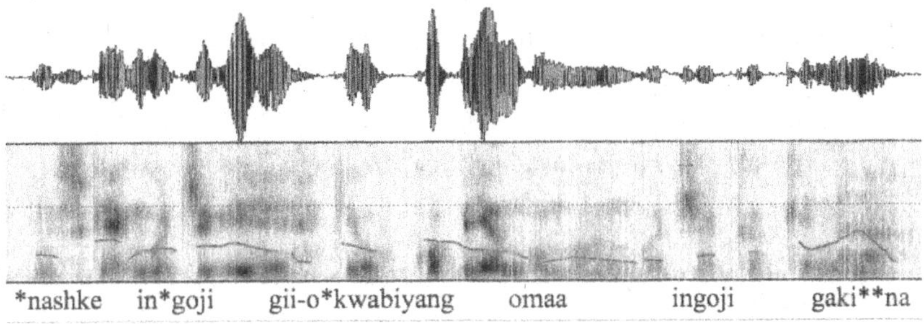

occurrence in §2.2(i); the pitch and waveform are given in Figure 4, which shows the pitch track of 2.2(i) until the start of 2.2; the rest of 2.2 has been omitted due to lack of pitch. There is also a pitch prominence on *gii-okwabiyang* and the discourse marker *nashke*. The pitch track confirms Fairbanks's (2016) observation that DM_1 attracts tonic stress; this is reflected by the pitch prominence on the second syllable of *nashke*.

This example illustrates the importance of an integrated prosodic and syntactic analysis. To see why, consider (1'), which gives the parse of the clause immediately after *nashke* as well as the following clause: the clause adjacent to *nashke* is an adjunct CP (in the conjunct mode) while the following clause is a root CP (in the independent mode). When this larger context is taken into account, it becomes

(1') Syntactic parse of §2.2 (see (1)), example of canonical DM1

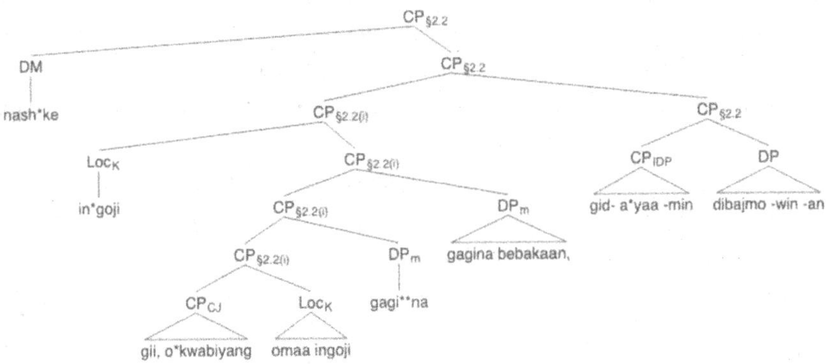

obvious that *nashke* scopes over the root CP, and that the adjunct CP has the status of a parenthetical. Thus, though *nashke* is clearly in P1 in (1'), it is not string adjacent to its host ($CP_{§2.2}$); this reflects the fact that the latter is modified by the adjunct $CP_{§2.2.(i)}$.

Now consider a P2 DM; we illustrate this with DM_2 *sa*. The pitch track and waveform appear in Figure 5; prosodically, *sa* attracts the max pitch.

As shown in (4'), which gives the parse of §4.1, as a second position element *sa* follows an XP, here the AdvP *akawe* 'first'. At the macro-level, (4') and (1') are

FIGURE 5. Pitch and waveform of §4.1: *akawe* ***sa*** *gidasemaa gidoodaapinaa*

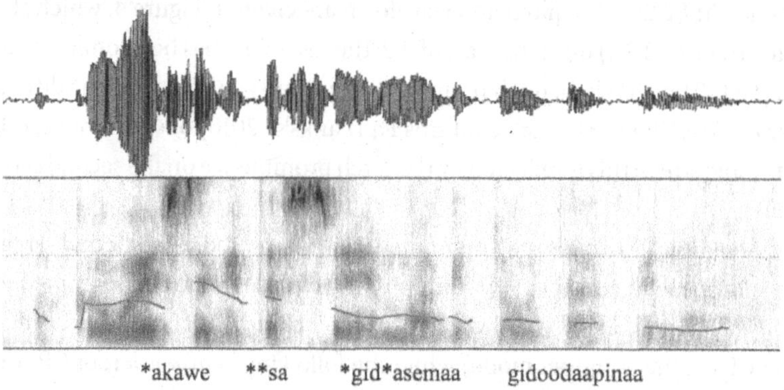

structurally similar inasmuch as both involve an independent mode root CP preceded by a conjunct mode adjunct CP. In Nancy Jones's text, this way of combining clauses is common, to the point that an independent mode root CP often marks the right margin of a complex CP. This exemplifies an asyndetic connection (Fairbanks 2016:183, fn. 9) where two clauses are juxtaposed without a connector; as Fairbanks (2016) observes, asyndesis is pervasive in Ojibwe oral narratives. However, it is often the case that the structural relation between the CPs can be recovered from other information, in this case from a contrast in clause type, specifically the contrast between the conjunct and independent mode.

(4') Syntactic parse of §4.1 (see (4)), example of canonical DM2

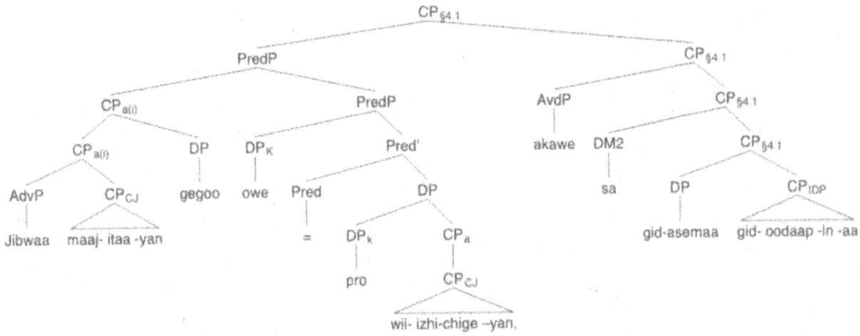

Discourse Markers in (Apparently) Non-Canonical Position

We now turn to DMs that do not obviously occupy P1 or P2. As we shall see, when the syntactic structures that host them are taken into account, these apparent counter-examples are in fact consistent with Fairbanks's classification. Consider first the placement of *anishaa* in (8), which at first glance occupies neither P1 nor P2. Figure 6 gives the prosodic coding, while Figure 7 shows the pitch track. *Anishaa* is a complex DM: it combines the P1 *aniish* ('well, after') with P2 *aa*, an allomorph of *naa* ('increase attitudinal force of speaker to utterance'); used together they align interlocutor expectations with those of the speaker (Fairbanks 2016:130). Prosodically, the locus of max pitch is the negator *gaawiin*, and there is also a pitch prominence on *awiiya* ('someone, anyone') and the DM *anishaa*.

FIGURE 6. Prosodic coding of §3.1b (see (8))

	OJIBWE	ENGLISH
§3.1b	‖ gawiin | **gaawiin *awiiya	'No, not (of) anyone
	[DM_1 **ani*sh**]= [DM_2 **aa**] **indaa-inendanzii** |	would I thus think to myself'

Example (8') gives the parse of §3.1b, which shows how DMs interact with other CP-adjoined XPs. Reading from left to right, §3.1 hosts §3.1a and §3.1b. We focus on §3.1b, which has a left-adjoined $PredP_{b(i)}$ and an independent mode root CP_b. The latter has four left-adjuncts: the negator *gawin*, the negative quantifier *gaawin awiiya* ('not anyone'), followed by the two DMs (*anish* and *-aa*). This articulated structure allows us to understand the tucking in of DMs relative to other left-dislocated XPs. This is not specific to Ojibwe; for similar observations on Meskwaki (Fox), see Dahlstrom (2003). Observe that, once again, the independent mode root CP

FIGURE 7. Pitch and waveform of §3.1b: *gawiin, gaawiin awiiya anishaa indaa-inendanzii*; (see (5) above)

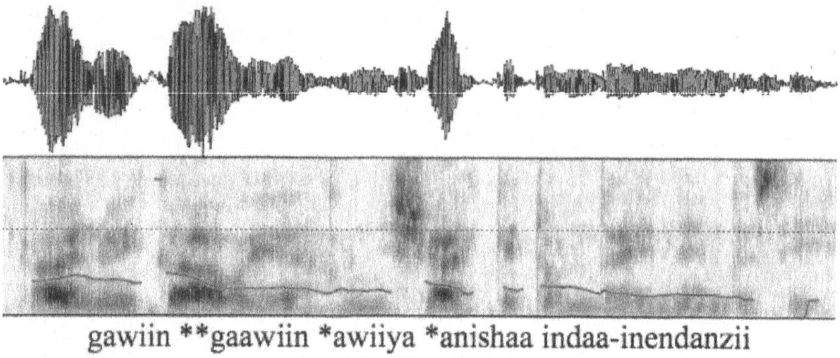

(8′) Syntactic parse of §3.1b (see (8))

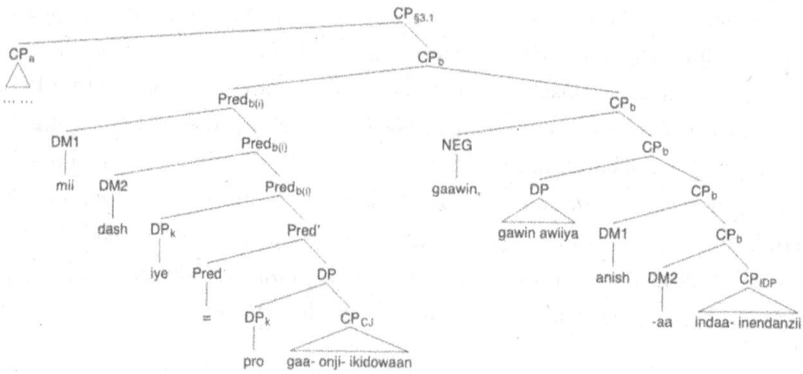

demarcates the right margin, and is preceded by a left-adjoined equative PredP (which hosts a relative clause).

Using Discourse Markers to Detect Structure

Not only is Fairbanks's (2016) characterization of Ojibwe DMs as occupying P1 or P2 consistent with the data in Nancy Jones's (2013) counseling speech, it can also be used to uncover subtle nuances in syntactic structure. We present two examples of how DMs can be used to detect structure. Our first breakthrough relating to prosody-syntax mapping—in particular how DM prosody guides parsing—came from §3.3, which has a sequence of two conjunct mode CPs, with the second introduced by DM_1 *nashke*; see (2) above. Based on the published

English translation, we treated this span as a single phrase, so the occurrence of DM_1 *nashke* was unexpected. However, listening to the audio revealed that the utterance contained two prosodic phrases, identifiable by a pause between *awe* and *nashke*. The next step was to recognize that *nashke* was in fact in P1, consistent with its max pitch. These two prosodic cues—pausing and max pitch—led us to reexamine the syntactic dependency between the CPs, which revealed themselves to be relative clauses, each hosted by a DP, with the two DPs related via equative predication; the structure is given in (2').

FIGURE 8. Prosodic coding of §3.3 (see (2))

	OJIBWE	ENGLISH
§3.3a	Minik ge**go gaa-izhi-dibaajimot awe	'What he speaks not much about,
§3.3b	‖ [$_{DM_1}$ na-**sh-ke] o*maa ge-niin |	look this is what here me too,
	*gaa-izhi-*gikinoo'amaagowaan	I was taught'

The last example that we consider presents an even more serious challenge to the view that DMs occupy P1 or P2 relative to the CP they are construed with. This concerns (9), whose pitch track is in Figure 10, and whose parse appears in (9'); anomalous is the occurrence of the complex DM *aaniishnaa* in sentence-final position. We conjecture that the unusual surface ordering of *aaniishnaa* accords with its canonical left-peripheral position, but only if one accepts that it attaches to an elided CP; [CP c] in (9').

Suggestive strands of evidence support the ellipsis analysis. First is the fact that the preceding CP (CP_a) is introduced by a complex DM: DM_2 *dash* in combination

FIGURE 9. Pitch and waveform of §3.3b: ***nashke*** *omaa geniin gaa-izhi-gikinoo'amaagowaan*; (see (2))

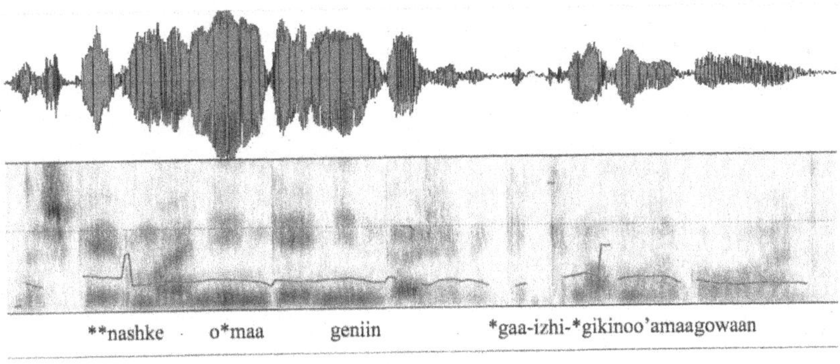

(2′) Syntactic parse of §3.3 (see (2))

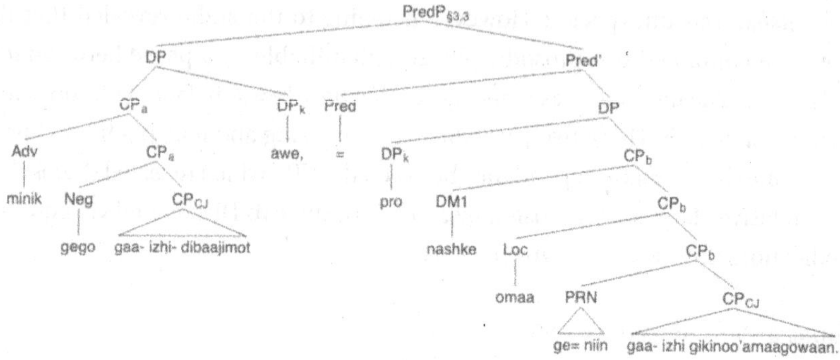

with the focus particle *wiin*. If *anishnaa* and *dash win* were to combine, this would yield the unattested sequence *[*anishnaa dash wiin* [CP...]]. Although DM strings are possible, they are structured in a particular fashion; examples are given in (14)–(16). In (14) we see a sequence of two P1 DMs (*aanissh mii*) followed by a P2 DM (*sa*). In (15), we see a sequence of three P2 DMs (*sha go naa*). And in (16), we see multiple occurrences of DM_1 *mii*, each of which introduces a distinct CP, yielding its characteristic sequencing effect. Crucially, in both (14) and (15), the DM sequences involve simplex expressions.

FIGURE 10. Pitch and waveform of §2.3: *gaawiin* ***dash win*** *awiyaa wikaa indaa-wetawaasii* ***aaniishinaa***; (see (9))

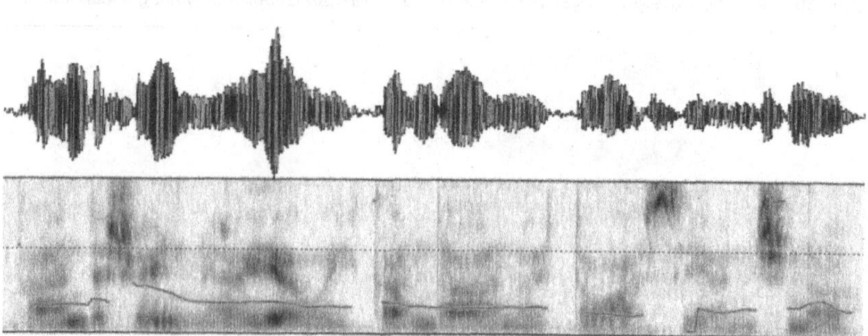

gaawiin *dash win awiyaa *wikaa indaa-weta**waasii aaniishi**naa

(9') Syntactic parse of §2.3 (see (9))

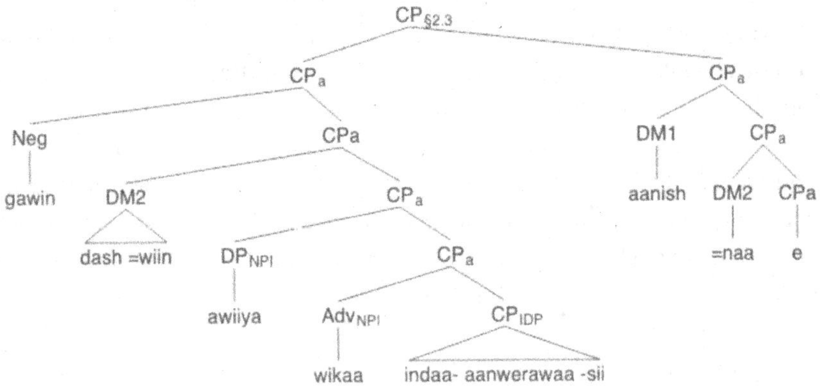

(14)

	P1	P1	P2		
"Aa haaw!"	**aaniish**	**mii**	**sa**	giwenh	gii-windmaadwaad
ok	well	so	EMPH.NVL	allegedly	PST-tell.RCP(3PL.PRX.CJ)

giwi ninwag,	"zhaadaa!"
DEM(3PL.PRX)	man.NA.PL let's.go

'"Okay!," well, it seems that those men told each other, "Let's go!"'
(SO1.33, from Valentine 2001:149 (53))

(15)

	P2	P2	P2	
gaawiin	**sha**	**go**	**naa**	indeapiitizisiin

'I'm not that old' (Fairbanks 2016:103)

(16)

P1	P2		
Mii$_a$	**dash**	gchi-gtaamgok	'**And$_a$** there was a great storm
mii$_b$-sh		gii-gnabaasninig iw wijimaanwaa	**and$_b$** it capsized their boat
mii$_c$	**dash**	gii-gbwnaabaagwewaad,	**and$_c$** they drowned,
mii$_d$	**dash**	gaa-wnji-wiiji-yaawaad maaba	**and$_d$** that's why this boy was
gwiiwzens niw ookmisan.			staying with his grandmother.'

(AD13.2, from Valentine 2001:151 (58))

Applying these observations to (9'), one possible reason why *anishnaa* is pushed into final position may be because it is not possible to combine complex DMs with one another. On this view, the unattested sequence in (17) would be prohibited because it would involve the interpolation of DM_1 and DM_2, as *anish* and *dash* are both drawn from the P1 set, and while *naa* and *wiin* are drawn from the P2 set. This is what makes the equivalent of (18a) impossible in Ojibwe. If so, then the solution adopted by the speaker of this text is to exploit CP ellipsis (18b), which places *anishnaa* in apparent sentence-final position. Although this is an admittedly abstract analysis, it has the virtue of making precise predictions about the contexts in which we expect to find sentence-final DMs.

(17) *P1 P2 P1 P2
anish-naa dash win
['And look, so then']

(18)	a. #	**'Look, and so then,**	it's not that I would ever disbelieve anyone'
	b.	**And so then,**	it's not that I would ever disbelieve anyone'
		'Look,	~~<it's not that I would ever disbelieve anyone>~~

Conclusion

Examining how the deployment of pitch on DMs structures the narrative is part of the larger question of how speakers recruit prosodic features and to what end. One potential weakness is the fact that the audio recording—even after two rounds of cleaning with Audacity—contains substantial background noise. This means that we could not rely on PRAAT's automatic pitch locator. Another limitation of our study is that, so far, it only examines one speaker on one occasion, and it is well known that the use of DMs varies across speakers and contexts, and so future work will study a wider range of data sets. In developing our analysis, we have drawn upon several analytic tools, including: (i) morphology, in order to develop conventions for tagging word classes (as there are currently no agreed-upon norms for classifying DMs)[6]; (ii) syntax, in order to develop diagnostics for how DMs are integrated into clause structure; (iii) information structure, in order to develop diagnostics that identify the left and right periphery of the clause; (iv) prosody, in order to track how it maps onto morphology, syntax, and discourse structure. While confirming previous classifications of Ojibwe DMs—in particular Fairbanks's (2016) contrast between P1 and P2 DMs—this approach has also yielded new insights. The most significant finding is that when DMs occur in non-canonical positions, this is attributable to independent syntactic factors. The specific cases we looked at involved the interaction of DMs with other CP-adjoined constituents (4), the interaction of DMs with equative PredPs (2), and the interaction of DMs with each other, which can force blocking effects (9). Further research will establish to what extent these represent general strategies. Another finding is the discovery—to our knowledge not noted elsewhere before—that DMs anchor to minimal utterances consisting of non-verbal predicates analyzed as PredP.

We end with a puzzle: although Ojibwe sentences are often accompanied by DMs, the latter are never obligatory; this is what Degand (2019:1) calls "the paradox of discourse markers." Fairbanks (2016:158) relates the optionality of Ojibwe DMs to the fact that the language uses asyndesis: "Ojibwe sentence[s] . . . may tolerate a total absence of any connectors at all and still remain grammatical" (Fairbanks 2016:158). This insight leads us to expect DMs to be compositional (in that they are additive), and this is what Fairbanks (2016:70) concludes: the meaning of a DM in combination with a proposition *p* should be a function of the meaning of the parts. Moreover, it predicts that the meaning of complex DMs should likewise be compositional. The hypothesized semantic compositionality of Ojibwe DMs also predicts that they will exhibit regular syntactic behavior. Treating DMs as regular expressions departs from most analyses of DMs, which treat them as exceptional relative to semantic force and syntactic integration (Schiffrin 1987, 2003; Brinton 1996). We look forward to testing the compositionality hypothesis in future work.

NOTES

1. Our research on prosody-syntax integration of DMs is part of a larger initiative aimed at using the *Dibaajimowinan* texts to develop resources for language researchers, teachers, and learners. It is funded by Queen's University Leaders' Fund. We are exploring ways of visualizing text presentation, with the goal of creating a flexible online interface where users select which information to display. This is why examples (1)–(9) and (12) have 6 lines: line 1 is the published text; line 2 is the transcription; line 3 is the segmentation; line 4 glosses in accordance with the *Ojibwe People's Dictionary*; line 5 glosses for cross-linguistic comparison; line 6 is our translation. (We use two more lines, not shown here, namely, the published translation and a literal translation.)

2. In Table 1, F2016 stands for Fairbanks 2016; J2013 stands for Jones 2013. Textual conventions: A paragraph is assigned a number preceded by J ("Jones"), e.g. J§1, J§2, J§3, J§4). Each sentence is assigned a sub-number, e.g. J§1.1 = paragraph 1, sentence 1. A complex sentence (a CP that contains several CPs) is assigned a letter, e.g. J§1.1a = paragraph §1, sentence 1, CP a. Non-root CPs—including both complement and adjunct CPs (temporal and manner adjunct CPs, relative CP) are assigned a Roman numeral, e.g. §1.1(i) = paragraph §1, sentence 1, adjoined CP (i). Conventions: ** = Max pitch prominence, * = pitch prominence, || = intonation break, 1 = 1st person, 2 = 2nd person, 3 = 3rd person animate, 0 = 3rd person inanimate, ∃ = existential quantifier, ADD = additive, ADV = adverb, APL = applicative, CJ = conjunct mode, D = determiner, CNTR = contrastive, DEG = degree, DISC = discourse, DM = Discourse Marker, DM = Discourse Marker, DM1 = Position 1 Discourse Marker, DM2 = Position 2 Discourse Marker, DEM = demonstrative, DETR = detransitive, DXS = deixis, EMPH = emphatic, EXP = expressive vowel length, FOC = focus, FUT = future, GNR = generic, INDF = indefinite, IC = initial change, IDP = independent mode, INTER = interactional, INV = inverse, IRR = irrealis, ITJ = interjection, LOC = locative, MNR = manner, NA = animate noun, NEG = negation, NI = inanimate noun, NMLZ = nominalizer, NPI = negative polarity item, NVL = novel, PL = plural, PROSP = prospective, PXL = proximal, PRN = pronoun, PC = particle, PFV = perfective, PRED = predicate, PV = preverb, QNT = quantifier, RED = reduplication, RT = root, SEQ = sequencer, SG = singular, TA = transitive animate verb, TMP = temporal, SEQ = sequence, TR = transitive, VCE = voice, WH = content interrogative.
3. Relative to the set of P1 DMs, ***mii*** is unusual in being a single syllable (CVV); all other P1 DMs are disyllabic (e.g. *nashke*, *aaniish*, *ahaw*). The data in Fairbanks (2016) clearly aligns ***mii*** with P1, but Rhodes (1998) presents the minimal pair in (i). *Mii* "is extremely common in narratives . . . [and] serves as a marker of normal discourse sequencing . . . [and] is a focusing element" (Valentine 2001:963). For exemplification see Rhodes 1998; Valentine 2001; and Fairbanks 2016.

(i) a. Walpole Ottawa (Rhodes 1998:287 (3a))
Gye go **mii** gii-aanzkonyeyaang. . . (B T9:15)
'And then we changed clothes . . .'

b. Manitoulin Island (Rhodes 1998:287 (4))
Mii gye goo gii-bskaabnaashkwindwaa.
'And then they were driven back.'

4. A possibility that we do not discuss is whether DMs are hosted by dedicated functional heads outside of the CP domain. For relevant discussion, see Wiltschko (2018). The discussion in the main text focuses on how DMs interact with other expressions that attach to CP, and treats all of them as CP-adjuncts.
5. See Déchaine (1997) for related discussion of how nominal predication is used as a scene-setting device in Plains Cree.
6. Many DMs seem to be tantalizingly bi-morphemic; e.g. ***-sh*** 'and, and then', which functions as a P2 DM, also occurs in many DMs, e.g. *(i)**dash*** 'and then', *mii**sh*** 'and then', *(i)nash**ke*** ~ *(a)**shke*** 'look!', *aanii**sh*** 'well then'. ***-sh*** is also found in adverbs (e.g. *ambegi**sh*** ~ *apegi**sh*** 'I wish', *awanji**sh*** 'persistently', *biini**sh*** 'until') and wh-words (*aanii**sh*** 'how', *awene**sh*** 'who' *(a)wegone**sh*** 'what', *aanapii**sh*** 'when').

REFERENCES

Audacity. https://www.audacityteam.org.

Baker, Mark C. 1996. *The Polysynthesis Parameter.* Oxford: Oxford University Press.

Brinton, Laurel. 1996. *Pragmatic Markers in English: Grammaticalization and Discourse Functions.* Berlin: Mouton de Gruyter.

Dahlstrom, Amy. 2003. Focus Constructions in Meskwaki (Fox). *Proceedings of the LFG03 Conference*, ed. by Miriam Butt and Tracy H. King, pp. 144–163. Stanford, CA: Center for the Study of Language and Information.

Déchaine, Rose-Marie. 1997. Nominal Predication in Plains Cree. *Papers of the 28th Algonquian Conference*, ed. by David H. Pentland, pp. 105–135. Winnipeg: University of Manitoba Press.

Degand, Liesbeth. 2019. The Paradox of Discourse Markers: Evidence from Production under Cognitive Load. Paper read at the 6th International Conference on Discourse Markers in Romance Languages, University of Bergamo.

Fairbanks, Brendan. 2016. *Ojibwe Discourse Markers.* Lincoln: University of Nebraska Press.

Jelinek, Eloise. 1984. Empty Categories, Case, and Configurationality. *Natural Language and Linguistic Theory* 2:39–76.

Jones, Nancy (Ogimaawigwa-nebiik, Ogimaakwewibiik). 2013. Gakina Dibaajimowin Gwayakwaawan. *Dibaajimowinaan: Anishinaabe Stories of Culture and Respect*, ed. by Nigaanigiizhig [Jim Saint-Arnold], pp. 9–10. Odana, WI: Great Lakes Indian Fish and Wildlife Commission.

Lieshout, Pascal van. 2003. PRAAT Short Tutorial: A Basic Introduction. https://web.stanford.edu/dept/linguistics/corpora/material/PRAAT_workshop_manual_v421.pdf.

Lochbihler, Brittany, and Éric Mathieu. 2016. Clause-Typing and Feature Inheritance of Discourse Features. *Syntax* 19(4):354–391.

Rhodes, Richard. 1998. The Syntax and Pragmatics of Ojibwe *mii*. *Papers of the 29th Algonquian Conference*, ed. by David H. Pentland, pp. 286–294. Winnipeg: University of Manitoba Press.

Russell, Kevin, and Charlotte Reinholtz. 1996. Hierarchical Structure in a Non-Configurational Language: Asymmetries in Swampy Cree. *Proceedings of the 14th West Coast Conference on Formal Linguistics*, ed. by José Camacho, Lina Choueiri, and Maki Watanabe, pp. 431–445. Stanford, CA: CSLI Publications.

Schiffrin, Deborah. 1987. *Discourse Markers*. Cambridge: Cambridge University Press.

Schiffrin, Deborah. 2003. Discourse Markers: Language, Meaning and Context. *The Handbook of Discourse Analysis*, ed. by Deborah Shiffrin, Deborah Tannen, and Heidi E. Hamilton, pp. 54–75. Malden, MA: Blackwell.

Valentine, J. Randolph. 2001. *Nishnaabemwin Reference Grammar*. Toronto: University of Toronto Press.

Wiltschko, Martina. 2018. Response Particles beyond Answering. *Order and Structure in Syntax 1*, ed. by Laura R. Bailey and Michelle Sheehan, pp. 241–279. Berlin: Language Science Press.

Put No Faith in the Foxes. They Are a Proud People. They Despise the French and All the Other Nations Also

Understanding Meshkwaki Social Landscapes through Semiotic Analysis of Ethnonyms

Erik D. Gooding

In the middle of the seventeenth century, as the French moved westward across the continent, they encountered the various Native groups that lived in what they claimed as New France.[1] Accumulating knowledge of the Indigenous peoples as they progressed, French military and government representatives, missionaries, trappers, traders, and settlers moved in waves through this new land. Either west of the Great Lakes in present-day Wisconsin, perhaps near Lake Winnebago, or north of the Great Lakes, a group of French traders came face to face with a small hunting party of an Indigenous group they had not yet encountered.[2] During this initial interaction it is conjectured that the French, using their limited knowledge of Ojibwe (speakers of which they had previously encountered), attempted direct communication. While we do not know what was said in detail, we do know that the French asked this group of hunters "from what group did they come?" History records that they responded with a variant of waakoohaki, which the French understood as 'fox'. Prior to this meeting, this group was known to the French by the Ojibwe exonym Otakaamiik 'people of the other shore', but following this meeting the French used their own exonym, Les Renards 'the Foxes'.[3]

Anthropologists, ethnohistorians, and linguists are extremely intrigued by this type of encounter. They have approached the study of these encounters, or events, from two perspectives, as a contextual event and as a performative event. Fogelson (1989), from a contextual perspective, would refer to this encounter/event as an activity "which occurs at a given time and place" (133). He further suggests that "Events are also considered to have properties and relationships" (133). From this contextual perspective we are able to examine events as "minimal units in historical discourse, [that] must be described, analyzed, ordered, and interpreted" (134). These events are embedded within the context of a culture or cultures, and can reflect historical and sociocultural processes.

Hymes (1962), from a performative perspective, would seek to analyze the various components of the encounter/event to understand its communicative aspects. From this perspective, we are able to examine these elements of communication in order to develop an understanding of the event's meaning(s).

In previous literature the interpretation of this event has been that the French inquiry was answered by clan identification, rather than a tribal identification.[4] This group, the people of the other shore, or the Foxes, refer to themselves as the Meshkwaki, meaning 'People of the Red Earth'. They are comprised of patrilineal exogamous clans, which also serve as ritual and naming units.[5] Today the Fox clan, along with the Bear, Wolf, Eagle, Thunder, Fish, and Swan clans, are active to some degree in the Meshkwaki community. Since this event in the 1600s, the Meshkwaki people have been referred to by a variety of exonyms, names that others refer to them by. However, the term 'Fox' or terms meaning 'Fox' have been the prevalent forms, including in the official U.S. government designation for the Meshkwaki, the Sac and Fox Nation of the Mississippi in Iowa.

This paper seeks not only to understand the greater processes of internal naming systems, endonyms, and external naming systems, exonyms, but also explores the reciprocal nature of naming events and their subsequent relationships. Through a semiotic analysis of this event, coupled with insight from Actor/Network Theory, a new deeper, thicker description and understanding of this first French-Meshkwaki encounter can be achieved.

Understanding 'Fox'

When the French individual addressed the Meshkwaki in his supposedly broken Ojibwe (Clifton 1978), I consider this a formal contextual and performative event. It occurred at a "given place and time," and the "properties and relationships" including its communicative elements must be considered.

A semiotic analysis of this event necessitates an understanding of the cultural sign systems at play, and this analysis understands ethnonyms as symbols with varying levels of indexical awareness. Following Silverstein (1998), this initial encounter is a performance in the context of social flux between humans in a lived reality in which identities are negotiated by the Meshkwaki and the French, and in the case of the Meshkwaki, a particular identity, that of 'Fox,' is projected. This projection is important to our reinterpretation. Why did this Meshkwaki answer with 'Fox'? What does it mean to be 'Fox'?

What if 'Fox' meant something more than simple clan affiliation to that small Meshkwaki hunting party meeting the French for the first time? A useful multifaceted concept to consider at this point is that of "voice," constructed by Bakhtin (1981, 1984), Hill (1985, 1986), Silverstein and Urban (1996); advanced by Parks and DeMallie (1992) and Dinwoodie (1998) among others; and one that I employed in Gooding 2004. For the purpose of this study, I employ Silverstein and Urban's (1996:8) denotation of voice, the "role inhabitance in discursive practices." At its most elementary level as assumed by Brown (1964), Clifton (1978), and Jones (1939), voice can be understood as the literal voice of the individual Meshkwaki who replied to the French inquiry. But a deeper understanding of Meshkwaki political organization reveals that no individual speaks for themself; instead, only individuals in certain roles can speak for the whole.[6]

Contemporary Meshkwaki refer to the often-cited quote of Peemosaaha, a Meshkwaki leader who angrily yelled "Lest ye forget the Fox are immortal" at the French leaders during a battle in 1712 near Detroit (Edmunds and Peyser 1993). Meshkwaki politics is based on consensus building from the bottom up. The leader could not, and would not, speak for the people without their consensus. Meshkwaki today do not see the quote attributed to Peemosaaha as a quote of Peemosaaha, but as a quote of the Meshkwaki people. He was simply acting in his role as a mouthpiece for the people.

A reconsideration of voice suggests that during their initial meeting with the French, the Meshkwaki man was not speaking as an individual who was a member of the Fox clan, as earlier scholars have claimed, but from within a state of social flux he was negotiating with the French from the perspective of his lived reality, as a representative of the Meshkwaki. He was in a specific role, perhaps a *mayaawoseewa* 'war party leader', and like Peemosaaha, his role allowed him to speak for the communal whole.

From this new understanding of the Meshkwaki voice at this event, the question "what does it mean to be Fox?" can be addressed. Meshkwaki political leadership consisted of a tripartite system with each *okima* 'chief' having specific duties and responsibilities. These three chiefs were the Bear chief, with the responsibilities of peace/internal leadership; the Fox chief, with the responsibilities of war/external leadership; and the Thunder chief, with the responsibility of declaring which of the two other leaders were in power. In some ways the Fox and Bear leaders acted like the classic southeastern Red/White organizations (see Gearing 1958).

By identifying himself as "Fox," the Meshkwaki individual was making a tribally sanctioned calculated political maneuver. All external political endeavors were the purview of the Fox *okima* with bottom-up authority ordained by the people. Beyond this declaration, this first encounter, this event, this performance in the context of social flux, also creates an actor-network, following the work of Latour (2005). Actor-network theory suggests that as actors enter into a relationship, they create a network between them with material and semiotic components that provide an ontological understanding of that relationship. This emergent network between the French and the Meshkwaki was re-created as well as reconfirmed through subsequent performances. This initial public act by the Meshkwaki actor, in his culturally defined role, informs the French actor of the nature of their relationship: we are "Fox," and provides the Meshkwaki interpretation of the nature of this newly created network: "We are antagonistic towards you." Ethnonyms, including this endonym, are enmeshed in histories and are indexical linkages to peoples and power relationships.

This new understanding of what it means to be "Fox" can shed light on other interpretations of Meshkwaki actions/inactions/interactions found in the historical record. Two examples can be reexamined here: la Potherie's (1994) observation of the actions of a Meshkwaki chief and Schenk's (1997) interpretation of Algonquian totems. First, la Potherie mentions two "extractions" (or divisions) among the Meshkwaki, the Red Earths and the Fox. La Potherie noted that Perrot visited the Meshkwaki in 1683 to negotiate peace between them and the Ojibwe, and to secure the release of an Ojibwe girl. Callendar described the situation:

> The chief of the Fox extraction holding this position as a replacement for his brother, whom the Ojibwe had recently killed, repeatedly rejected Perrot's request to smoke the calumet and come to terms. The Red Earth chief intervened, persuading him to settle the affair. (1994:111)

Callendar concludes that "While the behavior of the Red Earth chief resembled the moderating actions of the tribal or peace chief, the chief of the Fox extraction seems to have been acting from personal grievance over his brother's death rather than exercising the duties of a war chief" (1994:113). That is, I believe, because he was Fox, he could not have peace with the Ojibwe; that is not his responsibility. His job and his culturally sanctioned role was to be antagonistic, to seek conflict, and to succeed in conflict. While he very may well have been grieving the loss of his brother, it was the Red Earth extraction leader's responsibility to negotiate peace, not the Fox leader's.

Second, Schenk (1997) observes that "At the time of first contact each upper Great Lakes Algonquian village had a symbol, usually an animal, which is used to designate itself and which was used in turn by other groups to name them" (341). She notes that the totem employed by the Meshkwaki in a 1701 treaty of peace with the Iroquois was a "fox." Schenk further wrote, "The extended concept of totem, which was nothing more than a village or family naming system, had many functions in early Algonquian society. Not only was it the family name, but it served to regulate marriage and to establish a bond among relatives however distant" (343). She also speculates that over time the upper Algonquian peoples and their totems may have begun to take on some of the characteristics of central Algonquian clans. This is where the Meshkwaki stand out in her discussion, as the only central Algonquian in her data. Her interpretations of their motivations and use of the fox symbol are based on upper Algonquian understandings, not derived from an understanding of Meshkwaki-specific culture. The Meshkwaki, as was required in this context, were simply using their external symbol in dealing with the external world.

This semiotic approach to understanding the endonym 'Fox' illustrates the usefulness of this method, and suggests that a reexamination of all Meshkwaki exonyms could lead to a deeper understanding of the ever-changing Meshkwaki social landscapes.

Meshkwaki Ethnonyms

Native North America is full of ethnonyms from a variety of sources, from the groups themselves or from their friends or enemies, with forms either learned directly or from an indirect source. The nature of a tribal ethnonym is dependent upon the actors involved in the initial communicative event in which the emerging actor-network was created. In the case of the French-Meshkwaki example, the French directly asked the Meshkwaki for the name that they wished to be called. But in other cases, the group being named in an emergent proto-actor-network may not have been present. For example, the French already knew of the Meshkwaki when they met them—they had been previously made aware of them by the Ojibwe. That exchange, between the French and Ojibwe over the *Otakaamiik* 'people of the other shore' created an incomplete proto-actor-network, which was finalized when the French and the Meshkwaki came face-to-face. At that encounter, the ethnonym that the French used for the Meshkwaki changed from a borrowed term from the Ojibwe to the term given to them directly by the Meshkwaki, and the actor-network was fully established. In other completed networks, ethnonyms may not necessarily change from a borrowed proto-network form.

With each successive migration from their origin site near Lac St. Jean in Quebec, the Meshkwaki entered into new networks with new actors in new locations. As they negotiated these new relationships, the Meshkwaki either borrowed existing ethnonyms employed by other groups (either autonyms or exonyms), or they transformed a non-ethnonym into an exonym. I first provide selected examples of borrowed ethnonyms:

(1) The Meshkwaki adopted the autonym of other groups, such as Kickapoo (Callendar, Poe, and Pope 1978) and Shawnee (Callendar 1978c).

(2) The Meshkwaki adopted exonyms applied to a group by others. Examples of these include those borrowed from other Algonquian languages, such as Menominee (*manoominiwa* 'wild rice people') from Ojibwe (Spindler 1978) and Winnebago (*wiinipyeekohaki* 'people of the dirty water') from perhaps Potawatomi (Golla and Goddard 1978), as well as those borrowed from Siouan languages, such as the forms for Comanche, *patohka* 'enemy' (Parks 2001a), and the Sauk of Kansas and Nebraska, *nimaha* 'dirty water' (Goodtracks 1992), both from Chiwere.

Second, Meshkwaki-based forms follow:

(3) The Meshkwaki state that they were present when the Sauk were created, giving them the ability/authority to bestow their name on them, *asaakiwaki* 'people emerging' (Callendar 1978b).
(4) The Meshkwaki may have named other groups as well, including their term for the Potawatomi, *pehkineniihaki* 'aliens' (Clifton 1978).

Third, the Meshkwaki also transformed non-ethnonyms into exonyms, for example:

(5) Meshkwaki refer to the Dakota as *ashaaha*, a direct borrowing from Dakota *sháŋ* 'vagina' (Riggs 1992:440).

Among these exonyms are forms that are pejoratives (Dakota), forms that describe origins (Sauk), forms that describe another group's language and culture in relation to the Meshkwaki (Potawatomi), forms that describe a political stance (Comanche), forms that describe location (Shawnee), and forms that describe a key aspect of a group (Menominee).

In regard to ethnonyms applied to the Meshkwaki, four types are found: (1) those based on the endonym Meshkwaki, (2) those based on 'Fox', (3) those based on 'people of the other shore', and (4) those that refer to the Meshkwaki with the form for Sauk. Examples include:

(1) The Sauk and Kickapoo refer to the Meshkwawki as Meshkwaki, as do the Seneca in reference to the Meshkwaki group living among them (Hunter 1956).
(2) The Winnebago (Morse 1822), Shawnee (Voegelin 1938–1940), and Potawatomi (Gatschet 1878–1893) employ forms based on 'fox'. In addition, the Dakota borrowed the Winnebago form for their use (Riggs 1852).
(3) The Ojibwe call the Meshkwaki *otakaamiik* 'people of the other shore' (Jones 1911) and there is a secondary Menominee form *otaakaameew* (Bloomfield 1962).
(4) The Ioway (Goodtracks 1992) and Omaha (Fletcher and La Flesche 1911) refer to the Meshkwaki as Sauk.

Ethnonyms and Networks

Throughout history the Meshkwaki have created, negotiated, and renegotiated relationships with other groups. The ethnonyms employed by both actors within these networks are semiotic representations of these relationships, and can help us understand the nature of their relationship. Generally speaking, the Meshkwaki have participated in three types of networks.

First, the Meshkwaki-Dakota network represents an antagonistic network. The two ethnonyms employed in the network, the pejorative *ashaaha* used by the Meshkwaki towards the Dakota, and *bešdeke*, the borrowed form of the Winnebago *wašereke* 'fox' that the Dakota use for the Meshkwaki, illustrate the nature of their relationship. The previously examined usage of fox-related terms positions the Dakota, along with their Siouan relative the Winnebago, in political opposition to the Meshkwaki, while the use of a pejorative by the Meshkwaki indicates their contempt for the Dakota. This interpretation is supported their history of conflict (la Potherie 1911–1912; Hagan 1958). The majority of Meshkwaki networks are similar in nature to the Meshkwaki-Dakota network.

Second, the Meshwaki-Ioway network represents an ambivalent network. The Ioway refer to the Meshkwaki using their term for the Sauk *thake*, while the Meshkwaki use the term *aayahooweewa*, a form that has no meaning in Algonquian or Siouan languages (Parks 2001b). Neither employs the endonym of the other, while the Ioway's use of the Sauk form represents the Sauk's geographic and political positions between the Ioway and the Meshkwaki (Hagan 1958). Meshkwaki oral traditions recount the historic role of the Sauk as middlemen to the Ioway, as well as the Meshkwaki's ambivalence towards the smaller, weaker Ioway. This type of network was infrequent.

Third, the Meshkwaki-Kickapoo network represents a friendly network. Along with the Sauk and Mascouten, the Kickapoo speak a dialect of the language they share with the Meshkwaki. Both groups recognize their shared linguistic and cultural heritage, and each employs the other's endonym as its exonym. Friendly networks existed between the Meshkwaki and only their closest relatives, the Sauk and Kickapoo, although at times even these relationships were strained and contentious (Hagan 1958).

Conclusion

Ethnonyms are semiotic expressions of actor-networks that are framed within spatiotemporal contexts. The communicative act of identifying and/or naming through explicitly predetermined voices with specific roles establishes the nature and perspective of the actor-network, which is further re-created through subsequent performances. These natures, perspectives, and characters are all subject to reshaping as the voices or roles change or the conditions of the relationship are altered.

In the case of the Meshkwaki, they enter into networks with others, using a predetermined voice that indicates the nature and intent of their perspective, either antagonistic, ambivalent, or friendly, that is framed from their shared sociocultural understandings and history. Others react to their framing and establish networks from their own perspective. The totality of these networks becomes the essence of intertribal interactions. Understanding this approach to ethnonyms provides us with a method of interpretation that yields rich results, that allows us to revisit materials through ethnohistory, and to more accurately understand the complexity of social life in contested, ever-changing worlds.

NOTES

1. Examples for this paper were collected during fieldwork among the Meshkwaki community; from the *Handbook of North American Indians*, Northeast and Plains volumes (Callendar 1978a, 1978b); and from materials from the National Anthropological Archives. I would like to acknowledge members of the following Meshkwaki families: Bear, Brown, Buffalo, Davenport, Kapayou, Keahna, Lasley, Morgan, Pushetonequa, Snow, Wanatee, Whitebreast, and Youngbear, representing the Bear, Eagle, Fish, Fox, Swan, Thunder, and Wolf clans. I would also like to thank the anonymous reviewers for their comments, as well as the valued comments from Bret Salter. For more general information on the Meshkwaki and their ethnonyms, see Callendar (1978a) and Goddard (1978).
2. This composite reconstruction is based on accounts from Brown (1964), Clifton (1978), Jones (1939), and Meshkwaki Oral Traditions (MOT).
3. Meshkwaki terms follow the orthographic conventions from Goddard and Thomason (2014). For a discussion of the spelling and pronunciation of Meshkwaki and various orthographies, see Goddard and Thomason (2014:1–2). For overviews of the Meshkwaki

language in general, see Bloomfield (1925, 1927), Goddard and Thomason (2014), and Voorhis (1971).

4. See Brown (1964), Clifton (1978), and Jones (1939).
5. Goddard (1975) has clearly demonstrated that in the seventeenth century Meshkwaki clans were also residential village units.
6. Contemporary fieldwork on traditional cultural topics yields the same result: no one can speak for the group. Elders repeatedly emphasize this notion.

REFERENCES

Bakhtin, Mikhail M. 1981. *The Dialogic Imagination.* Austin: University of Texas Press.

Bakhtin, Mikhail M. 1984. *Problems of Dostoevsky's Poetics.* Minneapolis: University of Minnesota Press.

Bloomfield, Leonard. 1925. On the Sound System of Central Algonquian. *Language* 1(4):130–156.

Bloomfield, Leonard. 1927. Literate and Illiterate Speech. *American Speech* 2:432–439.

Bloomfield, Leonard. 1962. *The Menomini Language.* New Haven, CT: Yale University Press.

Brown, Richard Frank. 1964. A Social History of the Mesquakie Indians, 1800–1963. MA thesis, Iowa State University.

Callendar, Charles. 1978a. Fox. *Handbook of North American Indians*, vol. 15: *Northeast*, ed. by Bruce G. Trigger, pp. 636–647. Washington, DC: Smithsonian Institution.

Callendar, Charles. 1978b. Sauk. *Handbook of North American Indians*, vol. 15: *Northeast*, ed. by Bruce G. Trigger, pp. 648–655. Washington, DC: Smithsonian Institution.

Callendar, Charles. 1978c. Shawnee. *Handbook of North American Indians*, vol. 15: *Northeast*, ed. by Bruce G. Trigger, pp. 622–635. Washington, DC: Smithsonian Institution.

Callendar, Charles. 1994. Central Algonquian Moieties. *North American Indian Anthropology: Essays on Society and Culture*, ed. by Raymond J. DeMallie and Alfonso Ortiz, pp. 108–124. Norman: University of Oklahoma Press.

Callendar, Charles, Richard K. Poe, and Susan M. Pope. 1978. Kickapoo. *Handbook of North American Indians*, vol. 15: *Northeast*, ed. by Bruce G. Trigger, pp. 656–665. Washington, DC: Smithsonian Institution.

Clifton, James A. 1978. Potawatomi. *Handbook of North American Indians*, vol. 15: *Northeast*, ed. by Bruce G. Trigger, pp. 725–742. Washington, DC: Smithsonian Institution.

Dinwoodie, David W. 1998. Authorizing Voices: Going Public in an Indigenous Language. *Current Anthropology* 13(2):193–223.

Edmunds, R. David, and Joseph L. Peyser. 1993. *The Fox Wars: The Mesquakie Challenge to New*

France. Norman: University of Oklahoma Press.

Fletcher, Alice C., and Francis La Flesche. 1911. The Omaha Tribe. *27th Annual Report of the Bureau of American Ethnology for the Years 1905–1906*, pp. 27–262. Washington, DC: Government Printing Office.

Fogelson, Raymond. 1989. The Ethnohistory of Events and Nonevents. *Ethnohistory* 36:133–147.

Gatschet, Albert S. 1878–1893. Vocabularies, Texts, Notes: Shawnee, Potawatomi, Chippewa, Mainly 1878–1879. Manuscript No. 68 in National Anthropological Archives, Smithsonian Institution, Washington, DC.

Gearing, Fred. 1958. The Structural Poses of 18th Century Cherokee Villages. *American Anthropologist* 60(6):1148–1157.

Goddard, Ives. 1975. Fox Social Organization, 1650–1850. *Papers of the 6th Algonquian Conference*, ed. by William Cowan, pp. 128–140. Ottawa: National Museum of Man, Ethnology Division, Mercury Series Paper 23.

Goddard, Ives. 1978. Southeastern Ojibwa [Synonymy]. *Handbook of North American Indians*, vol. 15: *Northeast*, ed. by Bruce G. Trigger, pp. 768–770. Washington, DC: Smithsonian Institution.

Goddard, Ives, and Lucy Thomason. 2014. A Meskwaki-English and English-Meskwaki Dictionary, Based on Early Twentieth-Century Writings by Native Speakers. Petoskey, MI: Mundart Press.

Golla, Susan, and Ives Goddard. 1978. Winnebago [Synonymy]. *Handbook of North American Indians*, vol. 15: *Northeast*, ed. by Bruce G. Trigger, p. 706. Washington, DC: Smithsonian Institution.

Gooding, Erik D. 2004. Sing from the Heart, Sing for the People: An Ethnography of Dakotan Song and Singing, 1640–2000. PhD thesis, Indiana University.

Goodtracks, Jimm (compiler and editor). 1992. BJM *Ich^e Wawagaxe* IOM Dictionary. Boulder: Center for the Study of the Languages of the Plains and Southwest, Department of Linguistics, University of Colorado.

Hagan, William T. 1958. *The Sac and Fox Indians*. Norman: University of Oklahoma Press.

Hill, Jane. 1985. The Grammar of Consciousness and the Consciousness of Grammar. *American Ethnologist* 12(4):725–737.

Hill, Jane. 1986. The Reconfiguration of the Anthropology of Language. *Cultural Anthropology* 1:89–102.

Hunter, William A. 1956. Refugee Fox Settlements among the Senecas. *Ethnohistory* 3(1):11–20.

Hymes, Dell. 1962. The Ethnography of Speaking. *Anthropology and Human Behavior*, ed. by Thomas Gladwin and William Sturtevant, pp. 13–53. Washington, DC: Anthropological Society of Washington.

Jones, William. 1911. Algonquian (Fox). *Handbook of American Indian Languages*, ed. by Franz Boas, pp. 735–873. Washington, DC: Bureau of American Ethnology Bulletin 40.

Jones, William. 1939. *Ethnography of the Fox Indians*, ed. by Margaret Fisher. Washington, DC: Bureau of American Ethnology Bulletin 125.

la Potherie, Claude C. Le Roy Bacqueville. 1911–1912. History of the Savage Peoples Who Are Allies of New France. *Indian Tribes of the Upper Mississippi Valley and Region of the Great Lakes*, ed. by Emma H. Blair, pp. 273–372 in vol. 1, and pp. 11–136 in vol. 2. Cleveland: Arthur H. Clark.

Latour, Bruno. 2005. Reassembling the Social: An Introduction to Actor-Network-Theory. Oxford: Oxford University Press.

Morse, Jedidiah. 1822. A Report to the Secretary of War of the United States, on Indian Affairs, Comprising a Narrative of a Tour Performed in the Summer of 1820, under a Commission of the President of the United States, for the Purpose of Ascertaining, for the Use of the Government, the Actual State of the Indian Tribes in Our Country. New Haven, CT: S. Converse.

Parks, Douglas. 2001a. Comanche [Synonymy]. *Handbook of North American Indians*, vol. 13: *Plains* (2 vols.), ed. by Raymond J. DeMallie, pp. 902–905. Washington, DC: Smithsonian Institution.

Parks, Douglas. 2001b. Iowa [Synonymy]. *Handbook of North American Indians*, vol. 13 (2 vols.), ed. by Raymond J. DeMallie, pp. 445–446. Washington, DC: Smithsonian Institution.

Parks, Douglas R., and Raymond J. DeMallie. 1992. Plains Indian Narratives. *Boundary 2*, 19(3):105–147.

Riggs, Stephen. 1852. Grammar and Dictionary of the Dakota Language: Collected by Members of the Dakota Mission. Smithsonian Contributions to Knowledge 4. Washington, DC.

Riggs, Stephen R. 1992 [1890]. *A Dakota-English Dictionary*. St. Paul: Minnesota State Historical Society Press.

Schenck, Theresa. 1997. The Algonquian Totem and Totemism: A Distortion of the Semantic Field. *Papers of the 28th Algonquian Conference*, ed. by David H. Pentland, pp. 341–353. Winnipeg: University of Manitoba Press.

Silverstein, Michael. 1998. Contemporary Transformations of Local Linguistic Communities. *Annual Review of Anthropology* 27:401–426.

Silverstein, Michael, and Greg Urban. 1996. *Natural Histories of Discourse*. Chicago: University of Chicago Press.

Spindler, Louise S. 1978. Menominee. *Handbook of North American Indians*, vol. 15: *Northeast*, ed. by Bruce G. Trigger, pp. 708–724. Washington, DC: Smithsonian Institution.

Voegelin, Charles F. 1938–1940. Shawnee Stems and the Jacob P. Dunn Dictionary. 5 parts.

Indiana Historical Society, Prehistory Research Series 1(3):63–108, (5):135–167, (8):289–341, (9):345–406, (10):409–476. Indianapolis.

Voorhis, Paul H. 1971. New Notes on the Mesquakie (Fox) Language. *International Journal of American Linguistics* 37(4):238–243.

The Scattered Evidential System of Potawatomi

Robert E. Lewis Jr.

This paper provides an overview of the evidential system in Potawatomi.[1] Evidentiality is described by two core properties: (1) marking source of evidence and (2) membership in grammatical systems (Brugman and Macaulay 2015:201). An example that shows these properties of evidentiality comes from Cheyenne. Cheyenne has a four-way contrast in evidentiality in a suffix slot as shown in (1) from Murray (2016). In (1a), *-nėse* indicates the statement is hearsay. In (1b), *-neho* indicates the statement has a narrative source. In (1c), the morphologically complex *mó-. . .-he* indicates that the speaker infers the statement. Finally, in (1d), when no overt suffix is used, the statement was witnessed.[2]

(1) a. É-hoo'kòhó-nėse.
3-rain-RPT.SG.INAN
'It's raining, they say' or 'It's raining, I hear.'

b. É-hoo'kòhó-neho.
3-rain-NAR.SG.INAN
'It rained, it's told.'

c. Mó-hoo'kòhó-hané-he.
q+3-rain-NEG.INAN-INF
'It's raining, I gather' or 'It must be raining.'

d. É-hoo'kòho-Ø.
3-rain-WTN
'It's raining, I witnessed.' (Murray 2016:493–494)

In this paper I show that the evidential system of Potawatomi has the same functions as Cheyenne's, but these functions are "scattered" (Aikhenvald 2004:80) across three parts of the grammar "rather than existing in paradigmatic opposition to one another" (Brugman and Macaulay 2015:224). These three parts are a second-position enclitic slot, the dubitative mode inflection, and the particle *yédek*.

This paper is organized as follows. The next section describes Potawatomi's core evidential system. After that, I describe speaker certainty in Potawatomi and argue for similarities in evidentiality and epistemicity in Potawatomi. The following section explores the range of meanings available to the dubitative mode, and shows that it cuts across evidentiality and epistemicity. Next, I describe how dubitative inflection is being shifted to the particle *yédek*, and show that this shift captures meanings available for the dubitative mode laid out earlier. The final section concludes the paper.

Potawatomi Evidentiality

The evidential system in Potawatomi has the same functions as Cheyenne: hearsay, inference, and narrative. However, these functions are "scattered" across Potawatomi's grammar, to use the term from Aikhenvald (2004:80). Additionally, unmarked sentences do not indicate a specific evidential value, but are interpreted in context.

Hearsay: me

The second position enclitic *me* marks hearsay as in (2).[3] This is a unique enclitic slot. It is always the first enclitic when enclitics stack from left to right. The speaker in (2) was not a witness to the statement. Rather, the speaker heard it from someone else. Note that Potawatomi has three verbal orders: independent, conjunct, and imperative. The hearsay enclitic may appear with either the conjunct order as shown in (2b), or the independent order as shown in (3), but I am unaware of it ever appearing with the imperative order.

(2) Context: You just got back from a general council meeting.

a. Gde-mgejané.
gde-mgejané.
2-have.a.big.nose
'You have a big nose.'

b. I me ga-kedot o nJohn.

i	me	ga-kedo-t	o	nJohn.
that	HRSY	IC.PST-say.VAI-3SG.CONJ	that	John

'I heard that John said that.' (JT 2020-09-17)

(3) Context: You and I are driving around. We drive by and see that Donald is having a feast during hunting season.
Wgi-ntawé me.

w-gi-ntawé	me.
3-PST-kill.VAI.IND	HRSY

'I hear he killed something (a deer).' (JT 2020-09-17)

Inference: Dubitative Mode

The dubitative mode has been said to mark inferences (Lockwood 2017:132). Consider (4), where an independent order verb uses dubitative mode inflection. The sentence in (4) begins a story that would seem to preclude an inferential meaning because there is no previous evidence to base the inference on, but later in the story Jim Thunder follows (4) up with two pieces of evidence that led him to infer it: his elders had said so and he saw it written down.[4] The dubitative mode may appear in the independent or conjunct orders, but I am unaware of it ever appearing with the imperative order. Note that the conjunct dubitative mode takes a different form than the independent dubitative mode. The dubitative is discussed further below.

(4) Gi-manédgének zhena neshnabék ibe Wabeno wjiyegwan.

gi-mané-dgének	zhe	na	neshnabé-k	ibe	Wabeno
PST-many.VAI-DUB.3PL	EMPH	DM	neshnabé-PL	there	Wabeno

wji-yegwan.
from-direction
'There must have been a lot of Neshnabék towards Wabeno.' (Lockwood 2017:132, JT)

Since the dubitative mode inflection and the hearsay enclitic are not in the same grammatical category, they may be used together. There is no blocking. In (5), *me* appears in second position while the dubitative suffix *-dek* appears on the verb.

(5) Context: You were not home, but Virginia was. She tells you that John stopped by and he was looking for me. You see me later, and tell me the following:
nJohn me ggi bme ndewabmegwdek.
nJohn me g-gi-bme-ndewabmegw-dek.
John HRSY 2-PST-along-look.for.VTA.3>2-DUB
'I heard John must have come by looking for you.' (JT 2020-09-17)

Hearsay Enclitic in Narratives

The hearsay enclitic can also be used as a narrative evidential. First consider that in traditional narratives, the conjunct order verb inflection is used for main clause sentences (Buszard 2003:85). For example, (6a) is the first sentence of a traditional narrative about a raccoon, and as such it uses the conjunct order to establish narration. A narrator can then shift from the conjunct to independent order in order to background information, such as for settings, explanations, and evaluations (Buszard 2003:93). In (6b), the narrator shifts to the independent order for the main clause verb to provide background for the narrative. Note that there are still conjunct order verbs in (6b), but these verbs serve as subordinate clauses, not as the main clause.

(6) a. Ode yadsokan éspen é-bmebtot.
ode yadsokan éspen é-bme-bto-t
this story raccoon FCT-along-run.VAI-3.SG.CONJ
'This story is about the Raccoon running along.'

b. é-yé-bmebtot o éspen wgi-wabman amon é-gojnenet.
é-yé-bme-bto-t o éspen
FCT-while-along-run.VAI-3.SG.CONJ that raccoon

w-gi-wabm-an	amo-n	é-gojne-net.
3-PST-see.VTA-3SG>3OBV.IND	bee-OBV	FCT-hang.VAI-3OBV.CONJ

'While Raccoon was running along, he saw bees (a hive) hanging.' (Hockett 1937:31, JS 4.4)

Me can mark a narrative evidential in traditional narratives. An example of a narrative evidential use of *me* is given in (7). In (7a), the narrator, Alice Spear, uses the conjunct order verb and the particle cluster *i me se* 'once upon a time' to establish narration. Notice that *i me se* includes *me*. In general, *me se* introduces stories that are not personal narratives. Later in the narrative, Alice shifts into the independent indicative for the main clause in (7b) to provide background information. *Me* is used in (7b) to indicate that the background information follows the story line of the narrative. Both instances of *me* in (7) can be thought of as narrative evidential uses because the conjunct order establishes narration.

(7) a. I me se é-gi-dawat wéwidzhandejek

i	me	se	é-gi-da-wat	wéwidzhandejek,
that	HRSY	CONCL	FCT-PST-live-3PL	IC.be.siblings.3PL

'Once, there lived a bunch of brothers and sisters'

b. Wgi-wawyéjénan me ni wzheshéyen égi-sat zhiw bij-yegwan wzesanek.

w-gi-wawyéjénan	me	ni	w-zheshé-yen
3-PST-roll.VTA.IND.3SG>3OBV	HRSY	that.OBV	3-uncle-OBV

é-gi-sat	zhiw	bij-yegwan	wzesan-ek.
FCT-PST-put.VTA.CONJ.3SG>3OBV	there	inside	nest-LOC

'He rolled his uncle up round, it's told, and he put him in the nest.' (Hockett 1940:17, 36, AS 2.5)

Once again there is no blocking when the hearsay enclitic is used in narratives. Since *me* and narrative marking are not in the same grammatical category, they may be used together. The three evidential functions are summarized in Table 1. The functions are the same as Cheyenne, just "scattered" across the language's grammar. Unlike Cheyenne, however, sentences unmarked for evidentiality are not witnessed. They are unspecified for information source. Evidence for this comes from (6) where the evidential is not required in narratives, but only occasionally used as in (7).

TABLE 1. Evidential system of Potawatomi

HEARSAY	*me*
INFERENCE	dubitative inflection
NARRATIVE	conjunct order to establish narration + *me*

Speaker Certainty

There are some interesting similarities between evidentiality and epistemicity in Potawatomi. Specifically, Potawatomi uses the same elements of grammar for both: a second position enclitic slot and the dubitative mode.

Speaker Certainty and Mirativity

Ma occupies the same enclitic slot as the hearsay enclitic *me*.[5] The second position enclitic *ma* can be used for speaker certainty. Specifically, it corrects misunderstandings or clarifies competing options like a verum focus particle (Lohnstein 2016). For instance, the sentence in (8) asserts that it is the listener who the speaker is talking to, and not someone else as the listener has suggested.

(8) Context: You, Carla, and I are sitting in the conference room at the museum. You say *nenmewshen ι ndeswiwkwan* 'Hand me my hat (hat with a brim or a driver's cap).' I think you are talking to Carla and look at her. She doesn't move. When I look back at you, you say the following:
Héy! Gin ma gdenen.
Héy! gin ma gd-en-en.
Héy 2SG CER 2-say.VTA-1SG>2SG
'Hey! It's you I'm talking to.' (JT 2020-09-17)

Note that the speaker certainty enclitic may appear with either the independent order as shown in (8), the conjunct order as shown in (9b), or the imperative order as shown in (10).[6]

(9) Context: You just got back from a general council meeting.

a. Gde-mgejané.
gde-mgejané.
2-have.a.big.nose
'You have a big nose.'

b. I ma ga-kedot o nJohn.
i ma ga-kedo-t o nJohn.
that CER IC.PST-say.VAI-3SG.CONJ that John
'That's what John said (the speaker heard it from John).' (JT 2020-09-17)

Example (10) comes from a story where the hero turns into a horse. He tells an old couple, who are his owners, that they can sell him to a man who makes them an offer.

(10) Mojma dawén i niyow.
moj ma dawén i niyow.
even CER sell.VAI.IMP.2SG that 1.body
'Go ahead and sell me (to that man).' (Hockett 1937:47–48, 4.5)

The use of *ma* can sometime be assertive when the verb that it is used with has a negative connotation. In (11a), I asked a speaker whether he had a car. In (11b), he responded with an affirmative. He then added *gdebgwenos* 'you are dumb', and reinforced this statement with *ma*.

(11) a. Gde-wdodabyan né.
gde-wdodabyan né.
2-have.a.car.VAI Q
'Do you have a car?'

b. Ni gézhé. Gdebgwenos ma shna.
ni gézhé g-debgwenos ma zhe na.
of.course 2-be.dumb.VAI CER EMPH DM
'Of course, you are dumb.' (JT 2019-05-01)

The use of *ma* in (11b) is related to the fact that *ma* can also have a mirative function. In (12), *ma* is used with the verb *mbokshka* 'I'm broke' to indicate surprise on the part of the speaker. Jim Thunder notes that this statement might be used if someone thought they had some bills in their wallet and opens it to find no money there. Note that the use of *ma* 'speaker certainty' as a mirative marker is typologically rare. It is more common for an indirect evidential marker to indicate mirativity (Aikhenvald 2004:195).

(12) Mbokshka ma shna.
m-bokshka ma zhe na.
1-be.broke.VAI CER EMPH DM
'Oh, I'm really broke.' (JT 2017-06-07)

Speaker Uncertainty

A verb inflected in the changed conjunct dubitative mode and the particle *nemech* together mark speaker uncertainty.[7] Number (13) provides examples of the dubitative mode with the particles *nemech* and its present-day equivalent *mech/met.*[8] There are a range of meanings that these two elements can be translated with, including 'I don't know, I wonder.' Example (13a) comes from the coda of a story about a whale swallowing a boy. Both (13b,c) come from a story about when Potawatomis were living in Mexico.

(13) a. Nemech zhena zhi ga-bme-zhewébzegwén.
nemech zhe na zhi ga-bme-zhewébze-gwén.
not.know EMPH DM there IC.PST-along-happen.to.VAI-3SG.DUB
'I don't know what happened to him along there.' (Hockett 1940:5, 2.1)

b. Mech natso ga-yawagwén gi Neshnabék.
mech na tso ga-yaw-agwén gi Neshnabé-k.
not.know DM so.many IC.PST-be.VAI-3PL.DUB those neshnabé-PL
'I don't know how many Neshnabé people there were.' (Lockwood 2017:249, JT)

c. Mine o nJohn Mike met se natso gé wi ga-yawgwén i wpi.
mine o nJohn Mike met se na tso
and that John.Mike not.know CONCL DM so.many

gé wi ga-yaw-gwén i wpi.
also 3 IC.PST-be.VAI-3SG.DUB that when
'And John Mike, I wonder what age he was at that time.' (Lockwood 2017:253, JT)

Speculation

The dubitative mode has also been reported to mark speculation (Buszard 2003:25). In (14a,b), the dubitative mode is said to mark that the speaker is speculating rather than inferring as we saw the dubitative mode do in (4).

(14) a. Gnebech nwabmadek.
gnebech n-wabma-dek.
maybe 1-see.VTA.1>3-DUB
'Maybe I see him.'

b. Jo gnebech nwabmasidek.
jo gnebech n-wabma-si-dek.
NEG maybe 1-see.VTA.1>3-NEG-DUB
'I might not see him.' (Buszard 2003:25)

Table 2 summarizes the evidential and epistemic functions found in Potawatomi. These functions are both achieved by a second position enclitic or the dubitative mode inflection. Space does not allow for further discussion of whether this system could be reduced to one of an epistemic degree of certainty.

TABLE 2. Evidential and epistemic system of Potawatomi

		EVIDENTIAL	EPISTEMIC
ENCLITIC			
Hearsay	*me*	Yes	
Narrative	conjunct order to establish narration + *me*	Yes	
Speaker Certainty	*ma*		Yes
Mirativity	*ma*		Yes
DUBITATIVE MODE			
Inference	dubitative inflection	Yes	
Speaker Uncertainty	(*ne*)*mech* + conjunct dubitative inflection		Yes
Speculation	dubitative inflection		Yes

Dubitative Mode

Several different functions have been suggested for the dubitative mode. Buszard (2003) claims that there is a difference between the inference and the speculation functions in the dubitative mode based on tense, while Lockwood (2017) suggests the dubitative mode is strictly inferential. Earlier, I further complicated the picture by claiming that the dubitative mode expresses speaker uncertainty when used with *nemech*. In what follows I show that while tense has been suggested to contribute to the difference in interpretation for the dubitative mode, it is not predictive. Instead, I show that what order the verb is in and whether the verb is modified are predictive.

Tense

The dubitative mode has been claimed to have an evidential function in the past tense and an epistemic function in the present tense (Buszard 2003:25). Compare the inferential function in (15b) to the speculative function in (15a; repeated from (14a)).

(15) a. Gnebech nwabmadek.

gnebech n-wabma-dek.

maybe 1-see.VTA.1>3-DUB

'Maybe I see him.'

b. Ngi-wabmadek.

n-gi-wabma-dek.

1-PST-see.VTA.1>3-DUB

'I must have seen him.' (Buszard 2003:24)

However, Lockwood suggests that the dubitative mode "appears to be an inferential evidential" (2017:114, 192–193). He provides the present tense examples in (16a,b) and the past tense example in (16c).

(16) a. Gmesé gégo bwa-wzhetogwén gge-byéna.

g-mesé gégo bwa-wzheto-gwén g-ge-byéna.

1-sister something NEG-make.VTI-3SG.DUB 2-IMM-bring.VTA.2SG>3SG

'If your sister isn't doing anything, bring her over.' (Lockwood 2017:114, JT)

b. "O, mech ézhnagwdegwén," ndenéndem.

o, mech ézh-nagwde-gwén, nd-enéndem.

oh, not.know IC.how-look.VII-3SG.DUB 1-think.thus.VAI

'"Oh, I wonder what it looks like," I thought.' (Lockwood 2017:192, JT)

c. Mech wéwéne ga-zhenkazgwén.

mech wéwéne ga-zhenkaz-gwén.

not.know correct IC.PST-be.named.thus.VAI-3SG.DUB

'I don't know what his name really was.' (Lockwood 2017:192, JT)

While (16a) may show that the dubitative mode can have an inferential meaning in the present tense, (16b,c) express speaker uncertainty rather than inference. In other words, the dubitative mode in (16a) is evidential, while in (16b,c), it is epistemic. These examples allow us to conclude that tense does not predict the interpretation of the dubitative mode, since they contradict Buszard's claim that the dubitative mode is inferential (evidential) in the past but speculative (epistemic) in the present.

While tense is not predictive, what order the verb is in and whether the verb is modified are predictive. I turn to order and modification now.

Order

Unmodified independent order verbs in the dubitative mode convey inferential meanings as shown in (17).[9]

(17) a. Ngi-wabmadek.

n-gi-wabma-dek.

1-PST-see.VTA.1>3-DUB

'I must have seen him.'

b. Jo ngi-wabmasidek.

jo n-gi-wabma-si-dek.

NEG 1-PST-see.VTA.1>3-NEG-DUB

'I must not have seen him.' (Buszard 2003:25)

On the other hand, unmodified conjunct order verbs in the dubitative mode take on a variety of meanings. These meanings include 'whatever' and 'I don't know' as shown in (18). Example (18a) occurs in the context where some crows were about to eat a woman, but one of them told the others to wait and see what the chief says. Example (18b) occurs in the context where an older sister makes a negative comment to her younger sister about the old man who is her partner.

(18) a. Wa-kedgwén gge-zhechkémen.

wa-ked-gwén	g-ge-zhechké-men.
IC.FUT-say-3SG.DUB	2-IMM-do.thus.VAI-1INCL

'Whatever he says, we will do.' (Hockett 1940:23, AS 2.4)

b. "Wa-dodwagwén ni kewéziyen wannagzenjen" é-nat niw wshiméyen

wa-dodwagwén	ni	kewézi-yen
IC.FUT-do.with.VTA.3SG>3OBV.DUB	that.OBV	old.man-OBV

wannagzenjen	é-nat	niw
IC.look.dirty.3OBV	FCT-say.VTA.3SG>3OBV	that.OBV

w-shimé-yen
3-younger.sibling-OBV

'"I don't know what she'll do with that old dirty man," she said to her younger sister.' (Hockett 1940:53, AS 2.7)

Additionally, the dubitative mode is sometimes used in conditional clauses to convey an inferential meaning.[10] For example, in (19), a woman infers from the facts about a developing challenge that this challenge was what she saw in a dream when fasting. Statement (19) is uttered after a man issues a challenge to a group of women that they can have his pumpkins if one of them can throw him down.

(19) Gishpen i yawnegwén ndapwéwen égi-mkedékéyan, gwi-manétomen wabgonen.

gishpen	i	yawne-gwén	nd-apwéwen	é-gi-mkedéké-yan
if	that	be.VII-3SG.DUB	1-dream	FCT-PST-fast.VAI-1SG

g-wi-manéto-men	wabgon-en.
2-FUT-be.plenty.VTI-1INCL	pumpkin-PL

'If that's my dream when I fasted, we'll have plenty of pumpkins.' (Hockett 1940:2, AS 3.4)

Buszard-Welcher (1998), Buszard (2003), and Lockwood (2017) claim that the dubitative mode appears in independent and conjunct orders in Potawatomi. There is reason to question this, though. As Amy Dahlstrom points out (personal communication, 2019), the form I refer to as the changed conjunct dubitative in this paper bears a striking similarity to the interrogative participle in Meskwaki. In fact, there is reason to think that the changed conjunct dubitative is an interrogative participle.[11] One piece of evidence is that the immediate future tense and the modal in the changed conjunct dubitative take a participle form (gé- and *a-/da-*, respectively) rather than a verbal form (*géje-* and *aje-/daje-*, respectively).[12] In spite of this similarity, verbs in questions do not take interrogative participle inflection in Potawatomi as they do in Meskwaki. I leave these facts for future research, and refer the interested reader to Dahlstrom's (2019) paper on embedded questions in Meskwaki.

Modification

Independent order verbs in the dubitative mode can be modified by a doubt particle like *gnebech* 'maybe' to add speculation. In fact, Buszard notes that the negative dubitative "in the past tense, [is] often used with the particle *gnebech* 'maybe'" (2003:25).

(20) a. Gnebech nwabmadek.
gnebech n-wabma-dek.
maybe 1-see.VTA.1>3-DUB
'Maybe I see him.'

b. Jo gnebech nwabmasidek.
jo gnebech n-wabma-si-dek.
NEG maybe 1-see.VTA.1>3-NEG-DUB
'I might not see him.' (Buszard 2003:25)

However, conjunct order verbs in the dubitative mode express speaker uncertainty when modified with (*ne*)*mech*. In (21), the changed conjunct dubitative along with (*ne*)*mech* translate to 'I don't know, I wonder'.

(21) a. Mech wéwéne ga-zhenkazgwén.
mech wéwéne ga-zhenkaz-gwén.

not.know correct IC.PST-be.named.thus.VAI-3SG.DUB

'I don't know what his name really was.' (Lockwood 2017:192, JT)

b. O, mech ézhnagwdegwén.

o, mech ézh-nagwde-gwén.

oh, not.know IC.how-look.VII-3SG.DUB

'Oh, I wonder what it looks like.' (Lockwood 2017:192, JT)

In sum, there are a range of evidential and epistemic meanings inherent to the dubitative mode in the conjunct order, while in the independent order the data suggest that only an inferential meaning is available. Particles can then be used to modify the dubitative mode in both orders to achieve a specific meaning. The functions of the dubitative mode are summarized in Table 3.

TABLE 3. Functions of the dubitative mode by verbal order

	INDEPENDENT	CONJUNCT
EVIDENTIAL	inferential	conditional inference
EPISTEMIC		speaker uncertainty

As I show in the next section, the functions of the dubitative mode summarized in Table 3 also explain a shift in grammatical category for the dubitative mode as characterized by Lockwood (2017).

A Shift from Dubitative Inflection to Particles

Lockwood (2017) says that the dubitative mode is scarcely used in Potawatomi: "Evidentiality is now more often expressed with the particle *yédek* 'maybe, I wonder, must be' or *nmej* 'I do not know, I wonder'" (113–114).[13] Lockwood (2017) does not give a time depth, so I suggest using 1868 as a date of comparison as I have found that *nemech*, but not *yédek*, is given in Gailland's grammar of Potawatomi (Gailland 1868).

Lockwood's statement suggests *yédek* and *nemech* are on equal footing. While I agree that there is a shift from the dubitative inflection to the particle *yédek*, I do not find *nemech* to robustly participate in this shift. Furthermore, I find that *yédek* exhibits both evidential and epistemic functions while *nemech* exhibits only an epistemic function, as one would expect for a particle that expresses speaker doubt. Therefore, I posit that *yédek* was lexicalized as a dubitative particle while *nemech* has always been a particle expressing speaker uncertainty. This clearly follows from the range of inherent meanings available in the dubitative mode and the specific meaning of the particles.

Yédek

Yédek requires any accompanying verb to be in the conjunct order (Buszard 2003:65), and has a variety of meanings. It can mark inference based on sensory evidence or logical deduction as in (22), which is taken from a narrative about a young man. In the course of the narrative, the young man kills some game while he is being followed by another man. He returns home and sends his partner out to get the game. She looks for the game but cannot find it. She then gives up and returns home. It is at this point in the story that the narrator utters (22).

(22) I wi yédek géwi o nene égi-jag-gmodet i weyas.

i	wi	yédek	géwi	o	nene	é gi jag gmode t
now	CNTR	must.be	3	that	man	FCT-PST-all-steal.VAI-3SG

i	weyas.
that	meat

'Now, that man must have stolen all the meat.' (Hockett 1940:51, AS 2.7)

Yédek can also express speaker uncertainty. In (23), *yédek* is used to express uncertainty about how a young man would act at his in-laws' home. Statement (23) is uttered while the young man is still sleeping when an old man is ready to leave.

(23) I yédek na wa-bme-zhezheshnen ngoji mne'agbin.

i	yédek	na	wa-bme-zhezheshn-en	ngoji
now	must.be	DM	IC.FUT-along-lie.VAI-2SG	somewhere

mne'agbin.
stay.with.in.laws.VAI.1SG
'Is that how you're going to lie where your in-laws are at?' (Hockett 1940:46, 2.7)

With the modal, *yédek* also expresses speaker uncertainty, as seen in (24b). An older sister utters (24) as a negative comment to her younger sister about the old man who is her partner. Note in (24b) the use of the participle form of the modal (*a-*) instead of the verbal form (*aje-*).

(24) a. Wéte bzhe ode gtthe-babek byéwak wannagzet,

wéte	bzhe	ode	gtthe-babek	byéwak	wannagze-t,
good	EMPH	this	really-right.away	come.VAI.3SG	IC.look.dirty-3SG

'That dirty looking one came back this soon,'

b. gégo yédek a-bme-ntot

gégo	yédek	a-bme-ntot
something	must.be	MOD-along-kill.VTI.3SG>3

'I wonder could he have killed anything.' (Hockett 1940:49, 2.7)

In content questions, such as (25), *yédek* also expresses speaker uncertainty to form a conjectural question. A young girl utters (25) to the old man who is her partner when her parents come to pick her and her older sister up and take them home.

(25) Nije yédek wa-zhejkéyen?

ni	je	yédek	wa-zhejké-yen?
what	DM	must.be	IC.FUT-do.thus.VAI-2SG

'I wonder what you're going to do?' (Hockett 1940:55, AS 2.7)

Finally, at the end of a story, as in (26), *yédek* can mark a speculation to give an uncertain ending. Example (26) appears in the coda of a narrative about a young man, and the verb is inflected for the dubitative mode.

(26) Iw je yédek é-dawagwén ode wpi mégwa.

iw	je	yédek	é-da-wagwén	ode	wpi	mégwa.
now	DM	must.be	FCT-live.VAI-3PL.DUB	this	time	still

'And now they must be living there today still.' (Hockett 1940:64, AS 2.7)

Nemech

Nemech, or its present-day equivalent *mech/met*, can appear without a verb to express speaker doubt as in (27), which is taken from the coda of a story about Potawatomis in Mexico.

(27) I je nemech na i mzen'egen.

i	je	nemech	na	i	mzen'egen.
that	DM	not.know	DM	that	paper

'And I don't know about the treaty.' (Hockett 1940:5–6, JS 1.3)

Nemech can also be used together with *yédek* to express speaker doubt, as shown in (28a,b). A verb may follow as shown in (28c). Note that *yédek* does not appear without a verb except when occurring with (*ne*)*mech*.

(28) a. Mech yédek

mech	yédek
not.know	must.be

'I don't know.' (JT 2016-06-28)

b. Metsena yédek

Met	se	na	yédek
not.know	CONCL	DM	must.be

'I don't know./I'm not sure.' (JT 2016-05-17)

c. Mech yédek wa-zhewébzegwén.

mech	yédek	wa-zhewébze-gwén.
not.know	must.be	IC.FUT-happen.to.VAI-3SG.DUB

'I wonder what's going to happen to him.' (Lockwood 2017:114)

Without *yédek*, *mech* expresses speaker uncertainty, as (29) shows. Note that here *mech* occurs with a dubitative conjunct verb.

(29) Mech wéwéne ga-zhenkazgwén.

mech	wéwéne	ga-zhenkaz-gwén.
not.know	correct	IC.PST-be.named.thus.VAI-3SG.DUB

'I don't know what his name really was.' (Lockwood 2017:192, JT)

Finally, although the conjunct verb used with *nemech* seldom occurs in other than the dubitative mode, I have found four such instances (out of 25 instances of *nemech* in Hockett (1937, 1940)). One of these examples is given in (30), a narrative about how Natives used to doctor themselves.[14]

(30) a. Gi-gkéndan zhe wa-yot

gi-gkéndan	zhe	wa-yot
PST-know.VTI.3SG>3SG	EMPH	IC.FUT-use.VTI.3SG>3

'He knew what to use,'

b. nemech énapnét.

nemech	énapné-t.
not.know	IC.be.sick.VAI-3SG

'whatever sickness he had.' (Hockett 1940:6, AS 3.15)

I know of no present-day examples of (*ne*)*mech* appearing without the dubitative mode. In fact, when I asked speaker Jim Thunder about the example in (30), he insisted that I put the verb into the dubitative mode. This example is given in (31). Clearly, (31) contradicts the claim that the dubitative mode has been shifted to the particle (*ne*)*mech.*

(31) a. Wgi-gkéndan zhe wa-yot.

w-gi-gkéndan	zhe	wa-yot.
3-pst-know.VTI.3SG>3SG	EMPH	IC.FUT-use.VTI.3SG>3

'He knew what to use,'

b. mech zhe weyé énapnégwén.

mech	zhe	weyé	énapné-gwén.
not.know	EMPH	someone	IC.be.sick.VAI-3SG.DUB

'whatever sickness he had.' (JT 2019-10-09)

In sum, *yédek* has both evidential and epistemic functions while (*ne*)*mech* only has an epistemic function. Table 4 summarizes these functions via their translations.

TABLE 4. Functions of *yédek* and *(ne)mech*

	YÉDEK	*(NE)MECH*
EVIDENTIAL	'must have'	
EPISTEMIC	'I wonder'	'I wonder'
	'maybe'	
		'I don't know'
		'I'm not sure'
		'whatever'

Conclusion

The Potawatomi evidential system looks similar to that seen in Cheyenne: hearsay, inference, and narrative. These functions, however, are "scattered" across the language's grammar in a second-position enclitic slot, the dubitative mode inflection, and the particle *yédek*. Potawatomi sentences unmarked for evidentiality are not interpreted as witnessed as in Cheyenne, but are unspecified. Furthermore, many other Algonquian languages have an indirect evidential marker (Macaulay 2003; Dahlstrom 2020). In fact, the Potawatomi system is largely distributed like the one found in Meskwaki (Dahlstrom 2020), but with some clear differences that require a fuller explanation than can be given here.

This paper has also shown that epistemicity and evidentiality use the same grammatical categories in Potawatomi. I take this to mean that Potawatomi does not strictly differentiate between evidentiality and epistemicity. This finding adds credence to the claim that the division between evidentiality and epistemicity is a language-specific one (Brugman and Macaulay 2015:205).

Finally, this paper has shown that the dubitative mode is conditioned by what order the verb is in and whether the verb is modified. I have also shown that the range of meanings available to the dubitative mode is being shifted to the particle *yédek*, while (*ne*)*mech* only has epistemic functions, suggesting that it remains only a particle expressing speaker uncertainty as it has done since at least 1868.

NOTES

1. Migwétth Jim Thunder for all your help with the Potawatomi language! I would also like to thank Amy Dahlstrom, all of the conference participants of the 51st Algonquian Conference, and the anonymous reviewers for their helpful comments. All errors are my

own. I use the Wisconsin Native American Language Program (WNALP) writing system in this paper. All Potawatomi data comes from Hockett (1937, 1940) with speakers Alice Spear (AS) and Jim Spear (JS); Buszard (2003); Lockwood (2017), and language class with Jim Thunder (noted as JT Year-Month-Day). If no context is given for an example, that means that none was given in the source. I have added word final devoicing for oral stops in data from Hockett (1937, 1940).

2. Murray's examples are taken from Leman (2011). I use the following abbreviations: 1 = first person, 2 = second person, 3 = third person, AN = animate, DM = discourse marker, DUB = dubitative, CER = certainty, CNTR = counter-expectation, CONCL = conclusive, CONJ = conjunct, EMPH = emphasis, FCT = factive, FOC = focus, FUT = future, HRSY = hearsay, IC = initial change, IMM = immediate future, IMP = imperative, INAN = inanimate, INCL = inclusive, IND = independent, INF = inferential, IRR = irrealis, MOD = modal, NAR = narrative, NEG = negative, OBV = obviative, PL = plural, PST = past, Q = interrogative, RPT = reported, SG = singular, VAI = animate intransitive verb, VII = inanimate intransitive verb, VTA = transitive animate verb, VTI = transitive inanimate verb, WTN = witnessed, > = Act on.
3. Jim Thunder sometimes translates *me* as 'I hear', 'must have', 'supposedly', or 'I guess' given the context. *Me* is sometimes not an enclitic. I leave this to future research to work out.
4. This inference sounds like hearsay because Jim claims to have heard it from his elders, but hearsay is not his only source of information. He also saw it written down.
5. *Ma* is sometimes not an enclitic. I leave this to future research.
6. *Ma* with *moj* is defined as 'please, go ahead' in Hockett (1937, 1940).
7. This combination is also found in Ojibwe (Junker et al. 2018:449).
8. *Met* is the allomorph of *mech* used with *se*.
9. This may possibly be explained by referring to the independent order as an indexical clause anchored to the speaker. Specifically, indexical clauses (independent order) could have direct evidential force, while non-indexical clauses (conjunct order) could have indirect evidential force. In Plains Cree, independent order verbs indicate that the speaker was conscious of the event because they are indexical to the speaker (Cook 2014:91–109). Future research is needed to see if this holds for Potawatomi.
10. Conditional clauses require the conjunct order in Potawatomi, but the conditional does not modify the verb itself.
11. A reviewer pointed out that Littell et al. (2010) find evidentials in interrogatives result in conjectural questions. Notice that when *yédek* is used in content questions, as in (25), it results in a conjectural question. If conjunct dubitatives are conjectural questions too, the conjectural question interpretation would be attributed to dubitative and

interrogatives coming together, and not just another meaning of the dubitative.

12. Present-day speakers may have lost this distinction as *aje-* is frequently used in all forms.
13. This shift is not unique to Potawatomi. The further west one travels along the Cree-Innu dialect continuum, the more likely one is to find an evidential particle rather than evidential inflection (Junker et al. 2018:426).
14. The other three examples are found in Hockett (1940:64), (1940:5), and (1940:80).

REFERENCES

Aikhenvald, Alexandra Y. 2004. *Evidentiality*. Oxford: Oxford University Press.

Brugman, Claudia M., and Monica Macaulay. 2015. Characterizing Evidentiality. *Linguistic Typology* 19(2):201–237.

Buszard, Laura Ann. 2003. Constructional Polysemy and Mental Spaces in Potawatomi Discourse. PhD thesis, University of California, Berkeley.

Buszard-Welcher, Laura. 1998. Potawatomi Grammar Notes. Unpublished manuscript, University of California, Berkeley.

Cook, Clare. 2014. The Clause-Typing System of Plains Cree: Indexicality, Anaphoricity, and Contrast. Oxford: Oxford University Press.

Dahlstrom, Amy. 2019. Embedded Questions in Meskwaki: Syntax and Information Structure. *Papers of the Algonquian Conference*, ed. by Monica Macaulay and Margaret Noodin, pp. 69–85. East Lansing: Michigan State University Press.

Dahlstrom, Amy. 2020. An Overview of Meskwaki Evidentiality. *Papers of the Forty-Ninth Algonquian Conference*, ed. by Monica Macaulay and Margaret Noodin, pp. 81–98. East Lansing: Michigan State University Press.

Gailland, Rev. Maurice, SJ. 1868. Grammaire de la Langue Potêwatémie. Laura Buszard-Welcher Papers on the Potawatomi Language, Survey of California and Other Indian Languages, University of California, Berkeley.

Hockett, Charles F. 1937. Hockett Potawatomi Field Notebook IV. Laura Buszard-Welcher Papers on the Potawatomi Language, California Language Archives, University of California, Berkeley.

Hockett, Charles F. 1940. Hockett Potawatomi Field Notebooks I, II, and III. Laura Buszard-Welcher Papers on the Potawatomi Language, Survey of California and Other Indian Languages, University of California, Berkeley.

Junker, Marie-Odile, J. Randolph Valentine, and Conor Quinn. 2018. Evidentiality in Algonquian. *The Oxford Handbook of Evidentiality*, ed. by Alexandra Y. Aikhenvald, pp. 431–462. Oxford: Oxford University Press.

Leman, Wayne. 2011. *A Reference Grammar of the Cheyenne Language*. Raleigh, NC: Lulu Press.

Littell, Patrick, Lisa Matthewson, and Tyler Peterson. 2010. On the Semantics of Conjectural Questions. *Evidence from Evidentials*, ed. by Tyler Peterson and Uli Sauerland, pp. 89–104. Vancouver: University of British Columbia Working Papers in Linguistics.

Lockwood, Hunter Thompson. 2017. *How the Potawatomi Language Lives: A Grammar of Potawatomi*. PhD thesis, University of Wisconsin–Madison.

Lohnstein, Horst. 2016. Verum Focus. *The Oxford Handbook of Information Structure*, ed. by Caroline Féry and Shinichiro Ishihara, pp. 290–313. Oxford: Oxford University Press.

Macaulay, Monica. 2003. Negation, Dubitatives and Mirativity in Menominee. *Papers of the Thirty-Fourth Algonquian Conference*, ed. by H. C. Wolfart, pp. 217–240. Winnipeg: University of Manitoba.

Murray, Sarah E. 2016. Evidentiality and Illocutionary Mood in Cheyenne. *International Journal of America Linguistics* 82(4):487–517.

Gii-moozhiginigaazowag Miinawaa Gii-webinigaazowag (They Were Kidnapped and Orphaned)

Including Boarding School History in Anishinaabemowin Curriculum

Angela Mesic

"Gii-webinigaazowag."

'They were orphaned.'

"Gii-moozhaginigaazowag."

'They were taken/collected/kidnapped.'

"Ogii-gimoodi'aawaan."

'They were stolen by others.'

Alphonse Pitawanakwat and Howard Kimewon are two elders who attended boarding schools and were asked to talk about their experiences only in the Anishinaabemowin language. After they spoke about their experiences, they translated what they said into English (as shown above). When speaking of the boarding school experience in Anishinaabemowin, these elders use two different verb types to describe their experience as a form of kidnapping. The different verb forms in Anishinaabemowin allow a speaker to clarify what happened through conjugation of each verb. In the examples above, the speakers move from using animate intransitive verbs to transitive animate verbs. Through the use of these verb types it becomes clear that not only were humans stolen, but also the language was stolen. When speakers are not able to express themselves in their original language, emotions and some of the content can be lost.

In Anishinaabe culture, it is common to think in terms of the cardinal directions. Anishinaabe prayers often begin by greeting each of the winds: north, west, east, and south. Songs are often sung four times, once for each of these directions. There are four different verb types in Anishinaabemowin that describe what is happening in the world around us. By framing the boarding school experience in an Anishinaabe paradigm, it is understood that the language was taken, people were taken, and actions can be taken in response to this history. The four verb types allow us to question what is happening, and this forces us to see through an Anishinaabe lens of processing. As Indigenous-language instructors and researchers we must ask ourselves how we think about this state that we are in. There is existing research on both the cultural importance of boarding school history and the impact of historical trauma on current students and their success. This paper is a call for more research that combines these two fields. In this paper, I describe a small pilot study that aims to show this importance.

The boarding school system was cultural genocide. Students were severely disciplined when trying to express their culture—everything from wearing their hair long to speaking their native language was forbidden. This cultural and historical trauma has left many Native Americans feeling ashamed of their language, culture, and family. When students returned home to their reservation after years of being immersed in the horrors of boarding schools, many had extreme difficulty communicating with their families because they were no longer able to speak their language. Due to the boarding school system, the Anishinaabe language is in "severe danger" of being lost and is "spoken by grandparents and older generations" (Moseley 2010). The Anishinaabe language that was once spoken by every generation can attribute the enormous loss of language to the mandatory boarding school experience.

In the book *Ethnic Identity and the Boarding School Experience of West Central Oklahoma American Indians*, Sally McBeth (1983:133) states that language can express a system of social values and lend credence to a social group whose historical past was affected by a policy of cultural genocide. Language is considered a central part of any culture; therefore it was identified as a cornerstone of tribal identity and needed to be eradicated if assimilation was to be successful (Voyer 2006:39). The boarding school policy and the assimilation practices have greatly reduced the use of Indigenous languages to the extent that these languages are classified as either endangered or extinct. The 2010 United States Census Bureau estimated that there are approximately 8,371 Anishinaabemowin speakers in the states of Wisconsin, Michigan, and Minnesota (McCarty 2013:9). Other census data proclaimed that "Over 1 in 5 . . . people aged 65 and over spoke a [Native American] language . . . , while about 1 in 10 people aged 5 to 17 did so" (McCarty 2013:9).

As a multicultural community we must work together to teach this history in order to stop the destruction caused by assimilation and proactively research how this traumatic boarding school experience affects the views towards Indigenous-language learning. This history is extremely important for both Native and non-Native students to learn about. Lydia Whirlwind Soldier suggests that

> in order to help our children value and preserve our tribal languages, we must share with them what our people experienced because of the assimilationist ideology. Our children must realize the sadness and despair of losing what we had, so they may respond actively, saving what we have left. They then will come to understand and articulate the philosophical aspects and spiritual attachment we feel toward our language, the heart and mind of our culture. (Soldier 1993:24)

It has become increasingly important to consider historical trauma when assessing academic success. Historical trauma has been described as "trauma resulting from events such as mass genocide, oppression, victimization, or group trauma exposure inflicted on a collective group of people and carried through to subsequent generations" (Luger 2019:ix). The rates of success in the post-secondary level for Native American students remain far below those of non-Native students (Richard 2012:12). The Native American population has historically faced barriers to achieving a higher-education degree at predominantly white institutions. Some of these barriers consist of high school drop-out rates, inadequate college preparation, cultural differences, inadequate financial resources, fears about leaving the reservation, and loneliness and homesickness (Luger 2019:11). Native American students flourish in environments that incorporate Native culture, languages, and traditions (Luger 2019:11–12). Guinan (2016:16) states that in Canada, "as a result of ongoing efforts, the demographic recovery and decolonization of Indigenous peoples continues, and future political, economic, and cultural relations between settler and Indigenous cultures continue to evolve as the population, skills, and culture of Indigenous communities recover and increase." It is critical to use education in cultural recovery and survival through awareness of the history of cultural destruction during assimilation practices. By integrating teachings of the boarding school history, we are helping students of differing cultural backgrounds understand the big picture of why languages were lost and why it is important to revitalize them.

Positionality

It is understood that the traumatic events of the boarding school system that Native Americans faced for over a century have caused a reluctance to trust the white society. Research conducted by non-Native researchers has been perceived as dehumanizing, and in some cases has been misused or misconstrued to benefit the researcher rather than the Native American community (Voyer 2006:63). Stubben (2001) points out that multicultural competency is required when conducting research or working with reservation, rural, or urban Native Americans. Stubben suggests that

> a culturally competent researcher or service provider should (a) become known to and by the tribal community; (b) understand the particular tribal community that he or she is studying or working with in the terms of history, cultural norms, values, and even language, if required; (c) be culturally sensitive to the cultural differences that exist between the tribal community and the service provider or researcher; (d) have an understanding of his or her own cultural background; (e) respect the community enough to stop his or her research or reservice provision if it in any way may bring harm to the community; and (f) understand the value biases that he or she may possess. (2001:1476)

As a non-Native ally, I began my journey learning Anishinaabemowin as an undergraduate at the University of Wisconsin-Milwaukee (UWM) looking to learn more about the land where I am from and the language of the Indigenous people that occupy it. I have a strong interest in research with a focus on the psychology of learning and curriculum development, which led me to the Electa Quinney Institute of American Indian Education (EQI). At EQI, I assist in building the Anishinaabemowin curriculum. I currently am one of the instructors for the first-year Anishinaabemowin course at UWM and I provide online long-distance learning for Yale University. Through my experiences I have gained cultural sensitivity and credibility, and the opportunity to witness the culture, spiritual beliefs, and customs of the Anishinaabe people.

The Present Study

The pilot study described here attempts to quantify the connection between boarding school history and Indigenous-language classrooms. This small pilot study was completed by participants under the protocols of the Institutional Review Board (IRB) through the Electa Quinney Institute for American Indian Education. The methodology and questionnaires used to compile data are described, concluding with a discussion of what was learned about the connection between boarding school history and the Indigenous-language classroom. Throughout the explanation of this pilot study, the term "Native American" will be used consistently and whenever possible refer to the precise tribe in question.

The study consisted of three parts and was conducted in the first-semester Anishinaabemowin course and the Introduction to American Indian Studies course at UWM. The participants filled out a preliminary questionnaire, attended a lecture about the boarding school history, and then filled out a second questionnaire. I had two main hypotheses guiding the pilot study. First, I predicted a positive correlation between related family history of boarding school attendance and engagement in language revitalization. Second, I predicted a positive correlation between learning the history of Native American boarding schools and attitudes towards learning an Indigenous language and language revitalization.

Participants

Participants were enrolled in the first-semester Anishinaabemowin course or the Introduction to American Indian Studies course at UWM. Only one student was enrolled in both courses. Students enrolled in the Anishinaabemowin course attended in a synchronous online environment. They ranged from high school students to adult non-degree auditors. There were multiple family relationships present in the Anishinaabemowin course, consisting of an aunt and niece, grandmother and grandson, and mother and daughter. Both Anishinaabemowin and Introduction to American Indian Studies involve small classroom settings. Both courses are commonly taken to fulfill general education requirements, including world language and cultural diversity. A total of 60 participants completed the online surveys; 40 participants completed the preliminary questionnaire and 20 participants completed the subsequent questionnaire. The mean age of participants was 23.18 years. Demographic information of the participants is summarized in Table 1. Participants who completed the second questionnaire did not have to complete the preliminary questionnaire in order to participate. There were 19 out of 20 participants who completed the preliminary questionnaire as well as the secondary questionnaire. Data was collected via the UWM Qualtrics page.

Measures

Demographic Questionnaire

A questionnaire was distributed to gather information about each participant's basic demographic attributes, including age, gender, ethnicity, and education. The demographic questionnaire was provided at the same time as the preliminary questionnaire. See online Appendix A for full questionnaire.[1]

Preliminary Questionnaire

The preliminary questionnaire was used to examine whether participants knew about the boarding school history prior to attending the lecture, and if they were aware of how language use changed within the Indigenous communities. Participants were surveyed on the range of languages they spoke and the methods they used to learn them. Participants enrolled in the Anishinaabemowin course were asked to rate their experience attending a synchronous online class. This section contained 45 items rated on a five-point Likert scale ranging from 'strongly agree' to 'strongly disagree.' One item, for example, was "I feel determined learning an indigenous language of Wisconsin." See online Appendix B for full questionnaire.

Second Questionnaire

The second questionnaire was used to examine if participants thought it was important to learn how the boarding school history is connected to Indigenous languages. There were two open-ended questions asking if the Native American

TABLE 1. Demographic characteristics of the participants

AGE

18	*n* = 5	12.5%
19	*n* = 13	32.5%
20	*n* = 7	17.5%
21	*n* = 4	10.0%
22	*n* = 1	2.5%
25	*n* = 2	5.0%
26	*n* = 1	2.5%
30	*n* = 2	5.0%
35	*n* = 2	5.0%
40	*n* = 1	2.5%
41	*n* = 1	2.5%
57	*n* = 1	2.5%

GENDER

Female	*n* = 17	42.5%
Male	*n* = 23	57.5%

ETHNICITY

Ojibwe	*n* = 1	Finnish	*n* = 1
White Earth Anishinaabe	*n* = 1	Italian	*n* = 1
Oneida	*n* = 3	Asian	*n* = 2
Native American	*n* = 4	Polish	*n* = 1
White/Caucasian	*n* = 24	Russian	*n* = 1
Irish	*n* = 3	Sri Lankan	*n* = 1
Scottish	*n* = 1	Black/African American	*n* = 3
German	*n* = 2	Austrian	*n* = 1
Norwegian	*n* = 1	Danish	*n* = 1
Hispanic/Latino/a/x	*n* = 6		

EDUCATION

High school degree or equivalent	*n* = 8	20.0%
Some college but no degree	*n* = 27	67.5%
Associate degree	*n* = 1	2.5%
Master's degree	*n* = 2	5.0%
PhD or equivalent	*n* = 2	5.0%

Note: *N*=40. Participants could list all ethnicities that applied.

boarding-school history lecture had influenced their view on learning an Indigenous language and their view on language revitalization. See online Appendix C for full questionnaire.

Procedure

Participants first completed the demographics and preliminary questionnaires administered online through UWM Qualtrics. On average, it took participants about 20 minutes to complete both surveys.

After the preliminary questionnaire was closed, a day was scheduled for a lecture to the first-semester Anishinaabemowin course and the Introduction to American Indian Studies course. I began with a summary of facts about the Native American boarding school history, representing it in the American context as it affects Indigenous-language learning. During the lecture, it was stressed that it is important to know that many people did not choose to stop speaking their heritage language but instead were in a school where there was no choice. This history is not often included in American history books. The lecture showed examples of personal experiences by two elders who speak Anishinaabemowin, Alphonse Pitawanakwat and Howard Kimewon. These men were asked to only speak Anishinaabemowin and then collaborate on the translation. Students in the first semester Anishinaabemowin course were able to apply their knowledge of different verb types and introductory lessons to analyze the parts of each word in the sentences. A few of Pitawanakwat and Kimewon's statements along with their corresponding translations are as follows:

(1) Gii-odaapinamawaawaad odabinoojiimowaan.
'Their children were taken without permission.'

(2) Aangodinong gaawiin gii-piskaabiisiiwag, gaawiin geyabi danakiisiiwaad.
'Sometimes they did not return because they did not have a place to go.'

(3) Aanind gaa-zaagajiba'iwewaad mii igo gii-maajitaawaad bamendizowaad.
'When some of them left school they started to provide for themselves.'

(4) Giishpin gaa-bwaa-nisidotaman waa-pashanzhe'igwaa.
'If you didn't understand you would be strapped.'

After the boarding-school history lecture and personal-experience sentence examples, key takeaways from the lesson were explained. The objectives for students and participants were to understand the following points: (1) that the direct quotes from these survivors show the intensity of the experience and the desperation they felt as children, as well as how strong they had to be to survive; (2) a fully conjugated agglutinative language with pronouns attached to the verb is different from a language where the verb stands alone and the subject and object are made clear by separate pronouns and prepositional phrases; (3) that not everyone who attended a Native American boarding or day school had a bad experience and that the schools are different today; (4) how institutions and governments influenced language and culture decline; and (5) that many countries and communities are considering reconciliation and acknowledgment of Indigenous culture and language.

The final part of the lecture involved having the class learn the American Indian Movement song (https://ojibwe.net/songs/womens-traditional/aim-song). In the United States it was used as a song to focus attention on Native political issues. The American Indian Movement song was originally without words until a group of singers in Michigan received permission to add Anishinaabemowin lyrics to it. The lyrics connect speaking Anishinaabemowin with positive well-being and reiterates the need for continuous active language revitalization.

After the lecture was presented, the second questionnaire was opened for participants to complete. This survey was also administered online through UWM Qualtrics. On average, it took participants about ten minutes to complete the second survey.

Results

A positive correlation between family history of boarding school attendance and engagement in language revitalization was hypothesized. Seven participants noted an immediate or extended family member attended a Native American boarding school. Three of these participants had a positive view towards Indigenous-language learning and revitalization, while four did not report their views. Participants were given the opportunity to write about their family members' experiences and how this experience and history has impacted the development of their cultural identity. One participant wrote:

> My dad and his siblings went to day school. My great grandmother lived with them and spoke no English. My dad spoke Ojibwe [Anishinaabemowin] until he was six and went to day school and was told it was the devil's language and he would burn in hell if he spoke it. So, he avoided his grandmother and didn't speak to her at all for four years, he said. He was afraid of her and thought she was bad. He spoke to her for the last time when he was eleven and could barely understand anything she said. That's how Ojibwe was lost to my family.

Another participant reported:

> I feel like [the boarding school experience] contributed to the loss of our language. One of the last fluent Oneida speakers just passed away not too long ago, and that is kind of a scary feeling. Also, three girls' remains were just returned home to Oneida from a boarding school. I feel like a lot of Native people lost their identity as a Native person through their experiences at boarding schools.

A third participant explained,

> It certainly affected my family's participation in Anishinaabeg culture and language, at least in part. My grandfather has difficulty identifying as Native (despite having been born at White Earth, being an enrolled citizen, and living there his entire life), due to his parents' insistence that he not be identified as such. Uncle Henry's generation was the last in our family to have knowledge of the language, as far as I know. I am young enough to have been born to parents who were able to take some of the earliest Native Studies (though that likely wasn't what they were called in the 80s) courses in college, where they learned about the history of boarding schools as part of the process of forced assimilation, and worked to raise us with the understanding that not knowing our language wasn't our fault.

Participants being told stories about their family history of boarding school experience has most likely influenced their positive views towards Indigenous-language learning and revitalization. Through these experiences and history, we as language instructors must enrich and support intersecting identities and pedagogies within the multicultural classroom so everyone feels welcome and comfortable in the classroom.

A second hypothesis was that there would be a correlation between learning the Native American boarding-school history and a positive view towards learning an Indigenous language and language revitalization. When asked if participants felt that it was important to learn how the boarding school history is connected to Indigenous languages, eleven stated 'Strongly Agree,' seven stated 'Agree,' one stated 'Somewhat Agree,' and two stated 'Neither Agree nor Disagree.' Participants were asked to explain if learning the boarding school history influenced their view on learning an Indigenous language in an open-ended format. Only three students responded that learning this history had not influenced their view on learning an Indigenous language. One of these participants noted,

> Having been familiar with the history of boarding schools before taking this course, I'd say my opinion hasn't changed. But I will say for those who are less informed about the forced assimilation of the boarding schools, it is vital (if not mandatory) context for understanding the history of the language, and the importance of its acquisition in the present.

Other participants reported positive impacts towards language learning. One participant stated,

> The fact that indigenous languages are dying out really made me think. I am a native Spanish speaker and the thought of my native tongue dying out or forgetting my native tongue and losing contact with my roots really scared me. Language is very important, and it is very connected to who we are as people. This lecture made me realize that there was a time where people were getting their roots stamped out of them and that is never okay. I am more inspired to try to keep these languages alive.

Another participant responded:

> I think that it did change my view on learning an indigenous language. I was not very interested in learning an indigenous language but after the presentation and the explanations on why it is kind of a big deal to do so, I am much more interested in it. The presentation definitely put this topic on my radar.

There were two participants who were interested in learning Oneida. One responded, "Yes, because not many people know the history of Native languages. It is important to me to know this history because I am Oneida and in order to keep our language alive, we need to know its history." The other said, "I have always wanted to learn Oneida but after the presentation I want to even more."

The participants were asked in an open-ended format to explain if learning the boarding school history influenced their view on language revitalization. Three participants answered that it was not influenced, although one of these participants believed "it was already pretty strong in my experience, so not any more than it had already." One participant responded:

> I have taught the song I learned that comes from the Boarding School tradition for twenty-five years, sharing what I could about the boarding school situation with elementary children. I have been sharing it with my [University] students as well, but now I have even more reason to share the meaning behind it. I want to do more research into it and make sure that what I am presenting is truly accurate. I also want to help my [University] students understand why it is important that they teach it.

Another participant stated,

> The revitalization of Native American languages has always seemed important, and I understood that there was a major disconnect in language just because of the boarding school situation, but I didn't realize how many communities and generations upon generations of natives were affected by this.

Multiple participants said that they did not understand how in jeopardy some Indigenous languages were, and after learning about it during our lecture, it opened their eyes to what had happened and positively influenced their views towards revitalization. After reviewing the statements from each participant, it is clear how significant learning about the American Indian boarding school history is to positively influence students' views towards Indigenous-language learning and language revitalization.

Discussion

There are many reasons why it is important to do research on the language revitalization classes in American Indian Studies programs. Language revitalization classrooms rely on culturally informed pedagogy, methodology, and educational psychology, but may be limited because the optimal range of enrollment is no more than 20 students. Large lectures in American Indian Studies rely on the same culturally informed pedagogy, methodology, and educational psychology, and offer a larger sample for investigation of how students begin to think about the history of boarding schools. There is a strong need for more work to be done to connect educational research in language revitalization and Indigenous culture and history. Individuals involved in language revitalization and Indigenous studies need to collaborate. With respect to Algonquian languages, instructors whose communities have a smaller diaspora, such as the Menominee Nation, need to collaborate with other instructors within the larger Algonquian language diaspora.

One may believe that students who self-select into a language revitalization course would also take a culture and history course and vice versa. However, this is not the case. Many students study either language or history and culture, but not both. This happens because the Anishinaabemowin class and Introduction to American Indian Studies at UWM each satisfy general education requirements, including world language and cultural diversity. Since both classes check off multiple requirements, many students enroll in just one or the other. I have found that most of my students have no prior knowledge of language loss or the history of the specific Indigenous languages around them. We as language revitalization instructors need to teach this important history so students can understand the whole picture. Conversely, the history and culture instructors should also be providing examples of Indigenous-language texts to help students fully appreciate linguistic diversity and language loss. Students' ability to succeed with the language is affected when they do not understand the cultural implications. When students think Anishinaabemowin is a dead language, they do not excel as well as when they know the bigger picture. Bringing language revitalization efforts into the language classroom helps students to succeed.

The purpose of this pilot study was to examine the correlation between learning the history of the Native American boarding schools and attitudes towards learning an Indigenous language and language revitalization. During the pilot study, two hypotheses were assessed. The first was that there would be a positive correlation between family history of boarding school attendance and engagement with language revitalization. The second was that there would be a correlation between learning about Native American boarding-school history and having a positive view towards learning an Indigenous language and language revitalization.

All participants were asked the question "How do you feel learning an indigenous language of Wisconsin?" using a five-point Likert scale consisting of a set of adjectives to measure their interest in Indigenous-language learning and revitalization. The data from these answers suggests a positive view of Indigenous-language learning and revitalization.

Family boarding-school experience and understanding of the Native American boarding-school history are extremely important to consider when building an Indigenous-language course at a multicultural campus. We must create a positive, enriching space for our students. It is important for all students to know about this trauma within the Native American community to create a judgment-free space. Non-Native students may feel hesitant or awkward learning a new language that is not their heritage language. Native American students may feel more pressure and anxiety in learning their heritage language, and so it is imperative to make them feel less threatened and address these issues. One of three participants who did not identify their heritage stated in the preliminary questionnaire that they "Somewhat Agree" to feeling "Hesitant," "Worried," and "Overwhelmed" learning an Indigenous language of Wisconsin. This anonymous student could be Non-Native or American Indian. When every student understands this traumatic history, students from all backgrounds are more likely to be open-minded and supportive of one another. This creates a space where students are not afraid to ask questions, feel more confident speaking out loud, and feel more confident in their knowledge. The preliminary questionnaire asked, "How do you feel about your classmates having different backgrounds than you learning the same language? Please explain in detail." Participants who identified as Native American welcomed it. One participant said, "I feel good about it. I am happy that they care enough to learn our language." Another participant wrote, "I think everyone who lives on indigenous land should make the effort to learn indigenous languages."

One limitation to this study was that participants were not required to respond to any questions but rather were requested to answer. Participants could skip a question and Qualtrics would notify them that there was no answer selected and ask if they would like to continue. Many participants skipped the initial question "Are you currently enrolled in an Anishinaabemowin course at either the University of Wisconsin-Milwaukee or Yale University?" when beginning the section rating the Anishinaabemowin course experience. Thus it is possible that some participants rated their experience in the course despite not being enrolled.

Another limitation was that not every participant submitted an identification number. Due to this, we were unable to compare all submissions from the preliminary survey to the second survey.

A third possible limitation was that there was no preliminary survey question regarding the participant's thoughts on Indigenous-language learning and revitalization. It would have been helpful to have such a question to be able to evaluate whether there was a change in viewpoint. These potential limitations could skew the data and present different results than what we may see in the future.

Ethnicity demographics were not asked about in the second questionnaire, potentially also limiting the pilot study. In future studies, it would be beneficial to include a breakdown of participants' responses along ethnic lines. Knowing the identity of the participants in the second questionnaire would further this research by investigating whether non-Indigenous students who did not know about the boarding school history before the lecture had their attitudes towards learning an Indigenous language influenced.

As a new researcher, these limitations taught me how I can enrich this pilot study for future use by rewording questions to be more specific, adding more questions to the preliminary survey to include participants' initial thoughts on Indigenous-language learning and revitalization, and creating a more user-friendly format. This pilot study will be changed for future use and will be used in the upcoming Anishinaabemowin language class and in Introduction to American Indian Studies at UWM as well as the online distance-learning class for Yale University.

It is my hope that this pilot study can be reproduced to see how members of different communities evaluate Indigenous-language learning and language revitalization, and how family boarding-school experiences influence participants' perception. The outcomes from this pilot study found a shift in multicultural competency after the boarding school lesson was presented. These findings suggest a need for future research contextualized by the history of boarding schools and language loss.

NOTE

1. All three appendices can be found on the Algonquian Conference website, https://algonquianconference.atlas-ling.ca/eng/supplementary-materials/.

REFERENCES

A.I.M. Song. 2020. https://ojibwe.net/songs/womens-traditional/aim-song/.

Guinan, Dan. 2016. The Social Environment and Indigenous Student Success in a Canadian Post-secondary Institution. PhD thesis, Royal Roads University.

Luger, Elizabeth. 2019. The Impact of Historical Trauma on Alcohol Use and Academic Outcomes in American Indian College Students. PhD thesis, University of North Dakota.

McBeth, Sally. 1983. Ethnic Identity and the Boarding School Experience of West Central Oklahoma American Indians. Lanham, MD: University Press of America.

McCarty, Teresa L. 2013. Language Planning and Policy in Native America: History, Theory, Praxis. Tonawanda, NY: Multilingual Matters Ltd.

Moseley, Christopher (ed.). 2010. *Atlas of the World's Languages in Danger*, 3rd edition. Paris: UNESCO Publishing. http://www.unesco.org/culture/en/endangeredlanguages/atlas.

Pitawanakwat, Alphonse, and Howard Kimewon. 2019. Boarding School Lesson (oral), AIS 161, University of Wisconsin-Milwaukee.

Richard, Audrey L. 2012. Setting Good Footprints: Reconstructing Wholistic Success of Indigenous Students in Higher Education. MA thesis, University of Manitoba.

Soldier, Lydia Whirlwind. 1993. Lakota Language Survival and Restoration: Lessons from the Boarding School. *Tribal College: Journal of American Indian Higher Education* 4(4). https://tribalcollegejournal.org/lakota-language-survival-restoration-lessons-boarding-school/.

Stubben, Jerry. 2001. Working with and Conducting Research among American Indian Families. *American Behavioral Scientist* 44(9):1466–1480.

Voyer, Charlene. 2006. Assimilation of the American Indian: The Meaning of the Boarding School Experience. PhD thesis, Chestnut Hill College.

Exceptional Animates in Ojibwe

The Link between Gender and Classifiers

Cherry Meyer

Gender assignment in Ojibwe is relatively straightforward: i.e. nouns with notionally animate referents are assigned to the ANIMATE gender (1), while nouns with notionally inanimate referents are assigned to the INANIMATE gender (2).[1] There are exceptions to this generalization found only in the ANIMATE gender, i.e. nouns with notionally inanimate referents assigned to the ANIMATE gender (3).

(1) Animate Referent and ANIMATE Gender
ikwe 'woman', inini 'man', animosh 'dog', makwa 'bear', giigoonh 'fish'

(2) Inanimate Referent and INANIMATE Gender
waabigwan 'flower', ozid 'his/her foot', wiiyaas 'meat', nibaagan 'bed', izaaga'igan 'lake'

(3) Inanimate Referent and ANIMATE Gender
mitig 'tree', zesab 'nettle', asekaan 'tanned hide', miskomin 'raspberry', asin 'a stone'

Nouns of the type found in (3) are numerous and diverse enough to warrant a considerable amount of attention from speakers, learners, linguists, and anthropologists alike. The question is whether it is possible to motivate inclusion in the ANIMATE gender, along with humans and animals, of such a disparate group of nouns as pipes, beads, kettles, grain products, tobacco, trees, drums, rocks, feathers, money, cars, and nets, and do it in an elegant way. I propose an analysis of gender assignment whereby nouns like those in (3) are motivated by their compatibility with the semantics of one of five sortal classifiers, illustrated by the pairings in (4).

(4)	a.	mitig 'tree'	-	/-aatig-/	'long, narrow, rigid', i.e. stick-like
	b.	zesab 'nettle'	-	/-aabiig-/	'long, narrow, flexible', i.e. string-like
	c.	asekaan 'tanned hide'	-	/-eg-/	'long, wide, flexible', i.e. sheet-like
	d.	miskomin 'raspberry'	-	/-minag-/	'small, round', i.e. berry-like
	e.	asin 'a stone'	-	/-aabik-/	'mineral', i.e. metal, stone, glass

Additionally, some nouns may be assigned to the ANIMATE gender through analogical extension with nouns like those in (1) or (3). In the following sections, I describe the data collection and considerations of dialectal variation. I define and discuss gender assignment and sortal classifiers, before presenting the connection between them. I then discuss further considerations for the analysis, such as complexities arising from taxonomy, diachronic changes, dialectal variation, and analogical extension.

Data Collection and Dialectal Variation

Data for this project are drawn from fieldwork as well as dictionaries and grammars. Specifically, data for the classifiers comes from fieldwork conducted with speakers from the Sault Ste. Marie Tribe of Chippewa Indians, and several grammars and dictionaries (Baraga 1878; Rhodes 1985; Valentine 2001). Although the fieldwork and literature for the classifiers focuses on the Odawa dialect of Ojibwe, the claims made for classifiers hold across dialects. The data for the gender analysis is sourced from the online *Ojibwe People's Dictionary* (OPD; Nichols 2015), which is composed of words from 16 communities in Wisconsin, Minnesota, and north of the Canadian border in Ontario and Manitoba, comprising both the Southwestern and Saulteaux dialects. To avoid selectively picking and choosing nouns to support the analysis and in order to build a sufficiently large enough database, all "exceptional" nouns in the OPD were compiled, regardless of whether a corresponding INANIMATE form is listed from another community. The database contains 491 entries, all of which can be accounted for by the analysis. The "exceptional" nouns we are concerned with are, however, a source of dialectal variation. While this analysis cannot predict which nouns will be ANIMATE or INANIMATE in each speech community, it does provide a system of motivation. Dialectal variation is accounted for with a diachronic framework showing how the system came to be the way it is and the ways in which it is likely to vary.[2]

Gender Assignment

The term 'gender' comes from the Latin word *genus*, meaning 'kind' or 'sort' (*Online Etymology Dictionary* 2019). This type of noun categorization is defined by morphosyntactic agreement in associated elements outside of the noun (Corbett 1991:4, 105), i.e. other parts of speech associated with the noun vary their form to match the gender of the noun. In Ojibwe, demonstratives and verbs (Valentine 2001:124, 132) agree with nouns in gender.

In a gender system, every noun is assigned a single gender value. Gender assignment is the method by which nouns are allotted to different gender values within a language. The motivation for gender assignment may be based on the meaning of the noun, called semantic assignment, or phonological or morphological properties of the noun, called formal assignment. In Ojibwe, assignment is based on semantics.[3]

Sortal Classifiers

There are many kinds of classifiers. Classifiers generally are defined as free or bound morphemes occurring in specifiable morphosyntactic units that denote a property of the referent of a noun and may co-occur with the noun (Aikhenvald 2000:13; Grinevald 2000:64). The current typology of classifiers relies on identifying the part of speech to which the classifier is closest or attached (Grinevald 2000:62–63), e.g. classifiers adjacent to nouns are noun classifiers, classifiers that occur with numerals are numeral classifiers, etc. Classifiers serve to highlight or supplement the semantics of the noun (Aikhenvald 2000:319–330); the latter is shown in (5) with numeral classifiers in Yucatec Maya (Lucy 2000:329).

(5) *Numeral Classifiers in Yucatec Maya*

a. 'un-**tz'íit** há'as
one-1.dimensional.CL banana
'one banana fruit'

b. 'un-**wáal** há'as
one-2.dimensional.CL banana
'one banana leaf'

c. 'un-**kúul** há'as
one-planted.CL banana
'one banana tree'

Ojibwe has both verbal and numeral classifiers (Meyer 2019, 2020a). Within numeral classifiers, there are two subtypes. Mensural classifiers denote units of measurement, e.g. cups, gallons, rows, while sortal classifiers denote physical properties, e.g. shape, material, function. Both mensural and sortal classifiers are found in Ojibwe and they occur with different root forms of the numeral 'one' (Meyer 2020a).[4] There are traditionally five classifiers of the sortal type recognized in Ojibwe (Meyer 2020a; see also Valentine 2001:331).[5]

(6) *Sortal Numeral Classifiers in Ojibwe*

a. bezhigw-**eg** waabooyaan
one-sheetlike.CL blanket
'one (sheetlike) blanket'

b. bezhigw-**aabiig** naabkwaagan
one-stringlike.CL necklace
'one (stringlike) necklace'

c. bezhigw-**aatig** mtigoonhs
one-sticklike.CL stick.DIM
'one (sticklike) small stick'

d. bezhigw-**aabik** **zhooniyaa**
one-mineral.CL money
'one (mineral) dollar'

e. bezhgwa-**minag** sabaab
one-berrylike.CL ball.of.yarn
'one (berrylike) ball of yarn'

While classifiers form a distinct system of noun categorization that is separate from grammatical gender, the next section details how the two are also deeply entwined.

The Link between Gender and Classifiers

Nouns are assigned to the ANIMATE gender (1) when their meanings reflect animateness, (2) when their meanings reflect semantic compatibility with one of the five sortal numeral classifiers, or (3) through analogical extension with nouns assigned via the first two routes. To illustrate this proposed system of gender assignment in Ojibwe, a representative sample of the 491 "exceptional" nouns and those reflecting (un-exceptional) nouns with animate meanings are displayed below in figures. All nouns contained in the figures are listed as ANIMATE in the *Ojibwe People's Dictionary*. It is only necessary to account for the assignment of ANIMATE nouns, as all others are assigned to the INANIMATE gender by default.[6].

The figures are read as follows: The relevant semantic motivation, e.g. animacy or a sortal classifier, is located at the center. Arrows from the center to nouns represent direct motivation. Arrows from one noun to another represent an analogical extension. One noun may be responsible for the assignment of one or more nouns through analogical extension, but more often it seems that a group of nouns is responsible. In this case, an arc indicates the responsible group of nouns and the arrow(s) originate from there. Due to limitations of space, the figures show the assignment of a representative sample of nouns. For considerations of transparency, nouns not shown in the figures are directly motivated by animacy, a sortal classifier, or an analogical extension that has expanded to an entire cluster of nouns and constitutes its own motivation, e.g. playing cards. If a noun from the database is the single example of an analogical extension, i.e. the analogy did not expand to motivate the assignment of other nouns, it is included in the figures. This is to show that the role of analogical extension in the analysis is reasonably minimal.

In Figure 1, the semantic motivation at the center is Animateness. Many nouns are assigned based on this, e.g. all humans, animals, and spirits.[7] This motivation is salient and transparent, which is why the gender values are often labeled ANIMATE

FIGURE 1. Motivation from animateness: Imitation of animateness, playing cards, measurements of time, winter, gloves

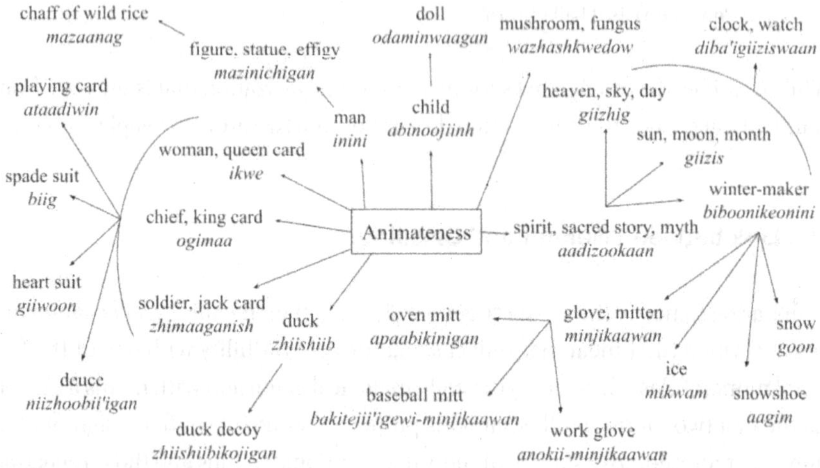

and INANIMATE. There are many analogical extensions stemming from nouns with animate meanings—for example, nouns referring to imitations of animate entities, e.g. statues, dolls, and decoys. Likewise, words for the queen, king, and jack cards are ANIMATE based on imitation. This cluster of ANIMATE nouns motivates all terms for playing cards being assigned ANIMATE gender, e.g. the numbered cards and suits.

On the right side of the figure, we have celestial bodies and winter, which are personified in mythology, e.g. Grandmother Moon and the Winter-Maker. As these are also used for measurements of time, e.g. day, month, and year, the cluster gives rise to the analogical extension that measurements of time are ANIMATE, explaining the assignment of *diba'igiiziswan* 'clock, watch'. Nouns associated with winter, e.g. *mikwam* 'ice', *agim* 'snowshoe', and *goon* 'snow', form another salient cluster by analogical extension.[8] Lastly in this figure, nouns referring to winter gloves and mittens motivate the assignment of all kinds of gloves and mittens in the ANIMATE gender, even those that have nothing to do with winter, e.g. *apaabikinigan* 'oven mitt'.[9]

The second figure has at its center the sortal classifier /-eg-/ 'sheetlike', which sometimes surfaces as /-iig-/ due to phonological conditioning (Valentine 2001:346). One important cluster here is different kinds of hides, which are used to make drums and lead to the analogical extension that all kinds of drums are ANIMATE.

FIGURE 2. Motivation from the sortal classifier /-eg-/ 'sheetlike': Hides, drums

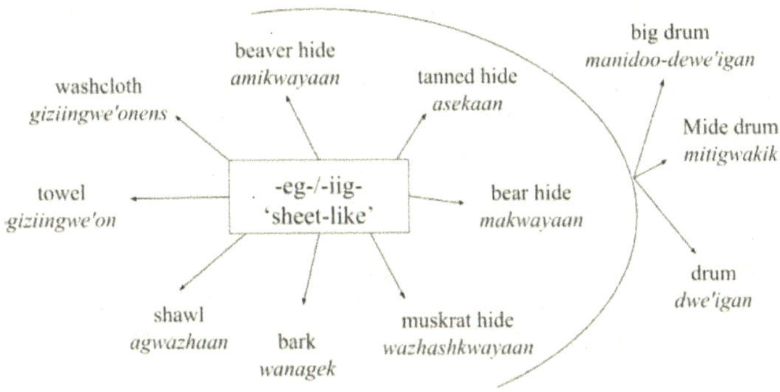

FIGURE 3. Motivation from the sortal classifier /-aabiig-/ 'stringlike': Nets, roots, sewing implements

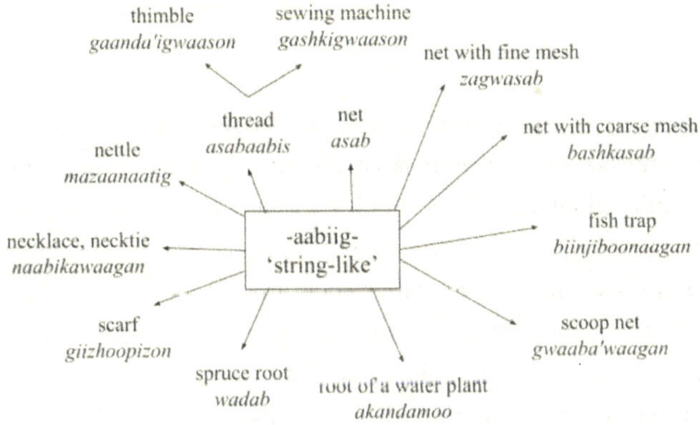

Also of note are nouns with different 'sheetlike' meanings, e.g., *wanagek* 'bark' and *agwashaan* 'shawl'.

The third figure shows assignments motivated by the sortal classifier /-aabiig-/ 'stringlike'. This includes some stringlike plants, e.g. *wadab* 'spruce root' and *mazaanaatig* 'nettle'; the fibers of the latter were used to make string. There is also *asabaabis* 'piece of thread' and importantly, *asab* 'net'. These words have a clear relation, and all kinds of nets are thus assigned to the ANIMATE gender.

The fourth figure is an important one, capturing a wide variety of nouns, the majority of which directly exhibit the 'sticklike' properties highlighted by the sortal classifier. This includes all kinds of trees and tree boughs. Many other nouns with sticklike meanings, such as *dewe'iganaak* 'drumstick', *ozhibii'igaanaak* 'pen, pencil', and *okaadaak* 'carrot', contain /-aak/. This morpheme, with the meaning 'sticklike',

FIGURE 4. Motivation from the sortal classifier /-aatig-/ 'sticklike': Trees, boughs, some body parts, some food

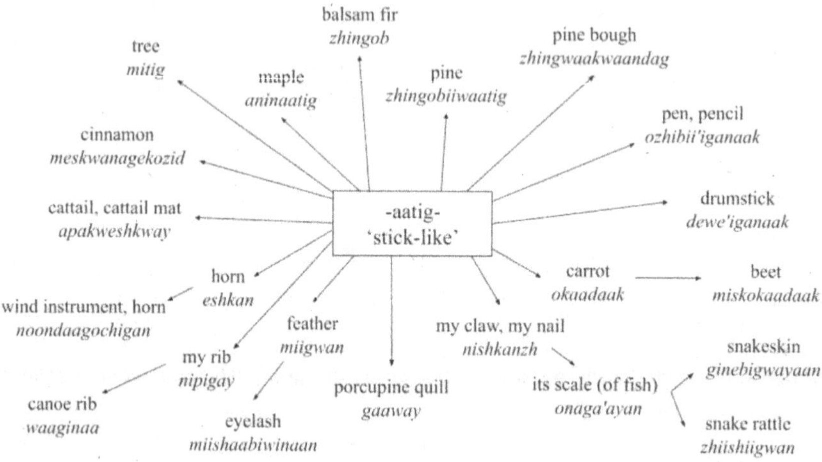

also functions as a verbal classifier (Meyer 2020a; see also Valentine 2001:346). One analogical extension, from *okaadaak* 'carrot' to *miskokaadaak* 'beet', is strengthened by the derivational relation, i.e. a beet is literally a 'red carrot', despite the bulbous shape.

Compatibility with this classifier accounts for the ANIMATE assignment of nouns such as *gaaway* 'porcupine quill', *miigwan* 'feather', and *nishkanzh* 'my claw/nail'. Many kinds of claws are sticklike, i.e. long, thin, and rigid, and the same noun is used to refer to nails, though we may not view nails as sticklike. The shape and consistency of nails is similar to that of scales, leading to the ANIMATE assignment of *onaga'ayan* and the subsequent analogical extension to *zhiishiigwan* 'snake rattle'.

The next figure (5) features the sortal classifier /-aabik-/ 'mineral' at its center. This classifier highlights a particular material, rather than shape and flexibility as the previous sortal classifiers did. It includes such nouns as *waabigan* 'clay', *asin* 'stone', and *akik* 'kettle'. The last of these gives rise to the analogical extension that metal containers for water are assigned to the ANIMATE gender; previously they would have been made of clay or birch bark. Nouns with meanings related to currency are also ANIMATE, since the currency used by Europeans was made of metal. The cluster of nouns with the semantics of currency is so numerous that it forms its own analogical extension for ANIMATE assignment, applying to nouns with currency meanings that are not even metal, e.g. *mazina'igani-zhooniya* 'paper money'. Finally, since all kinds of rocks and stone are ANIMATE, and pipes were made

FIGURE 5. Motivation from the sortal classifier /-aabik-/ 'mineral': Stones, metal water containers, money, pipes, tobacco

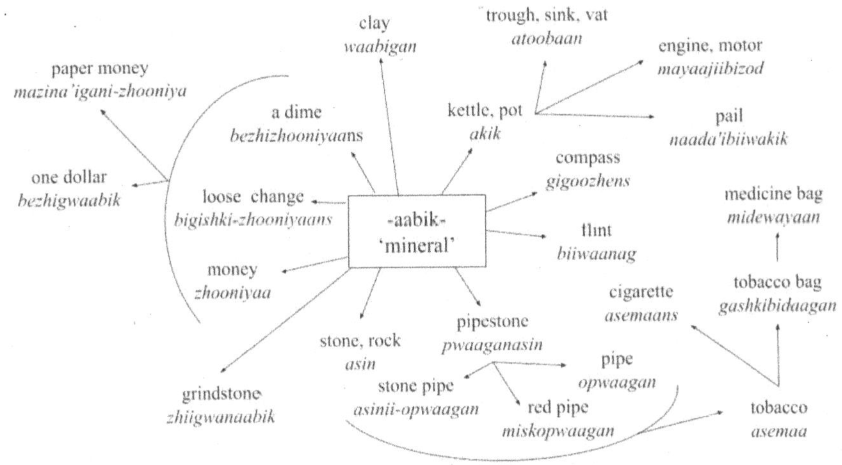

of stone and used with tobacco, this sortal classifier also accounts for all kinds of pipes and tobacco as ANIMATE.[10]

The final figure, (6), showing motivation from the sortal classifier /-minag-/ 'berrylike', is very full. There are three groups of nouns showing 'mixed' gender assignment: plants, food, and body parts. We have seen already that plants assigned to the ANIMATE gender can be accounted for mostly by compatibility with the sortal classifier /-aatig-/ 'sticklike', as can some food and body parts, and a few other plants with /-aabiig-/ 'stringlike'. The sortal classifier /-minag-/ 'berrylike' accounts for the rest of the food and body parts, as well as shells and beads.

The body parts fitting these semantics are all small and round.[11] It seems that *ninishiwag* 'my testicles' may have motivated the analogical extension to nouns referring to and associated with reproductivity. Another small, round body part, which resembles testicles but serves a very different purpose, is *wiinzhinaa* 'castor sac'. These are found on beavers of both sexes, and are responsible for the secretion of a fatty, yellowish substance called castoreum. Beavers use castoreum for marking their territory and adding additional waterproofing to their fur. This substance was highly prized by European traders, and it is still used in food and perfume manufacturing for its vanilla-like qualities. An analogical extension from the derivationally related *wiinzhinaa* motivates the assignment of *amiko-wiinin* 'beaver fat' to the ANIMATE category, despite all other kinds of fat being INANIMATE.

FIGURE 6. Motivation from the sortal classifier /-minag-/ 'berrylike': A lot of food including corn and grain products, food-producing bushes, beads, a lot of body parts including reproductive organs

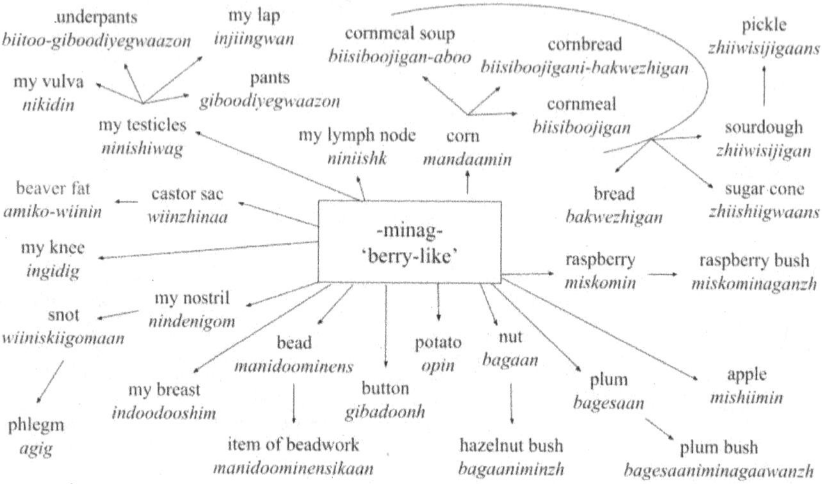

A comparison of nouns often employed to illustrate the lack of transparency in assignment is between ANIMATE *wiiniskiigomaan* 'snot' and *agig* 'phlegm' and INANIMATE *zikowin* 'saliva' and *zhishigagowaan* 'vomit'. These differing assignments are due to the origin of these bodily fluids, and the availability of an analogical extension to the former but not the latter. *Nindenigom* 'my nostril' seems to always be ANIMATE, motivated by its small, round shape and compatibility with the sortal classifier /-minag-/. Snot and phlegm are both mucus mixed with viruses, bacteria, and other particulates needing to be expelled by the body, so they look alike and often co-occur. An analogical extension from *nindenigom* motivates the ANIMATE assignments of 'snot' and 'phlegm', while no such motivation exists for 'saliva' and 'vomit'.

Focusing on *mandaamin* 'corn', the kernel of which is certainly berrylike, we see that all corn products are also ANIMATE by analogical extension. Prior to the introduction of wheat products, grain products were made of corn. Later, this analogical extension continued for all kinds of wheat products, e.g. *bakwezhigan* 'bread'. While *zhiiwisijigaans* 'pickle' is not itself a wheat product, the noun is formed by adding the diminutive to *zhiiwisijigan* 'sourdough', so that a pickle is literally called 'a little sourdough'.

Further Considerations: Multiple Motivations, /-isag-/, and Taxonomic Effects

First, note that some nouns may have multiple motivations for assignment to the animate gender. For example, *mitigwaagim* 'ski' could be animate through association with winter or the classifier /-aatig-/ 'sticklike'. Likewise, *zhiishiigwaans* 'sugarcone' could be animate through association with grain products or *zhiishiigwan* 'snake rattle'. This is not a problem for the analysis, since more motivation leads speakers to the same conclusion, i.e. assignment to the animate gender.

Second, there is one more classifier that explains the assignment of a group of nouns to the ANIMATE gender, which is /-isag-/ 'worked wood' (Figure 7). Its most recent usage, however, was mensural and not sortal. Baraga (1878:311) records its usage for measurements of barrels, kegs, and boxes, with the mensural numeral root for 'one'. More specific mensural classifiers have since replaced it, e.g. /-makak-/ 'box', and it is currently only a verbal classifier. The semantics are compatible with a sortal usage, and given that it accounts for nouns with meanings of canoe parts and cars, it is plausible that it functioned as a sortal classifier in the distant past.

Readers may wonder about several nouns that are expected to be ANIMATE by this analysis, but are actually INANIMATE. These include *wiigwaas* 'birch bark', *asabaab* 'thread', *mitig* 'stick', *bigiw* 'tar', *miin* 'blueberry', and *misan* 'firewood'. The reason these nouns are INANIMATE, despite perfectly fitting the semantics of the sortal classifiers, is because they name the category as the superordinate term, i.e. as a hypernym.[12] Similar nouns that are ANIMATE represent instances of the category as subordinate terms, i.e. hyponyms. For example, the superordinate term *mitig* 'stick' is INANIMATE, while specific kinds of sticks, e.g. *dewe'iganaak* 'drumstick', *gaaway* 'porcupine quill', and *miigwan* 'feather', are ANIMATE.[13] This effect of taxonomy is not uncommon in gender assignment (Zubin and Köpcke 1986).

These nouns also appear to be the lexical origin for the relevant classifier forms, though further diachronic data is needed to confirm this (see (7)).[14] The change from a noun to a classifier is accompanied by phonological reduction and the addition of premedial, e.g. /aa-/, or post-medial material, e.g. /-ag/ (Valentine 2001:332).

FIGURE 7. Motivation from the sortal classifier /-isag-/ 'worked wood': Canoe parts, cars

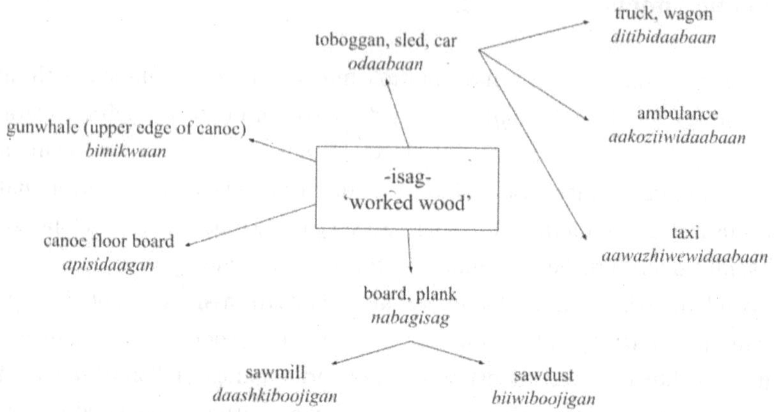

(7) Lexical Origin of Sortal Classifier Forms

a.	wiigwaas 'birch bark'	>	/-iig-/ 'sheetlike'
b.	asabaab 'thread'	>	/-aabiig-/ 'stringlike'
c.	mitig 'stick'	>	/-aatig-/ 'sticklike'
d.	bigiw 'tar'	>	/-aabik-/ 'mineral'
e.	miin 'blueberry'	>	/-minag-/ 'berrylike'
f.	misan 'firewood'	>	/-isag-/ 'worked wood'

An instance of a category, i.e. hyponym, may serve as the lexical origin for a classifier, and in the process become a hypernym.[15] For example, the noun *miin* 'blueberry' refers to a specific kind of berry and is a hyponym. When speakers use it as the classifier /-minag-/, the semantic range broadens to refer to berry-shaped referents, transforming it into a hypernym. Mithun (1986:391) discusses this process, noting that the lexical origins of classifiers are not necessarily the most prototypical instances of the category, but the most frequent.[16]

Dialectal Variation

The apparently "exceptional" nouns under discussion are a source of dialectal variation. This variation is the result of differing perceptions and analogical extensions being conventionalized in different speech communities, the fading of the sortal classifier system, and the productivity of the gender system. The variability in assignment of *ingidig* 'my knee', and *miishaabiwinaan* 'eyelash', for example, are attributable to a difference in the salient characteristics of these body parts encoded in the language. 'Knee' is ANIMATE in communities where the salient aspects of its shape were small and round, making it compatible with /-minag-/. In other communities, the salient aspects of its shape were different, maybe as more of a cap or half of a round than fully round, and the noun is INANIMATE there. Similarly, 'eyelash' may be perceived as similar to a feather, and the analogical extension from that noun (rather than direct motivation from a sortal classifier as with 'knee') motivated its ANIMATE assignment.[17] Other communities did not make this analogy and the noun is INANIMATE there. The variability results from the differing perspectives encoded in the language, not a singular, objective reality (see Lakoff 1987 for more discussion of how human experience affects our creation of categories). It is not the case that there is an insurmountable difference in how speakers in various communities literally perceive knees and eyelashes, and that they are incapable of perceiving them otherwise. The reality is less rigid; there are simply multiple ways these body parts could be perceived and encoded in the language, and different communities settled on slightly different representations in the language.

Some variation may also be observed in the cluster of body-part nouns motivated by reproductivity. *Nishiwag* 'my testicles' is ANIMATE due to compatibility with the sortal classifier /-minag-/ 'small, round'. Possibly bolstered by *doodooshim* 'breast', which is also directly motivated by compatibility with the sortal classifier /-minag-/ and is part of the (female) reproductive system, a noun cluster motivated by associations with reproductivity emerged, which may or may not include nouns with referents like 'vulva', 'penis', 'my lap, (front of) thigh', 'pants', and 'underpants'. Note that *nibwaam* 'my thigh (back of)' is INANIMATE. Both ANIMATE and INANIMATE nouns for 'penis' exist in different dialects. It seems the more traditional term, *wiinag*, remained INANIMATE, since it did not match the shape requirements for /-minag-/, but more recent or slang terms may be ANIMATE, e.g. *baashkzigan*, based on compatibility with the more recent and salient motivation from reproductivity.

Valentine (2001:116–118) writes that the Eastern and Odawa dialects differ from others in that nouns for money are INANIMATE. For some communities, it was salient that money was made of metal, a mineral material, and thus all money terms are assigned to the ANIMATE gender, while for other communities it was not. This leads to the question of how analogical extension can be reined in, to which I offer three constraints. First, only those extensions that resonate with speakers will become conventionalized. An analogical extension can start with a single "Trojan horse" noun (Corbett 1991:98–99), which is assigned by a new analogical extension, but then opens the door for similar nouns, e.g. *akik* 'kettle'. Secondly, a derivational relationship is often visible between nouns leading to analogical extension, e.g. *zhiiwisijigan* 'sourdough' and *zhiiwisijigaans* 'pickle'. Third, cross-linguistically, many of the extensions shown here are common, e.g. celestial bodies personified in mythological stories and thus categorized with humans or animates (Corbett 1991:10). The more analogical extensions there are in gender assignment, the less transparent it becomes. This leads newer speakers to change it to match salient motivations.

Another reason some other nouns are not ANIMATE in certain communities despite fitting the semantics of the sortal classifiers is that the sortal classifier system seems to be fading.[18] In the list of sortal classifiers (6), it should be noted that (6d) /-aabik-/ 'mineral' no longer functions as such and has instead become lexicalized as the morpheme for 'dollar' (Meyer 2020a). Speakers rejected its use with a huge list of semantically compatible nouns, e.g. pot, kettle, doorknob, windowpane glass, boulder, belt buckle, stove, etc., even commenting for the last, "It sounds like there's a dollar on the stove." A narrowing of semantics may be indicative of the fading of a classifier system (Grinevald 2000:85). Indeed, it seems the classifier /-isag-/ underwent a similar change earlier, from sortal numeral classifier, to mensural numeral classifier, to not functioning as a numeral classifier at all.

The fading of the sortal classifier system affects the system of gender assignment such that the motivation from the sortal classifiers is no longer salient for speakers. Newly coined nouns that are semantically compatible with sortal classifiers are not ANIMATE, and it is possible that some older nouns that are compatible may be recategorized as INANIMATE, in accordance with (unconscious) regularization of assignment. This may explain why the Eastern and Odawa dialects differ from others in that nouns for stones and hides are INANIMATE (Valentine 2001:116–118).

Currently, the salient motivations for assignment are noun clusters like those listed earlier, e.g. pipes, beads, kettles, grain products, tobacco, trees, drums, feathers, reproductivity, cars, nets. That the gender assignment system has continued to change is a sign that it is a productive and dynamic system. Aikhenvald (2000:313) says, "The productivity, or vitality, of a system is measured by its ability to accept and classify new members, and reanalyze and extend the semantic range of a noun categorization device over time." The system of gender assignment, like other aspects of grammar, is largely unconscious, though some speakers may have conscious insight into current motivations.

Further diachronic research is needed to determine exactly why certain nouns show variation. This analysis predicts that the nouns most likely to show variation are those motivated solely by compatibility with sortal classifiers that have not been reanalyzed as one of the aforementioned noun clusters (e.g. stone), those that are the result of an extension that failed to solidify in certain communities (e.g. money terms), as well as those that constitute less central, more unique analogical extensions, e.g. *miishaabiwinaan* 'eyelash'.

Conclusion

There has been much discussion and theorizing about the apparently "exceptional" nouns of semantic gender assignment in Ojibwe and across the Algonquian family, i.e. those that have inanimate referents but ANIMATE gender (e.g. Greenberg 1954; Hallowell 1955, 1960, 1976; Black 1969; Darnell and Vanek 1976; Black-Rogers 1982; Straus and Brightman 1982; Corbett 1991; Dahlstrom 1995; Goddard 2002; Quinn 2001, 2018). It has been shown here that there is no need to consider these nouns as exceptional, once the role of sortal classifiers and a small amount of analogical extension are taken into account. Nouns may be assigned to the ANIMATE gender if their meaning is (1) animate, (2) compatible with one of the sortal classifiers, or (3) associated through analogical extension with a noun assigned via the first two routes. Dialectal variation is the result of differing analogical extensions in different speech communities, as well as the fading of the sortal classifier system in combination with the productivity of the gender system. While this analysis seems to account for gender assignment in Ojibwe quite well, further detailed research on gender and classifier systems within particular Algonquian languages and across the language family (e.g. Goddard 2002 for gender, Biedny et al. 2021 for classifiers) will illuminate whether this approach is applicable to other Algonquian languages.

NOTES

1. Many thanks to speakers Elizabeth and Leonard Kimewon, and my mentor Susan Askwith, for teaching me about the language, as well as my advisers Amy Dahlstrom, Salikoko Mufwene, and Itamar Francez, for their guidance and feedback. Thanks are

also due to the undergraduate assistants who contributed through the Sapir Scholars Program: Anand Abraham, Anna Whitney, and Garrett Johnson. All errors are my own.

2. For further discussion of the history of predictability vs. motivation, the interested reader is referred to Lakoff (1987:65, 96) and Dahlstrom (1995:52–53).
3. For a review of the history of semantics in gender assignment as it relates to Algonquian languages, readers are referred to Corbett (1991:20–24); Dahlstrom (1995); and Meyer (2020b). For a more detailed discussion of gender and classifiers in Ojibwe, as well as relevant cross-linguistic data, readers are referred to Meyer (2020b).
4. Mensural classifiers are used with *ngo(dw)*- 'one'. Sortal classifiers are used with *bezhigw*- 'one'. Both forms are traceable to Proto-Algonquian (Rhodes and Costa 2003:181–183).
5. Examples (6a–c) and (6e) were provided by speakers during field work, while (6d) is from Baraga (1878:312). The sortal classifier /-aabik-/ in (6d) no longer functions as such, since it cannot appear with overt nouns. It has become lexicalized for expressing dollar amounts (Meyer 2020a). This is discussed below under Further Considerations.
6. Inanimate is also considered the unmarked gender, used to determine agreement when there is no associated noun, or the gender of the referent of the noun is unknown or unspecified (Goddard 2002:221–224).
7. A reviewer notes that *aadizookaan* 'spirit, sacred story, myth' may be animate when referring to spirits and inanimate when referring to stories. This is compatible with semantic assignment and motivation based on animacy, since spirits are animate referents and stories are not.
8. An independent noun for 'winter' does not exist; *biboon* is a verb meaning 'it is winter'. When expressing measurements of time, preverbs are used, e.g. *ningo-biboon* 'one winter' and *ningo-giizis* 'one month'.
9. Note that *apaabikinigan* also exists as an inanimate noun meaning 'potholder'. When the noun referent is no longer a glove or mitten, the assignment differs. For more discussion on such animate/inanimate noun pairs, termed 'lexical recategorization', see Meyer (2020b).
10. A reviewer notes that asin 'rock' may be inanimate for some speakers if the rock is large and stationary. Treatment of this noun herein is limited to its entry in the OPD, which is only animate. A full discussion of potential effects of size and utility are outside the scope of this paper, but Goddard (2002:217–220) discusses this in regard to the assignment of hides in Meskwaki.
11. The body parts motivated by /-minag-/ 'berrylike' also come in pairs, though this may simply be caused by natural human symmetry.
12. Mithun (1986:387) observes that in prototypical classifier systems, classifiers serve as

hypernyms.

13. A word derived from *mitig* 'stick' is *mitigoons* 'small stick'. A small stick may be an instance of a stick, but the referent may not be considered sufficiently distinct, resulting in the same inanimate assignment as *mitig*. This is compatible with the fact that use of the diminutive is not usually accompanied by a change in gender.
14. Cross-linguistically, classifiers most often develop from nouns (Mithun 1986:388–391; Aikhenvald 2000:353). Grinevald (2000:61) also states that classifiers have a clear lexical origin.
15. A term for a hypernym that is simultaneously a hyponym is 'autohyponym' (Horn 1984).
16. A reviewer noted that inanimate *manoomin* 'wild rice', translated literally as 'good berry', contains the morpheme /-min/ 'berry' and asked whether this would be a hypernym or a hyponym. While *manoomin* has some berrylike qualities in the way it grows, it does not meet the relevant shape criterion for compatibility with the classifier and is neither. In other words, the morpheme /-min/ in nouns is not the same morpheme as /-min-/ in the classifier /-minag-/, though they are historically related. The former is potentially applicable to referents with any berrylike qualities, while the latter requires a berrylike shape, hence its compatibility with many inedible referents. This is similar to how English has two related morphemes /un-/. One prefixes to adjectives and gives the opposite meaning, e.g. *unpainted*. The other prefixes to verbs and reverses an action, e.g. *unlock*. Something must first be locked in order to be unlocked, but it does not need to first be painted in order to be unpainted.
17. A reviewer points out that *nimaamaa* 'my eyebrow' also shows variation across communities. While not part of the OPD database, this can be accounted for the same way as *miishaabiwinaan* 'eyelash'.
18. The use of verbal classifiers and mensural (numeral) classifiers is alive and well. This claim is limited to sortal (numeral) classifiers.

REFERENCES

Aikhenvald, Alexandra Y. 2000. *Classifiers: A Typology of Noun Categorization Devices*. Oxford: Oxford University Press.

Baraga, Frederic. 1878. *A Theoretical and Practical Grammar of the Otchipwe Language for the Use of Missionaries and Other Persons Living among the Indians*. Montreal: Beauchemin & Valois.

Biedny, Jeremy, Matthew Burner, Andrea Cudworth, and Monica Macaulay. 2021. Classifier Medials across Algonquian: A First Look. *International Journal of American Linguistics*

87(1):1–47.

Black, Mary B. 1969. A Note on Gender in Eliciting Ojibwa Semantic Structures. *Anthropological Linguistics* 11(6):177–186.

Black-Rogers, Mary B. 1982. Algonquian Gender Revisited: Animate Nouns and Ojibwa 'Power'—an Impasse? *Research on Language and Social Interaction* 15(1):59–76.

Corbett, Greville. 1991. *Gender*. Cambridge: Cambridge University Press.

Dahlstrom, Amy. 1995. Motivation vs. Predictability in Algonquian Gender. *Papers of the 26th Algonquian Conference*, ed. by David H. Pentland, pp. 52–66. Winnipeg: University of Manitoba.

Darnell, Regna, and Anthony L. Vanek. 1976. The Semantic Basis of the Animate/Inanimate Distinction in Cree. *Research on Language and Social Interaction* 9(3–4):159–180.

Goddard, Ives. 2002. Grammatical Gender in Algonquian. *Papers of the 33rd Algonquian Conference*, ed. by H. C. Wolfart, pp. 195–231. Winnipeg: University of Manitoba.

Greenberg, Joseph H. 1954. Concerning Inferences from Linguistic to Nonlinguistic Data. *Language in Culture: Conference on the Interrelations of Language and Other Aspects of Culture*, ed. by Harry Hoijer, pp. 3–10. Chicago: University of Chicago Press.

Grinevald, Colette. 2000. A Morphosyntactic Typology of Classifiers. *Systems of Nominal Classification*, vol. 4: *Language, Culture, and Cognition*, ed. by Gunter Senft, pp. 50–92. Cambridge: Cambridge University Press.

Hallowell, Alfred I. 1955. *Culture and Experience*. Philadelphia: University of Pennsylvania Press.

Hallowell, Alfred I. 1960. Ojibwa Ontology, Behavior and World View. *Culture in History: Essays in Honor of Paul Radin*, ed. by Stanley Diamond, pp. 19–52. New York: Columbia University Press.

Hallowell, Alfred I. 1976. Contributions to Anthropology: Selected Papers of A. Irving Hallowell. Chicago: University of Chicago Press.

Horn, Laurence. 1984. Ambiguity, Negation, and the London School of Parsimony. *Proceedings of NELS 14*, ed. by Charles Jones, pp. 108–131. Amherst: GLSA, University of Massachusetts Amherst.

Lakoff, George. 1987. Women, Fire and Dangerous Things: What Categories Reveal about the Mind. Chicago: University of Chicago Press.

Lucy, John. 2000. Systems of Nominal Classification: A Concluding Discussion. *Systems of Nominal Classification*, vol. 4: *Language, Culture, and Cognition*, ed. by Gunter Senft, pp. 326–341. Cambridge: Cambridge University Press.

Meyer, Cherry. 2019. The Status of Classifying Morphemes in Ojibwe. *Papers of the 48th Algonquian Conference*, ed. by Monica Macaulay and Margaret Noodin, pp. 159–172. East

Lansing: Michigan State University Press.

Meyer, Cherry. 2020a. Numeral Classifiers in Ojibwe. *Papers of the 49th Algonquian Conference*, ed. by Monica Macaulay and Margaret Noodin, pp. 115–132. East Lansing: Michigan State University Press.

Meyer, Cherry. 2020b. Noun Categorization in Ojibwe: Gender and Classifiers. PhD thesis, University of Chicago.

Mithun, Marianne. 1986. The Convergence of Noun Classification Systems. *Noun Classes and Categorization*, ed. by Colette Craig, pp. 379–397. Philadelphia: John Benjamins.

Nichols, John D. 2015. *Ojibwe People's Dictionary* (OPD). https://ojibwe.lib.umn.edu.

Online Etymology Dictionary. 2019. https://www.etymonline.com/search?q=gender.

Quinn, Conor. 2001. A Preliminary Survey of Animacy Categories in Penobscot. *Papers of the 32nd Algonquian Conference*, ed. by John D. Nichols, pp. 395–426. Winnipeg: University of Manitoba.

Quinn, Conor. 2018. Productivity vs. Predictability: Evidence for the Syntax and Semantics of Animate Gender in Four Northeastern-Area Algonquian Languages. In *Gender and Noun Classification*, ed. by Éric Mathieu, Myriam Dali, and Gita Zareikar, pp. 249–265. Oxford: Oxford University Press.

Rhodes, Richard A. 1985. *Eastern Ojibwa-Chippewa-Ottawa Dictionary*, vol. 3: *Trends in Linguistics: Documentation*, ed. by Werner Winter. Berlin: Walter de Gruyter.

Rhodes, Richard A., and David J. Costa. 2003. The History of Algonquian Number Words. *Essays in Algonquian, Catawban, and Siouan Linguistics in Memory of Frank T. Siebert, Jr.*, ed. by Blair A. Rudes and David J. Costa, pp. 181–215. Algonquian and Iroquoian Linguistics Memoir 16. Winnipeg: University of Manitoba Press.

Straus, Anne Terry, and Robert Brightman. 1982. The Implacable Raspberry. *Research on Language and Social Interaction* 15(2):97–137.

Valentine, J. Randolph. 2001. *Nishnaabemwin Reference Grammar*. Toronto: University of Toronto Press.

Zubin, David, and Klaus-Michael Köpcke. 1986. Gender and Folk Taxonomy: The Indexical Relation between Grammatical and Lexical Categorization. *Noun Classes and Categorization*, ed. by Colette Craig, pp. 139–180. Philadelphia: John Benjamins.

Constellational Visions

International Configurations of Survivance in Gerald Vizenor's *Hiroshima Bugi*

Maral Aguilera-Moradipour

In *As We Have Always Done* (2017), Michi Saagiig Nishnaabeg scholar Leanne Betasamosake Simpson explains that constellations convey Anishinaabe notions of relationality—the view that relationships, not discrete subjects, are the primary state of existence.[1] Through a close reading of Gerald Vizenor's *Hiroshima Bugi: Atomu 57* (2003), this paper contemplates Vizenor's writing about survivance as a practice of relationality. He does so through the evocation of stars and stones that symbolize Anishinaabe stories and cosmology in a way that resonates with the cosmologies of the Japanese and Ainu as an enactment of Anishinaabe internationalism.

Although Vizenor grounds survivance (the practice of active presence in the face of domination) in Anishinaabe epistemology, his novel offers the term as a useful way of thinking about liberation between peoples—in particular, between Anishinaabeg, other Indigenous peoples of North America, the Ainu, and the Japanese. Specifically, I demonstrate how Vizenor extends his concept of survivance to Anishinaabe and non-Anishinaabe peoples often separated by considerable time and space, thereby enacting relationality. Like constellations composed of distant celestial entities whose light reaches our eyes sometimes long after a star has died, such relationality between people transcends linear notions of both dimensions.

In *Manifest Manners*, Vizenor (1994:vii) characterizes survivance as "an active sense of presence, the continuance of native stories, not a mere reaction or a survivable name. Native survivance stories are renunciations of dominance, tragedy, and victimry."[2] Survivance, then, is a practice co-constituted through what Vizenor calls "natural reason"—embodied, relational, place-based knowledges and ways of knowing—and speaks to Indigenous continuance.[3] Survivance includes practices like the continuance of Anishinaabe stories and storytelling, reliance on and relationships with nonhuman entities in the natural world, and maintenance of Anishinaabemowin. Within these practices, survivance is the inherent capacity of Anishinaabe society to withstand and outlast any form of domination, exploitation, or deracination. Although it is relevant to the colonial moment, survivance preexists colonialism in the form of Anishinaabe relationality, which is rooted in the relationships to time and place that enable Anishinaabeg to move through one time to another, through one geolocation to another. Anishinaabe poet and scholar Margaret Noodin provides a helpful starting point for conceptualizing this relationality, in the form of a story that she synopsizes. This story follows Nanabozho and his brother, who was a stone. In a version shared by Noodin in *Bawaajimo: A Dialect of Dreams in Anishinaabemowin Language and Literature* (2014:165), the stone-brother becomes jealous of Nanabozho's stories of worldly travels and the teasing he receives about "his permanence and inability to be anywhere but one place." Cunning proves itself a family trait as the stone-brother offers Nanabozho a way to destroy him, but ultimately tricks Nanabozho into helping him. After Nanabozho follows the instructions to toss the stone into a fire followed by an ice-cold shower, his stone-brother is not destroyed but shattered and scattered all over the earth.

Vizenor often uses the term 'stone' to refer to tribal tricksters, stories, and himself. Significantly, tricksters are linked to stones. While I elaborate on tricksters more broadly below, here I consider stones' manifold meanings. In *The Heirs of Columbus* (1991:9), Vizenor's main character states that his "stories are stones." In *Postindian Conversations* (1999:130–131) he states: "I am a stone, and stones are native stories . . . Everywhere there are stones of that first fire of the tricksters." And in *Griever: An American Monkey King in China* (1990), he associates the Anishinaabe Trickster with the Monkey King, a Chinese trickster, through the Monkey King's birth via stone. About this latter connection, Vizenor (1993:50) states: "the beginning of life comes from something substantial, like a rock."[4] As Noodin expertly shares in *Bawaajimo*, Anne M. Dunn tells a story in which the first storyteller is a stone.[5] These stone stories, which for Noodin provide the foundations for Anishinaabe literary studies, inform my approach towards and methodology for reading the novel. Indeed, in an interview a decade before the publication of *Hiroshima Bugi*, Vizenor (1993:51) refers to the story in which "the trickster-stone bursts" and says that "today every stone from anywhere on this world is metaphorically from that first break-up of the trickster."

Following the trajectories of stardust and stone in *Hiroshima Bugi* through the circuitous journey undertaken in the protagonist Ronin's narrative is not simple. So, I offer a brief sketch to contextualize my analysis of relationality in the novel. Ronin Ainoko Browne is the 57-year-old son of an Anishinaabe World War II veteran and Japanese (possibly Ainu) boogie dancer. He was born in Japan, moved to America as a young teen, and returns to Japan to fulfill his father's vision and to destroy the symbols of "fake" or "nuclear" peace, which are sites memorializing the atomic bomb. We learn that his mother, Okichi, abandoned him to an orphanage for the mixed (*hafu*) kids of the war and that the White Earth Nation adopted him in his teens. He lived there well into adulthood until he went in search of his father. His father, Orion "Nightbreaker" Browne—who is unaware that he has a son—worked in Nevada at a nuclear test site after returning from the war and subsequently departs for the Mississippi headwaters and finally to Nogales, Arizona, to stay at the Hotel Manidoo, a hotel for Indigenous war veterans. Manidoo Envoy, an *Anishinaabenini* from Leech Lake who is also a connoisseur of Japanese culture, becomes Nightbreaker's roommate at the Hotel.[6] Because Nightbreaker dies several days before Ronin arrives at the hotel to finally meet his father, Manidoo Envoy is the one to receive Ronin. After Ronin's departure for his adventures in Japan, it is Manidoo Envoy and the other Native vets at Hotel Manidoo who receive the boxes of Ronin's writings from Miko, a hostess and Japanese shaman, and put them together into a book. In this book, Manidoo Envoy provides the explanatory companion segments to Ronin's chapters. Given these meanderings, it is not surprising that Ronin bears different names at different times. Through his many nominal and physical transformations and his cunning—or trickster moves—Ronin arrives in Japan to forge relationships with the Japanese and Ainu and deface the symbols of fake peace, victimry (a term that Vizenor uses throughout his novel), and domination.

I contend that in *Hiroshima Bugi*, Vizenor shatters the stone through language and casts one of its pieces across the world to Japan, where it transforms in its new location, like the tiny stones Nanabozho tosses into the air that turn into butterflies in a story shared by Basil Johnston (n.d.). These stone shards or pebbles capable of transformation are stories that can be considered nodes of Anishinaabe thought that, as an embodied practice—as with all matter—have a natural frequency of vibration. I extrapolate from this physical property for my reading of the novel and suggest that when in alignment with another body, or story, that shares this natural frequency, the second entity begins to vibrate in tandem. Each entity maintains its distinct integrity, but both resonate in recognition of a shared or compatible quality. This is what I call READING FOR RESONANCE.

Reading for resonance means recognizing compatibility without conflation and respecting locational difference—a crucial quality of constellations. Accordingly, Vizenor's scattered stones elicit storied resonances in their new locations in time and space while extending his concept of survivance outwards from an Anishinaabe center. In so doing, they unsettle the processes of settler colonialism and domination for both Anishinaabe and non-Anishinaabe peoples. At the same time, Vizenor models how other peoples can mobilize from within their own cosmologies and localities in imagining alternative ways of cohabiting the Earth. I argue that Vizenor's work connects overlapping and dismembering systems of power and domination to reveal to the grounded, careful reader the interlocking ways in which systems of dominance operate. Through the stories of stone, *Hiroshima Bugi* conveys the risks of violating relationality between human beings and other entities. Furthermore, the concept of shattering stone can be applied to other formative moments that radiate outwards and form their own nodes or resonances. In this way, the stone provides not just a literary genealogy but also a reading model. A place-aware reading of his novel, focusing on the motif of rivers that weave through the named and implied places within their watersheds, enables readers to envision a world in which relationality, a concept underpinned by natural reason, is honored.

Stars, Stones, and Stories

The image that Vizenor conjures of a first fire of tricksters that manifests stones brings to mind the explosion of another primordial fire, namely, a dying star. From the explosion of a dying star comes dust and gas and the formation of a nebula. Under the right conditions, this dust and gas come together to birth new stars and planets. Elements like silicon, carbon, and others that make up the stone on the

Earth were at one time stardust—from a first fire of creation. *Hiroshima Bugi*'s protagonist, Ronin Browne, is the progeny of Orion Browne. His father's first name calls to mind the Orion Nebula and traces his trickster lineage to the stars and the most ancient creation stories of many of the world's peoples. It also summons the Orion constellation, which, in one understanding from Anishinaabe star knowledge, in the spring shares many of the main identifying stars as a Nanabozho constellation, notably in pointing to the east.[7] While the figure in the constellation is pointing to another important Anishinaabe constellation, more generally, he is pointing eastward, which is the direction of Orion and Ronin's travels from Anishinaabe territory. Moreover, in *Ojibwe Giizhig Anang Masinaa'igan* (*Ojibwe Sky Star Map Constellation Guidebook*)*: An Introduction to Ojibwe Star Knowledge*, Lee et al. (2014:27) explain that the "the main body of Biboonikeonini–Wintermaker overlaps with the Greek Constellation Orion." and signals the time when "winter-only stories are told . . . because a person knows the winter spirits are there" (2014:26). In another view, Orion as Biboonikeonini thus creates a literary climate in which Nanabozho is present and stories about him are appropriate—traditionally, his name and stories are not to be said during other seasons. The name is significant because it underscores the flow of both Orion's and his son's travels and is also a reference to their literary and cosmological inheritance.

Moreover, in regards to this inheritance, although Orion Browne is never named as a descendant of the Brownes from Vizenor's earlier works, his last name and belonging to the White Earth Reservation signal his kinship, and thus Ronin's, to the tribal tricksters of *The Trickster of Liberty* (1988:xii), one of whom states, "The trickster is never in a name, tribal tricksters are in our consciousness." Ronin continues that consciousness both temporally and across novels, repurposing the English language to transmit the vibrations of Anishinaabe stars, stones, stories, and storiers into contemporary contexts and across oceans.

The original Trickster, Nanabozho,[8] as Johnston (1994:17–20) explains, "was a supernatural being" sent by Kitche Manitou to "teach the Anishinaabeg" through his "paradox[ical]" capacity as both "physical and spirit being." Within Anishinaabe cosmology, Nanabozho is clearly a spirit and teacher and not an archetype or literary device; however, Nanabozho embodies and teaches certain modes of thinking within Anishinaabe thought. Noodin (2014:175–178) asserts that Vizenor "rewrites the colonial language that has been used to describe the Anishinaabe," and she argues that tracing the genealogy of Vizenor's usage of "trickster" through the specific Anishinaabe personage enables literary analysis from "an Anishinaabe perspective" and points to "the raw power of transformation and possibility" in Vizenor's trickster novels. Vizenor (1988:x) states that "tribal tricksters are embodied in imagination and liberate the mind" through narratives that "contradict, unsettle, and unglue the creeds" (1987:294). Through embodied imagination, *Hiroshima Bugi* unsettles and unglues creeds of nationhood that are built on racialism and separatism as premises for domination. Vizenor foregrounds survivance as both a basis of Anishinaabe society and a practice counter to racialist and separatist thought that underpin societies of dominance. It follows that the crossblood trickster storiers in Vizenor's works, such as Ronin, are not venerating racial or cultural hybridity. They challenge what Vizenor (1988:x) calls the "translated trickster" figure of the Eurocentric scholarly imagination in which the Anishinaabe are a vanishing tragic race of "Indians"—by death, assimilation, or blood dilution. Therefore, Vizenor's tricksters and Trickster narratives unsettle colonial, anthropological, tragic "translations" of Anishinaabe peoples and thought as only Anishinaabe if they are historically fixed, static, and pure. Anishinaabe stories and society are dynamic and engage with other beings and societies in a distinctly Anishinaabe way.

With *Hiroshima Bugi*, Vizenor casts one of the stones of Anishinaabe stories across the ocean and into Hiroshima, wherein survivance reverberates through the novel as embodied by Ronin and generated through his trickster logic. Within the opening sentences, Vizenor (2003:1) evokes the image of stone as storyteller when Ronin, sitting at the site of the atomic bomb dome, beckons an unidentified addressee to "Come closer to the stone" and "stay overnight [so that] . . . you may see a theater of human horseweeds and perfect memories. This is our new story" (Vizenor 2003:2). By addressing the audience in the second person, the text leaves readers initially to assume that Ronin is speaking to them, thus indicating that the story demands an active listener. An active listener who comes closer to the "stone" can see it as "the planting" of a story within a story, which Noodin (2014:74) identifies as an "essential trait in oral stories" and a technique used in Anishinaabe stories to connect to "other archetypes that may help listeners anchor the story to Anishinaabe" epistemology. By coming closer to the stone or anchoring *Hiroshima Bugi* to Nanabozho as a philosophical impetus—that is, by using a trickster logic or mode—the audience can witness Ronin's "new story," which is the "theater of human horseweeds and perfect memories" (Vizenor 2003:2). I discuss "perfect memories" in the next section, but at this point it is helpful to note that horseweeds were the first plants to grow in the scorched ruins of the atomic bomb and became a source of sustenance for the starving survivors. At one level, Vizenor's metaphor suggests that the trickster mode sustains survivance or a theater of presence and continuance in the face of domination and destruction.

First Resonance: Form and the Constellation of Turtle Island Storiers

In *Hiroshima Bugi*, Vizenor animates the presence and creativity of oral storytelling practices using textual strategies such as nonlinear plot development, the gaps between what is told by co-narrators, and communal discourse. The novel is structured through the constellation of Anishinaabe and other Indigenous storiers of Turtle Island, and in one view is the relational story of three Indigenous characters: Ronin, Nightbreaker, and Ranald MacDonald. Vizenor (2003:22) calls this interwoven story "perfect memories," which I define as a collective vision generated by survivance. The novel begins with Ronin in the atomic ruins. Fifty-eight years after the Americans dropped the bomb on Hiroshima, Ronin stages a number of acts of survivance by subverting the monuments of "fake peace" erected by militarism, colonialism, and dominance. The narrative moves back and forth through time and space and interweaves the life of Ronin with that of Nightbreaker, and with the real-life sailor from the 1800s, Ranald MacDonald, the son of a Chinook mother and Scottish father.

This interwoven quality gestures toward the communal narrative. Vizenor (1988:x) explains that "narrative voices are corporeal in the oral tradition" and this corporeality is carried into the trickster narrative as "a wild venture in communal discourse." The active, corporeal reader is part of the communal discourse and "implies the author, imagines narrative voices, inspires characters, and salutes tribal tricksters" (Vizenor 1988:xi). Each chapter is narrated first by Ronin, then, under the heading Manidoo Envoy, by the unnamed Anishinaabe veteran. Ronin's accounts are sparse, poetic, and literary and often contextualized, problematized, or expanded by Manidoo Envoy's lengthy, citation-filled sections.

Vizenor fashions what Anishinaabe writer and scholar Kimberly M. Blaeser (1999:62) identifies as a practice in Indigenous literature to use "multiple voices to create a cacophony of reality" and demands an active listener or audience who can fill in the gaps and create connections and thus emulates the "often participatory" traditional oral storytelling practices. Moreover, the Manidoo Envoy explains that Ronin sent his journal to the Hotel Manidoo, where it was used by the Native storier veterans to communally produce the novel through their "perfect memories" (Vizenor 2003:9). The novel is not only co-narrated, but it has been communally composed through this practice that Ronin learns from the hotel's Indigenous inhabitants. These co-narrations and collective compositions are also Anishinaabe constellations insofar as the image or story is relationally produced. Perfect memories, then, are the result of a practice of communal composition that challenges dominant, singular narratives of history and anthropology and transcend time and space.[9]

Ronin took the practice of perfect memories across the ocean and "created perfect memories of his father on the road of visions, and that was how he returned with his father, a visionary union, to Japan" (Vizenor 2003:22). Perfect memories are co-created in *waabi* 'vision.' Johnston (1994:119) explains that in Anishinaabe cosmology, visioning is the "capacity" that distinguishes humans from other creatures and casts them as "moral beings" animated by the necessity "to seek and fulfill vision" born of each individual's "innermost being." As an incorporeal faculty, visions are not spatially or temporally restricted. Consequently, Ronin demonstrates how perfect memories offer a mode of constellation or being in relationship that is not restricted by systems of colonial mediation such as military occupations or colonial explorations. Perfect memories are an Anishinaabe mode of survivance comparable to how Simpson (2017:213) interprets Jarret Martineau's (nêhiyaw and Dene Suline) "resistant constellations as flight paths to the future," not as a future TIME but as A WAY OF LIVING THE "FUTURE" NOW in the fugitive spaces outside of the reach of colonialism. Nightbreaker's vision was to trace MacDonald's trip to Japan. He learned Japanese "because he was fascinated by the adventures of Ranald MacDonald, who was a native and, ironically the first teacher of English in Japan" (Vizenor 2003:21–22). Nightbreaker planned to carry out his vision by "shadow[ing] MacDonald in Japan" (Vizenor 2003:122). However, as Ronin explains, "The war recast his adventures, and my father served as a military interpreter in the occupation in Tokyo . . . My father inspired me to carry out his vision of the journey. MacDonald was in custody most of the time he was in the country, so my rove was on the paths he and my father might have taken, first with the Ainu in Hokkaido, and then the ghost parades in Hiroshima" (Vizenor 2003:122). As a member of the occupation forces, Nightbreaker was unable to build meaningful relationships with the Japanese or Ainu—the Indigenous peoples of northern Japan. Similarly, MacDonald wanted to foster kinship relations with the Japanese, as he thought Japan was where "North American Indians originally came" from (Vizenor 2003:140); but his ability to interact with Japanese society was heavily inhibited by the Japanese suspicion of European invaders. In this context, his presence was mediated through his proximity to English—a colonial tongue. Manidoo Envoy asserts that MacDonald thought that, as an English teacher, he could make himself "something of a personage" among the Ainu, who he presumed to be "similar to the Indians and probably ignorant" (Vizenor 2003:140). MacDonald's motivations constitute a troubling mélange of ideas of kinship, white supremacy, and empire. Ronin, by contrast, uses trickster modes to bypass imperialist mediations and makes his way to the Ainu. Having attacked manifestations of "fake peace," it is only among the Ainu as they tell their stories of "natural reason" (Vizenor 2003:122) that Ronin first feels the presence of his father and MacDonald and a resulting, genuine "peace" (Vizenor 2003:124). This is a peace whose flight path came from the constellation of Indigenous visions that lead to the creation of perfect memories.

Expanding Resonance: Aligning Stars through Natural Reason

In this final section, I examine how Vizenor recognizes natural reason as resonance between Anishinaabe and Shinto worldviews and uses this premise to co-create and imagine with a distant people what human life that respects the natural and spiritual worlds can look like. Traditionally, Shinto shrines honor nature and kami spirits (Vizenor 2003:157). Vizenor positions Shinto as a Japanese form of natural reason when the novel describes it as "a native persuasion," "a sense of presence" with a relational understanding of land, human, and nonhuman beings as kin that is compatible with an Anishinaabe worldview but whose "participants . . . for a time, surrendered to a fascistic emperor" (2003:63). However, the Yasukuni Jinja, a Shinto shrine not located in nature or the site of kami spirits, is a monument to Japanese Empire that reveres military men and racial superiority at the expense of the *hibakusha* survivors of the atomic bomb and others. Ronin's "desecration" (Vizenor 2003:117) of the Yasukuni Jinja is a trickster move to UNSETTLE and UNGLUE conceptions of racialist nationhood. The Manidoo Envoy includes this attack as one of Ronin's "tricky moves" through which "the illusions of peace were converted into stories of survivance" (Vizenor 2003:13), where the stories belong to the *hibakusha* and occupation orphans—not the Anishinaabe.

Ronin pronounces the shrine, and by extension Shinto, "misused by the emperors and then by the militarists" (Vizenor 2003:143). In the middle of discussing the Yasukuni Jinja, Vizenor (Vizenor 2003:117) jarringly juxtaposes the fake peace in Japan with the fake peace of settler colonialism in the United states when the Envoy notes: "the shrine was founded in 1868, the same year that the United States government established the White Earth Reservation."[10] Supporting this dual, complex critique of dominance as manifested by American and Japanese imperialisms, Ronin enters the shrine in Nightbreaker's U.S. military regalia with an Imperial chrysanthemum seal on his helmet to the tune of U.S. military hymns such as "From the Halls of Montezuma," whose lyrics trace American conquest from the Americas to Africa (Vizenor 2003:165). Ronin's composite costume and his choice in music within the context of the shrine hold Japan accountable for its colonialism, but also for its neglect of their responsibility to denounce American domination; in this way, he also holds the United States accountable as a global force of domination—and also one that continues to occupy the lands of Indigenous nations such as the Anishinaabe. This parallel suggests that America is also a nation of "fake peace," and the existence of reservations is a testament to this.

The parallel between two imperial powers is characteristic of the novel's narrative structure insofar as its trickster structure can be understood to expose and unglue creeds of domination. Trickster as a narrative structure employed by Vizenor can also be understood as a form of what Simpson (2017) calls Anishinaabe internationalism, which includes Anishinaabe relations with other-than-human nations (56), relationships with "different Indigenous nations" of Turtle Island (58), and relationships with other global relations, such as with the "Black Radical Tradition" or "revolutionary movements in the Global South" (2017:56–66). Simpson elucidates how Nanabozho teaches Anishinaabe internationalism and its ethical frameworks when, after the creation of the world, Nanabozho "walked the world to understand their place in it, [Nishnaabeg] place in it, to create face-to-face relationships with other nations and beings" (2017:56). These relationships can involve "shar[ing] and generat[ing] story, ceremony, song, and *action*" (Simpson 2017:57). This is what the stone, Ronin, does as Vizenor generates Anishinaabe literature that creates international relationships through the sharing of survivance. Speaking specifically to Vizenor's long engagement with Japanese thought and literature, Noodin (2014:164) asserts that he "compar[es], contrast[s], and weav[es] two compatible threads of tradition together . . . in an international context and . . . demonstrates how a detailed knowledge of another culture can enhance the understanding of one's own."

Situating this novel in Japan, Vizenor looks at a culture whose cosmology, like the Anishinaabeg, is premised in natural reason, one whose philosophical roots have been violated through the adoption of racialist and separatist postures, thus becoming ordered by systems of dominance. Japanese colonialism in Asia, as experienced by the Ainu but also by others—including the Koreans, the erasure of the Ainu, the abandonment of the *hibakusha* and Japanese children fathered by foreign occupiers, and the exile of lepers—is shown to result from racialist notions of nationhood that betray Shinto. By contrasting racialism as the basis for national identity to Japanese ontologies such as Shinto, Vizenor elucidates why natural reason must be understood as a living practice and not a reified, decontextualized doctrine. As Noodin has observed, Vizenor (2003:166) uses an international context with the Japanese to enhance his, and his community's, understanding of Anishinaabe culture. Ronin and Manidoo Envoy's criticism of the American Indian Movement within the Yasukuni Jinja survivance episode as "racial simpletons and paranoid separatists" serves as the author's reminder and warning to his own nation, the Anishinaabeg.[11] It is a reminder that Anishinaabe nationhood is not based in philosophies of racial superiority but in survivance. Unlike the Japanese, whom Vizenor suggests were led astray by their own leaders, Vizenor's conception of Anishinaabe survivance suggests that the Anishinaabe should be cautious not to internalize Eurocentric notions of race and nationhood. To do so would be to accept an anthropological view of themselves. Instead, Vizenor's novel suggests that Anishinaabe nationhood is constituted by Native stories of survivance and not some purist idea of race or anthropologically fetishized, fossilized rituals. He insists that Anishinaabe ontology and epistemology are vitally dynamic, creative, and resilient. These qualities (not race or hybridity) demonstrate that Anishinaabeg are a distinct people with philosophies that can participate in transforming the world in response to the needs and concerns of the present day.

Conclusion

Vizenor's extensions of survivance in *Hiroshima Bugi* create constellations of relationality through the resonances between the experiences and work of characters and historic storiers separated by time and space. Vizenor may conceptualize survivance in distinctly Anishinaabe terms, yet in doing so he models how both Anishinaabe and non-Anishinaabe peoples can mobilize from within their own knowledges and localities against forces of domination, such as white supremacy and colonialism, to imagine and enact different kinds of international relations.

Importantly, by elaborating survivance in this spirit, Vizenor shares valuable ideas across nations or cosmologies, which is something that has long been denied to Indigenous peoples, and imagines how a different world can be co-created.

NOTES

1. Simpson writes, "Constellations are place-based relationships and land-based relationships are the foundation of Indigenous thought" and that "Constellations exist only in the context of relationships; otherwise they are just individual stars" (2017:214–215).
2. Following Vizenor, I use 'victimry' in this paper.
3. Vizenor defines and discusses natural reason throughout his extensive corpus. In *Hiroshima Bugi*, Manidoo Envoy says, "Natural reason is an active sense of presence, the tease of the natural world in native stories[,] . . . the use of nature, animals, birds, water, and any transformation of the natural world as direct references and signifiers in language" (Vizenor 2003:36).
4. In this interview, Vizenor shares a version of the Nanabozho and his stone-brother story that Noodin uses in *Bawaajimo*. It is in reference to how and why he embedded that story within *Dead Voices*.
5. Anne M. Dunn is an "Anishinabeg grandmother and an elder storyteller," as described on the back cover of her book *Winter Thunder* (2001).
6. *Anishinaabenini* means 'Anishinaabe man'.
7. Anishinaabe cultural advisor Joseph Bert Sutherland teaches that in the spring, these stars make up the Nanabozho constellation that points to the east and the "Bagone Giizhig" constellation (also known as the Pleaides constellation) from which the Anishinaabeg come to the Earth. He explains that with the first snowfall this constellation "changes to the . . . [B]iboonkeonini" (Mishkiki 2019). He gave me permission to share this teaching here (Joseph Bert Sutherland, personal communication, 2019).
8. Spelling, and presumably pronunciation, varies by writer, and he is also called Nanabush (for example by Basil Johnston).
9. Linda Lizut Helstern (2008:165) in "Shifting the Ground: Theories of Survivance in *From Sand Creek* and *Hiroshima Bugi: Atomu 57*" examines Perfect Memory from the perspective of individual agency as a form of survivance that centers the body in assisting "individuals . . . to see that they have the power to perform or not perform the roles in which they have been cast."

10. Interestingly, the Yasukuni Jinja was founded in 1869 (Yasukuni Jinja n.d.). Vizenor's tweaking of historical data at the service of the story is a kind of perfect memory-making. Creating perfect memories is not an endeavor to capture or recover historical fact so much as it is a practice of healing from past and ongoing traumas and fashioning something different. This practice, as Ronin demonstrates, includes the fulfillment of collective vision through action.
11. For decades, Vizenor has been a vocal critic of the AIM and has preferred "serious Native intellectual discourse combined with less visible grassroots activism" (Noodin 2014:152). Noodin provides a more nuanced perspective on this difference when she argues that the "stereotypes AIM embraced and used to their advantage are the very aspects of Native American Identity that Vizenor rejects" (2014:152).

REFERENCES

Blaeser, Kimberly M. 1999. Writing Voices Speaking: Native Authors and an Oral Aesthetic. *Talking on the Page: Editing Aboriginal Oral Texts*, ed. by Laura J. Murray and Keren D. Rice, pp. 53–68. Toronto: University of Toronto Press.

Dunn, Anne M. 2001. *Winter Thunder: Retold Tales*. Duluth, MN: Holy Cow! Press.

Helstern, Linda Lizut. 2008. Shifting the Ground: Theories of Survivance in *From Sand Creek* and *Hiroshima Bugi: Atomu 57*. *Survivance: Narratives of Native Presence*, ed. by Gerald Vizenor, pp. 163–188. Lincoln: University of Nebraska Press.

Johnston, Basil. [n.d.]. Butterflies. *Nanabush Trails*. www.nanabushtrails.com/butterflies.htm.

Johnston, Basil. 1994. *Ojibway Heritage: The Ceremonies, Rituals, Songs, Dances, Prayers and Legends of the Ojibway.* Toronto: McClelland & Stewart.

Lee, Annette Sharon, William Peter Wilson, and Carl Gawboy. 2014. *Ojibwe Giizhig Anang Masinaa'igan (Ojibwe Sky Star Map Constellation Guidebook): An Introduction to Ojibwe Star Knowledge*. Minnesota: Native Skywatchers.

Mishkiki. 2019. Nanaboozhoo. https://www.facebook.com/Mishkiki.Org/posts/nanaboozhoo-is-pointing-to-a-cluster-of-stars-known-as-the-pleiades-the-pleiades/437735297024614/.

Noodin, Margaret. 2014. *Bawaajimo: A Dialect of Dreams in Anishinaabemowin Language and Literature.* Ann Arbor: Michigan State University Press.

Simpson, Leanne Betasamosake. 2017. *As We Have Always Done.* Minneapolis: University of Minnesota Press.

Vizenor, Gerald. 1987. Interview with Joseph Bruchac. Follow the Trickroutes: An Interview with Gerald Vizenor. *Survival This Way: Interviews with American Indian Poets*, ed. by Joseph Bruchac, pp. 287–310. Tucson: University of Arizona Press.

Vizenor, Gerald. 1988. *The Trickster of Liberty: Native Heirs to a Wild Baronage*. Norman: University of Oklahoma Press.

Vizenor, Gerald. 1990. *Griever: An American Monkey King in China*. Minneapolis: University of Minnesota Press.

Vizenor, Gerald. 1991. *The Heirs of Columbus*. Middletown, CT: Wesleyan University Press.

Vizenor, Gerald. 1993. Interview with Larry McCaffery and Tom Marshall. Head Water: An Interview with Gerald Vizenor. *Chicago Review* 39(3/4):50–54.

Vizenor, Gerald. 1994. *Manifest Manners: Narratives on Postindian Survivance*. Lincoln: University of Nebraska Press.

Vizenor, Gerald. 1999. *Postindian Conversations*. Lincoln: University of Nebraska Press.

Vizenor, Gerald. 2003. *Hiroshima Bugi: Atomu 57*. Lincoln: University of Nebraska Press.

Yasukuni Jina. [n.d.]. History. www.yasukuni.or.jp/english/about/history.html.

Adapting the CEFR to Algonquian Languages

Cécile Planchon, Marie-Odile Junker, John O'Meara, and Claire Owen

Ever since it was released by the Council of Europe almost 20 years ago, the *Common European Framework of Reference for Languages* (CEFR) has slowly but surely established itself as the go-to tool for second-language teaching, assessment, and pedagogical design all around the world.[1] In Canada, as the demand is increasing for Indigenous-language teaching and proficiency assessment, this framework seems also to be used by default.[2] However, because it was originally designed for robust European languages with a strong written tradition, some of the starting premises are not applicable to languages with much fewer speakers and fewer resources, such as Indigenous languages.

An adapted CEFR focused on Indigenous languages would provide a valid and reliable tool for assessing learner proficiency, and would also provide an important tool for guiding the development of robust curriculum that would support policy goals for achieving success in Indigenous-language learning.

In this article, we provide a tool to streamline learners' proficiency assessment for teachers of Algonquian languages and any scholar with interest in language revitalization, curriculum design, or documentation aimed at language instruction. We have designed a modified version of the CEFR, which should be better suited to assess Algonquian languages.[3] We first provide an overview of the CEFR itself before delving into the situation of Indigenous languages in Canada. Then, based on a two-step trial we conducted by looking into two series of textbooks and consulting language experts, we identify some key concerns (necessary rescaling, limited exposure, generational changes, lack of written history or resources, registers and styles, dialectal variations). Finally, using input from language specialists and inspired by a similarly revised framework for the Romani language in Europe, we propose a revised and annotated version of the CEFR template to open the discussion.

What Is the CEFR?

The *Common European Framework of Reference for Languages: Learning, Teaching, Assessment* (CEFR) is a set of guidelines used to describe proficiency in a foreign language across Europe and, increasingly, around the world (including Canada). Launched by the Council of Europe in 2001, it is currently available in 40 languages and was updated in 2018. The CEFR identifies six broad levels of competency, grouped in pairs: A1-A2 (basic user), B1-B2 (independent user), and C1-C2 (proficient user) summarized in their Global Scale.[4] Interim skill levels are indicated by a plus sign (+) where an individual may have surpassed the previous level but does not quite meet the criteria for the next one. More recently, the addition of an official "Pre-A1" category acknowledges certain language milestones appropriate for true beginners, primarily simple formulaic language or memorized forms. Each level contains general descriptors that cover five domains of competency: listening, reading, spoken interaction, spoken production, and writing (see Self-Assessment Grid in Appendix 1). Finally, it addresses spoken performance by providing the Qualitative Aspects of Spoken Language Use Table,[5] which outlines different qualitative aspects of language use (range, accuracy, fluency, interaction, and coherence) to assess spoken production at different levels of competency.

The CEFR also addresses the notions of plurilingualism and pluriculturalism, which would apply to most Indigenous-language speakers in Canada as they usually also speak English and/or French, as well as the issue of minority and endangered languages. The latter takes the shape of a curriculum framework specifically drawn up for the Romani language. This adapted framework aims at providing a common basis to develop educational material throughout Europe "to strengthen the growth of Romani," which is "in danger of disappearing" (Little and Simpson 2008:3–4).

In our view, this framework also offers an interesting alternative for Indigenous languages because it is designed to accommodate three different sociolinguistic situations: children who do not speak Romani at home, children who are not fluent in Romani but whose parents and grandparents are, and children who are fluent in Romani but need to develop their skills (Little and Simpson 2008:7). It also uses only the first four CEFR levels (A1 to B2) to assess proficiency in Romani, and offers activities designed around 11 themes closely related to the learners' daily life and Roma culture (such as "myself and my family," "my community," "festivals and celebrations," "travel and food," or "hobbies and the arts").

Algonquian Languages: Living but Endangered

Algonquian languages, like most Indigenous languages in North America, are in a distinctive situation in that they are in most cases spoken by a very limited number of individuals who usually live in small communities, quite distant from one another (Drapeau 2000). This situation of limited transmission and diffusion directly impacts the volume of resources available, from teaching material to literary works.

Because of their small pools of speakers, their sociocultural representation is extremely circumscribed, which makes them very vulnerable to language abandonment (Dorian 1998; Fishman 2011) triggered by language shift towards a more dominant language. Bilingual by default and necessity (education, access to media, etc.), a large number of Algonquian speakers live in a constant state of diglossia where the forced cohabitation of their mother tongue and the language of the majority slowly erodes the vitality of their native language.

In Canada, Cree and Ojibwe are, along with Inuktitut, the "only viable languages with large [enough] population bases [that their] long-term survival is likely assured" (Norris 2007:27; also McMillan 1994:224). However, this relatively positive evaluation masks the variation in vitality of these languages.[6] Cree cannot be taken as a single speech community as there are many languages, each with several dialects, that are part of what is a large dialect continuum (MacKenzie 1980), with limited mutual intelligibility as distance increases. Cree speakers live in very distant communities ranging from Alberta to the Atlantic Ocean, and do not interact much with each other, especially when also separated by provincial legislation. There is no "agreed upon standard version of the Cree language" (Brittain and MacKenzie 2010:2–3), although there are regional spelling standards. In the northern part of

Western Canada and in Quebec, many Cree languages are still passed on as a mother tongue to children, taught at school, and spoken in most contexts in the communities. In other parts, there is no more transmission to children, and when there is no standard writing system, nor printed resources or oral recordings, the language can be severely endangered. The situation is similar with Ojibwe and Oji-Cree, and vitality must be evaluated on a community-by-community or regional basis.

In this article, we take examples from the following languages: East Cree, spoken in Eastern James Bay; Innu, spoken in Quebec and Labrador; Atikamekw, spoken in Quebec; Nishnaabemwin or Odawa/Eastern Ojibwe, spoken on Manitoulin Island in Ontario; Oji-Cree (Severn Ojibwe), spoken in Northern Ontario; and Eastern Swampy and Moose Cree, also spoken in Ontario. Oji-Cree, East Cree, Innu, and Atikamekw are for the most part still passed on to children, but this is no longer the case for the other languages considered here. Working with a sample of languages with such varying degrees of vitality compelled us to find ways to adapt the numerous CEFR grids to allow for a better fit.

Methodology

What would an adapted CEFR framework look like for it to fit the reality of Algonquian languages? We explored some existing Algonquian language-learning textbooks/courses to determine what elements worked in favor of an adaptation and what looked like issues to be addressed. We followed the introduction of new grammatical elements such as verb classes or verbal inflection, the use of conjunct order verb forms across verb classes, obviation, etc., to see if the teaching progression could easily be converted to CEFR levels. We also looked at the domains of use and the expected proficiency outcomes for different levels of instruction to verify if they could be matched to CEFR descriptors.

To further strengthen our findings, we solicited feedback from L1 and L2 language teachers about the CEFR Self-Assessment Grid (Appendix 1). Our discussion took place during a language resource development workshop held at Carleton University in April 2019, with six expert language professionals (with experience as language teachers, curriculum developers, and lexicographers), fluent in four different Algonquian languages with various levels of vitality. Each expert was given a copy of the grid in the colonial language they mastered (English or French), and was asked to use it to rate language proficiency in their classes or more generally in their communities. While some of them only teach first-language speakers, others work with both first- and second-language speakers. They were asked to annotate their grid individually and to indicate which descriptors they felt were adequate or inadequate, attainable or unrealistic. We then held a group discussion on each cell and compiled all the comments. We held a second discussion the following day to clarify and confirm our findings.

CEFR and Algonquian Languages: Key Considerations

To get an idea of the potential benefit of CEFR for Algonquian languages, we selected two of the most advanced textbooks we could find: *Spoken Cree* (SC) by Ellis (2000, 2004, 2016)[7] (covering the Moose and Eastern Swampy Cree languages spoken in northern Ontario) and the series on Severn Ojibwe by Beardy (1996a, 1996b, 1997; also spoken in northern Ontario),[8] both aimed at six semesters of University-level courses (i.e. 216 instructional hours).

While these textbooks were developed without reference to the CEFR framework or other assessment tools, some of their activities, themes, and tasks can be matched with existing CEFR rubrics.[9] The introductory levels focus on essential components of Ojibwe or Cree grammar, most notably noun gender and its interaction with verb classes. They both provide sufficient content for students to attain the CEFR A1 level across the board. The Listening, Reading, and Writing categories emphasize entry-level achievement of elementary language tasks. However, depending on the language, the scope of the vocabulary learned in the course would limit the responses that learners could give, since the Spoken Cree course introduces three times the amount of words as the Severn Ojibwe course.[10]

Intermediate Ojibwe (Beardy 1996b) and *Advanced Ojibwe* (Beardy 1997) substantially increase the complexity of grammatical concepts, in particular the use of VTA (transitive verbs with animate objects), of conjunct order verb forms across all verb classes, obviation, noun possession, and a broader range of vocabulary areas including colors, body-part terms, currency and cost, and environmental vocabulary. SC II and SC III do the same, with domains of use having to do with life in a Cree village, but SC III also aims at a higher literacy level with reading texts in syllabics (legends, biblical stories, treaties in translation), using various orthographic conventions (pointed or non-pointed syllabics).

Necessary Rescaling

We estimate that *Intermediate Ojibwe* and *Spoken Cree II* provide sufficient content for learners to achieve CEFR level A2, while *Advanced Ojibwe* and SC III provide sufficient content for learners to achieve CEFR level B1, perhaps B1+ or B2 for SC III. As far as we know there is no Indigenous textbook series that would lead to achieving the C (1, 2) level.

The C level is indeed problematic for Indigenous languages. While it is designed for second-language learners, it should be roughly equivalent to what a native speaker can do. In the context in which CEFR was developed, such an ideal speaker could be defined as an 'educated native speaker of a language with a strong and rich written tradition and whose intergenerational transmission was NOT disrupted by colonialism.' A highly proficient Indigenous speaker, however, would rarely, if ever, fit this description. Since the start of colonization in North America, there has always been disruption of intergenerational transmission, in addition to massive changes in lifestyle. All experts consulted noted that comprehension of elders' speech was difficult for them (i.e. vocabulary and knowledge of life in the bush).

The same conclusion came from the evaluation of the CEFR Self-Assessment Grid (Appendix 1) by our language experts. Indigenous-language learners increasingly expect to develop proficiency in reading and writing skills. Yet, our preliminary work with experienced Indigenous-language teachers in reviewing the CEFR documents revealed their awareness of the challenges involved in learners achieving advanced proficiency levels (C levels) in these areas, which is reflected in the revisions that were made in the proposed adaptation of the CEFR levels. They determined that the grid descriptors were applicable in all the areas highlighted

TABLE 1. Indigenous-language experts' assessment of the Self-Assessment Grid

	A1	A2	B1	B2	C1	C2
UNDERSTANDING						
LISTENING						
READING						
SPEAKING						
SPOKEN INTERACTION						
SPOKEN PRODUCTION						
WRITING						

in gray in Table 1. However, they felt the areas displayed in black showed problems of relevance and required adjustments to their descriptors.

Echoing our findings with the textbooks, the C level was considered a non-target for all the languages involved, except for the Speaking category, since our experts were living proof that such a level of fluency could be reached. However, the consensus was that it was unlikely new learners could attain this level.

Limited Exposure

Mastering skills like Listening or Spoken Interaction/Production requires a certain number of hours of study and exposure (O'Grady 2018:329–330). Because English- or French-speaking learners of an Algonquian language will face completely new vocabulary, word structure, syntax, and pronunciation, it is likely that they will require significantly more hours of study to reach CEFR targets than would English-speaking learners of a Germanic or Romance language. Estimates suggest that the latter would require approximately 1,060–1,200 cumulative hours of study to reach the C2 level in a language with significant grammatical differences from their own (Alliance Française n.d.).

Although there are no estimates of required hours of study for a speaker of English or French to learn an Algonquian language, it is reasonable to assume that the number would be substantially higher. Therefore, the issue of hours of study in postsecondary program and course design for Indigenous languages requires further investigation, given its likely impact on levels of achievement. And it is all the more so since, contrary to learners of languages widely spoken, it is very difficult, even impossible, for learners of some Algonquian languages to interact with speakers outside the classroom, either because there are too few of them or because they simply do not exist.

Vitality

A key premise of the CEFR is that languages are robust and safe. However, this is not always the case with any given Indigenous language. When the language is endangered, the proficiency level of teachers cannot be taken for granted (O'Grady 2018:330), nor can the speakers' competence in all domains of use. Then comes the question of intergenerational transmission, home use, and community use in everyday interactions. The reality that language shift might be happening now, or has already happened (Burnaby 1981), cannot be overlooked. Hence, a revised CEFR for Algonquian languages should consider the vitality of the target language.

Dialects

Dialect variation affects B1–C2 for Listening and almost all Reading levels. Whenever there is no standard orthography, even if written material exists, the lack of consistency and the multiple orthographic systems are a huge barrier for a learner attempting to develop and practice reading skills. A good case study for understanding where the problem lies is Innu, a language whose speakers have agreed, after 40 years, on one standard orthography (Baraby 2003), but where mutual intelligibility declines as the distance between the communities increases. East Cree has fewer mutual intelligibility problems, partly solved at the written level by two standard orthographies (one for each larger dialectal group), allowing a little more transparency in the writing system than Innu. For Ojibwe dialects, the lack of standardization in writing increases challenges. Most writing systems in other Algonquian languages that we know of, even when well-established, are not consistently written by speakers, and writing conventions show a range of variation (Fiero 1985).

Written Language

There is a common asymmetry between oral proficiency and literacy among Indigenous speakers: people can read but not write, or they can speak but not read or write. Many elders are at a C2 level for speaking, but only reach A1 for writing. It is important to note that even if the language has a standardized orthography, it is most likely recent and not yet mastered by most of the population. Reading at an advanced level for such languages would thus imply familiarity with several (past) orthographic systems and high awareness of the phonemic principles governing dialectal variation. Syllabaries sometimes cause people to become fixated on mechanical learning of the syllabary, but without developing proficiency in reading whole texts or fluency in writing. For example, a few communities do have a newspaper available in the language, but very few younger speakers have the necessary proficiency to read or understand it. Thus, it becomes difficult to use a descriptor like "I can read articles or reports concerned with contemporary problems in which the writers adopt particular attitudes or viewpoints" (CEFR, Reading B2) as a baseline if none of the targeted audience is able to read a newspaper. Therefore, Reading descriptors are affected at all levels and Writing descriptors were unanimously declared non-applicable at the C levels by our experts.

Register and Styles, Cultural Norms

The question of style is mentioned in the Self-Assessment Grid for writing skills at the C levels, where the descriptors ("I can select a style appropriate to the reader in mind" (C1) and "I can write summaries and reviews of professional or literary works" (C2)) were ruled out by our experts. The issue of styles and registers intersects with the paucity of written material and written literary tradition. Knowledge of cultural norms is what would determine proper use of the language, and thus descriptors for Understanding and Reading at the B2, C1, and C2 levels would have to be redeveloped to include language-specific norms. During our discussions, language teachers brought up the theme of politeness, highlighting how different the norms are between the Algonquian language they speak and English or French.

Scarcity of Language Resources

Access to pedagogically useful written and spoken language resources varies by language and dialect, with modest but increasing availability of materials. Questions of dialect variation and acceptance of orthographic standards often have an impact on the acceptance and utility of materials. Cree and Anishinaabemowin (Ojibwe) reflect this reality, with both having local standards for the use of syllabic and alphabetic writing systems. As of today, and to the best of our knowledge, there are very few monolingual films or TV shows in any Algonquian language that would allow someone to practice their listening skills. Therefore, Listening at B1, B2, and C1 levels are affected. For example, at B1, the descriptor that states "I can understand the main points of many radio or TV programs" was crossed out because there are no such programs to listen to. Some radio shows do exist; for example, some hockey tournaments are broadcast in Innu or Cree, but they are usually not available on the web for on-demand listening. Moreover, compared to the vast resources available for European languages, there is very little production of literature, podcasts, films, or videos conceived IN an Algonquian language today. If any, they are often translations from French or English or are not readily usable as pedagogical material.[11]

The general shortage of written material affects Reading at all levels: in A1, it was suggested to replace "reading catalogues" with picture books. Simple everyday material such as advertisements, brochures, menus, and timetables were crossed out (A2), as they are usually not produced or available in the language. The few that do exist are often the result of translation, with inconsistent quality, which means that they may not be appropriate for language learning. Our experts decided that "Short, simple personal letters" (or e-mails) could remain as part of the A2 Reading descriptor, though. From B2 onwards, the descriptors apply to languages with literary traditions and were thus hardly applicable. Written production in the language, when it exists (see the Cree school board book catalogue), tends to be limited to elementary-school readers and children's books.[12]

Our Proposal: An Adapted Version of the CEFR Self-Assessment Grid

In view of all the different issues we identified, as well as the concerns and limitations expressed by our experts pertaining to the C levels, we decided to emulate the approach put forth by the group who worked on the Romani language (Little and Simpson 2008).

We worked at adapting the current CEFR Self-Assessment Grid descriptors to make them fit better within the reality experienced by these Indigenous communities. Our first decision was to limit our grid to four levels, that is from A1 to B2, skipping the C levels altogether as they were not considered realistically attainable. We then eliminated all mentions in the descriptors of material that is not easily accessible or available, such as "catalogues," "television programs," "films," "broadcasts," "contemporary literary prose," or "literary works," and instead selected replacements (e.g. "picture books" or "postcards") suggested by our specialists.

While the Romani framework offers 11 different grids, one per theme, each perfectly adapted to topic-specific activities and skills, we decided to focus our work on one general grid, mostly based on the different aspects of current Indigenous daily life, in keeping with the grid of descriptors they drew for Romanipe (Little and Simpson 2008:23–24).

The descriptors we chose are a mix of the original descriptors, those of the Romanipe grid, and input from our specialists and ourselves (see our revised version in Appendix 2). We tried to use broad-enough wording to encompass learners of all ages—not exclusively children, as was done for Romani—and made sure to keep a constant link with the Indigenous languages and cultures. For instance, the descriptor for Listening B1 mentions "I can listen to a talk about my community history or traditions" instead of a radio or TV program as it is in the original CEFR grid. Speaking-Production B2 reads "I can retell a familiar legend in phrases or simple sentences" when the original refers to educational background or past/present jobs.

This version is only a preliminary template, aimed at gathering as much feedback from teachers and other language experts as possible. As a prospective tool valuable at the policy level and at the curriculum-design level, it will require testing on a much broader scale. Whether it is about necessary adjustments to the descriptors, a reflection about the benefit of such a tool in real-life classrooms, or a need for more community/language-specific grids, we welcome constructive criticism to open the discussion on the importance of assessment in Indigenous languages.

The aim of this first attempt is to garner enough attention and generate a group dynamic to join forces and come up with an Algonquian language CEFR.

APPENDIX 1. The CEFR Self-Assessment Grid

		A1	A2	B1
UNDERSTANDING	LISTENING	I can recognise familiar words and very basic phrases concerning myself, my family and immediate concrete surroundings when people speak slowly and clearly.	I can understand phrases and the highest frequency vocabulary related to areas of most immediate personal relevance (e.g. very basic personal and family information, shopping, local area, employment). I can catch the main point in short, clear, simple messages and announcements.	I can understand the main points of clear standard speech on familiar matters regularly encountered in work, school, leisure, etc. I can understand the main point of many radio or TV programmes on current affairs or topics of personal or professional interest when the delivery is relatively slow and clear.
	READING	I can understand familiar names, words and very simple sentences, for example on notices and posters or in catalogues.	I can read very short, simple texts. I can find specific, predictable information in simple everyday material such as advertisements, prospectuses, menus and timetables and I can understand short simple personal letters.	I can understand texts that consist mainly of high frequency everyday or job-related language. I can understand the description of events, feelings and wishes in personal letters.
SPEAKING	SPOKEN INTERACTION	I can interact in a simple way provided the other person is prepared to repeat or rephrase things at a slower rate of speech and help me formulate what I'm trying to say. I can ask and answer simple questions in areas of immediate need or on very familiar topics	I can communicate in simple and routine tasks requiring a simple and direct exchange of information on familiar topics and activities. I can handle very short social exchanges, even though I can't usually understand enough to keep the conversation going myself.	I can deal with most situations likely to arise whilst travelling in an area where the language is spoken. I can enter unprepared into conversation on topics that are familiar, of personal interest or pertinent to everyday life (e.g. family, hobbies, work, travel and current events).
	SPOKEN PRODUCTION	I can use simple phrases and sentences to describe where I live and people I know.	I can use a series of phrases and sentences to describe in simple terms my family and other people, living conditions, my educational background and my present or most recent job.	I can connect phrases in a simple way in order to describe experiences and events, my dreams, hopes and ambitions. I can briefly give reasons and explanations for opinions and plans. I can narrate a story or relate the plot of a book or film and describe my reactions.
WRITING	WRITING	I can write a short, simple postcard, for example sending holiday greetings. I can fill in forms with personal details, for example entering my name, nationality and address on a hotel registration form.	I can write short, simple notes and messages relating to matters in areas of immediate needs. I can write a very simple personal letter, for example thanking someone for something.	I can write simple connected text on topics which are familiar or of personal interest. I can write personal letters describing experiences and impressions.

B2	C1	C2
I can understand extended speech and lectures and follow even complex lines of argument provided the topic is reasonably familiar. I can understand most TV news and current affairs programmes. I can understand the majority of films in standard dialect.	I can understand extended speech even when it is not clearly structured and when relationships are only implied and not signalled explicitly. I can understand television programmes and films without too much effort.	I have no difficulty in understanding any kind of spoken language, whether live or broadcast, even when delivered at fast native speed, provided I have some time to get familiar with the accent.
I can read articles and reports concerned with contemporary problems in which the writers adopt particular attitudes or viewpoints. I can understand contemporary literary prose.	I can understand long and complex factual and literary texts, appreciating distinctions of style. I can understand specialised articles and longer technical instructions, even when they do not relate to my field.	I can read with ease virtually all forms of the written language, including abstract, structurally or linguistically complex texts such as manuals, specialised articles and literary works.
I can interact with a degree of fluency and spontaneity that makes regular interaction with native speakers quite possible. I can take an active part in discussion in familiar contexts, accounting for and sustaining my views.	I can express myself fluently and spontaneously without much obvious searching for expressions. I can use language flexibly and effectively for social and professional purposes. I can formulate ideas and opinions with precision and relate my contribution skilfully to those of other speakers.	I can take part effortlessly in any conversation or discussion and have a good familiarity with idiomatic expressions and colloquialisms. I can express myself fluently and convey finer shades of meaning precisely. If I do have a problem I can backtrack and restructure around the difficulty so smoothly that other people are hardly aware of it.
I can present clear, detailed descriptions on a wide range of subjects related to my field of interest. I can explain a viewpoint on a topical issue giving the advantages and disadvantages of various options.	I can present clear, detailed descriptions of complex subjects integrating sub-themes, developing particular points and rounding off with an appropriate conclusion.	I can present a clear, smoothly-flowing description or argument in a style appropriate to the context and with an effective logical structure which helps the recipient to notice and remember significant points.
I can write clear, detailed text on a wide range of subjects related to my interests. I can write an essay or report, passing on information or giving reasons in support of or against a particular point of view. I can write letters highlighting the personal significance of events and experiences.	I can express myself in clear, well-structured text, expressing points of view at some length. I can write about complex subjects in a letter, an essay or a report, underlining what I consider to be the salient issues. I can select style appropriate to the reader in mind.	I can write clear, smoothly-flowing text in an appropriate style. I can write complex letters, reports or articles which present a case with an effective logical structure which helps the recipient to notice and remember significant points. I can write summaries and reviews of professional or literary works.

Source: https://rm.coe.int/CoERMPublicCommonSearchServices/DisplayDCTMContent?documentId=090000168045bb52

APPENDIX 2. Self-Assessment Grid, adapted for Algonquian languages

		A1	A2	B1	B2
UNDERSTANDING	LISTENING	I can understand words related to my family, daily activities, items of clothing and food, the main celebrations and commemorations, songs, dances, legends of my community and other leisure/ sporting activities.	I can understand simple instructions given about my daily life at home/ in the community. I can understand simple explanations of matters of most immediate personal relevance. I can understand the main points and purpose of a simple legend or story.	I can understand a story or account about my family or community. I can listen to a talk about Indigenous history, traditions or way of life and understand the main points.	I can understand in detail an extended talk about Indigenous life, history or culture, as well as reasonably familiar issues that arise in the modern world.
	READING	I can recognize and understand basic words related to my family, daily activities, items of clothing and food, the names of familiar legend characters and songs on a poster, flash card, menu or in a picture book.	I can read and understand short texts, (e.g. a familiar legend, story, personal narrative), with very familiar words of high frequency. I can read and understand simple texts about daily life, history or traditions. I can understand short simple personal letters or e-mails.	I can read and understand an account of Indigenous people past and present experiences. I can understand texts that use high frequency everyday language. I can understand the description of events, feelings and wishes in personal letters.	I can read and understand a detailed description of daily life issues. I can read and understand an account of the experiences of a person or group from my community in which they express a specific viewpoint. I can read and understand a biographical text about a well-known person or a legend character.
SPEAKING	INTERACTION	I can ask for basic items in the home. I can respond nonverbally or with single words or very brief answers to questions about my daily life (family, home, activities, likes and dislikes, and experiences) provided the other person is ready to repeat or reformulate things at a slower rate of speech. I can greet and respond to greetings appropriately.	I can ask and answer simple questions about familiar topics and activities (crafts and hobbies, typical events and community activities). I can handle very short social exchanges, but not enough to keep the conversation going myself.	I can ask and answer a range of questions about aspects of Indigenous life and culture. I can answer questions about my life and how I see the traditions of my culture. I can enter unprepared into conversation on topics that are familiar, of personal interest or pertinent to everyday life (e.g. family, hobbies, work, travel and current events).	I can interact with a degree of fluency and spontaneity that makes regular interaction with native speakers quite possible. I can discuss in detail the traditions of Indigenous communities and their impact on daily life. I can take an active part in discussion in familiar contexts, while expressing and supporting my opinions.

		A1	A2	B1	B2
SPEAKING	PRODUCTION	I can use key words or basic phrases to describe my family, home, activities, job, likes and dislikes.	I can use a series of simple phrases and sentences to describe my family and community, my living conditions, my educational and/or professional background. I can retell a familiar story in phrases or simple sentences.	I can connect phrases in a simple way in order to describe personal experiences, events or feelings. I can briefly give reasons and explanations for opinions and plans. I can narrate a legend, a story or an aspect of Indigenous life, history or culture and describe my reactions.	I can present clear, detailed descriptions on a wide range of subjects related to my field of interest, highlighting the significant points. I can explain a viewpoint on a topical issue and debate the validity of various opinions. I can share my experience about learning an Indigenous language and illustrate the talk with examples taken from different varieties of the language.
WRITING		I can copy or write words or lists related to my family members, daily activities, items in the home, food and clothing as well as important events or legends. I can write a short, simple postcard, for example sending holiday greetings.	I can write short texts using familiar vocabulary to describe an aspect of Indigenous history or tradition, or to give a brief summary of a familiar legend, story or personal narrative. I can write short, simple notes and messages relating to personal or very familiar matters. I can write a very simple personal letter.	I can write simple connected texts on topics which are familiar or of personal interest. I can write letters describing personal experiences and impressions.	I can write clear, detailed texts on a wide range of subjects related to my interests. I can write an essay or report, debating the validity of a particular viewpoint. I can write content highlighting my personal viewpoint of certain events and experiences.

NOTES

1. Contributor Roles and Acknowledgments: Planchon: research, writing, editing, final revision; Junker: conceptualization, funding (SSHRC grant # 435-2014-1199, NRC), research, writing; Owen and O'Meara: research, writing. *Mikwetc* to Nicole Petiquay, Jeannette Cocoo, Véronique Chachai, Mary Ann Corbiere, Loretta Assinewai, Yvette Mollen, Mimie Neacappo, and Katie Martunizzi.
2. It has become the default benchmarking norm for many institutions, such as the Université de Montréal, which uses the CEFR levels for all its language courses, including the Algonquian language Innu (https://centre-de-langues.umontreal.ca/cours-et-horaires/cours/innu/).
3. It is important to note that we briefly explored other frameworks aside from the CEFR, but they were not all relevant. For example, the Canadian Language Benchmarks scale was designed for adult second-language learners of English and French, focusing on the needs of immigrants for integration into Canadian society and the workplace. Another, NEȾOLNEW, is a relatively new (2016) assessment tool for Indigenous languages in British Columbia, developed collaboratively by community members and researchers in education/linguistics. However, this tool functions best in a specific context such as the Mentor-Apprentice learning model, especially where the language may be severely endangered. Rather than a template for standard linguistic benchmarks, it serves more as a motivational tool, with "can do" statements and individual learning goals. In the United States, the ACTFL offers three grids of performance descriptors for language learners that are much closer to the CEFR ones. Each grid covers one mode of communication (Interpersonal, Interpretive, or Presentational) across three ranges of performance (Novice, Intermediate, and Advanced). It was, however, predominantly created for English-speaking learners from the U.S. to answer very specific needs for standardized tests.
4. Council of Europe (2001), *Common European Framework of Reference for Languages: Learning, teaching, assessment*, Global scale - Table 1 (CEFR 3.3): Common Reference levels https://www.coe.int/en/web/common-european-framework-reference-languages/table-1-cefr-3.3-common-reference-levels-global-scale.
5. Council of Europe (2001), *Common European Framework of Reference for Languages: Learning, teaching, assessment*, Qualitative aspects of spoken language use - Table 3 (CEFR 3.3): Common Reference levels https://www.coe.int/en/web/common-european-framework-reference-languages/table-3-cefr-3.3-common-reference-levels-qualitative-aspects-of-spoken-language-use.
6. According to Statistics Canada 2016, an estimated 96,575 speak Cree; 28,130 speak

Ojibwe, 15,585 speak Oji-Cree, and 11,360 speak Montagnais-Naskapi. https://www12.statcan.gc.ca/census-recensement/2016/as-sa/98-200-x/2016022/98-200-x2016022-eng.cfm.

7. Earlier versions of *SC I* and *SC II* were published in the 1960s and then entirely revised.
8. Severn Ojibwe (Oji-Cree) is spoken in northern Ontario (Valentine 1994). Teaching materials for Severn Ojibwe courses for University language learners were prepared in the mid-1990s (Beardy 1996a, 1996b; Beardy 1997). The introductory-level text is an adaptation of an earlier text prepared in the 1980s (Mitchell et al. 1988). All three volumes are written in a roman orthography developed for varieties of Ojibwe in northern Ontario. It is similar to that in Nichols and Nyholm 1995, the main difference being the treatment of consonant clusters.
9. It is highly likely that time spent in class and with the textbook would be the primary—and for some, only—sources of Ojibwe or Cree language content.
10. Ojibwe: 1,122 (Introductory 354, Intermediary 320, Advanced 448) vs. Spoken Cree 4,580 (Introductory 1,280; Intermediary 1,680; Advanced 1,620). The SC number includes 94 morphemes (medials and finals), some of which are repeated in dependent nouns, given in the third person. Otherwise all entries are types, not inflected tokens, thus confirming the large and rich vocabulary of the SC textbooks.
11. The 2019 Canadian federal election leaders' debate was dubbed in several Algonquian languages and made available on YouTube, but with only one voice for all four leaders, and as a translation product—not ideal for language learning.
12. To access the Cree School Board catalogue, see https://www.eastcree.org/cree/en/catalogue/.

REFERENCES

Alliance Française. [n.d.] https://afleeds.org.uk/faq.

Baraby, Anne-Marie. 2003. The Process of Spelling Standardization of Innu-aimun (Montagnais). *Indigenous Languages across the Community*, ed. by Barbara Burnaby and Jon Reyhner, pp. 197–212. Flagstaff: Northern Arizona University.

Beardy, Tom. 1996a. *Introductory Ojibwe: Parts One and Two in Severn Dialect*. Thunder Bay, ON: Lakehead University.

Beardy, Tom. 1996b. *Intermediate Ojibwe: Parts One and Two in Severn Dialect*. Thunder Bay, ON: Lakehead University.

Beardy, Tom. 1997. *Advanced Ojibwe: Parts One and Two in Severn Dialect*. Thunder Bay, ON: Lakehead University.

Brittain, Julie, and Marguerite MacKenzie. 2010. The Future of Cree. *Research Report: Cree School Board Language of Instruction Evaluation.* Chisasibi, QC: Cree School Board of Quebec. https://www.eastcree.org/pdf/Brittain_MacKenzie_2010_The_Future_of_Cree.pdf.

Burnaby, Barbara. 1981. Language Shift in Northern Ontario. *Papers of the Twelfth Algonquian Conference,* ed. by William Cowan, pp. 114–120. Ottawa: Carleton University.

Council of Europe. 2001. *Common European Framework of Reference for Languages* (CEFR). https://rm.coe.int/1680459f97.

Dorian, Nancy. 1998. Western Language Ideologies and Small-Language Prospects. *Endangered Languages: Language Loss and Community Response,* ed. by Lenore A. Grenoble and Lindsay J. Whaley, pp. 3–21. Cambridge: Cambridge University Press.

Drapeau, Lynn. 2000. *Les langues autochtones du Québec.* Quebec: PUQ.

Ellis, C. Douglas. 2000. *Spoken Cree, Level 1: West Coast of James Bay.* Edmonton: University of Alberta Press.

Ellis, C. Douglas. 2004. *Spoken Cree, Level 2: West Coast of James Bay.* Edmonton: University of Alberta Press.

Ellis, C. Douglas. 2016. *Spoken Cree, Level 3: West Coast of James Bay.* Edmonton: University of Alberta Press.

Fiero, Charles. 1985. Style Manual for Syllabics. *Promoting Native Writing Systems,* ed. by Barbara Burnaby, pp. 95–104. Toronto: OISE Press.

Fishman, Joshua A. 2011. *In Praise of the Beloved Language: A Comparative View of Positive Ethnolinguistic Consciousness.* Contributions to the Sociology of Language, vol. 76. Berlin: Walter de Gruyter.

Foreign Service Institute. Foreign Language Training. U.S. Department of State. https://www.state.gov/foreign-language-training/.

Little, David, and Barbara L. Simpson. 2008. *A Curriculum Framework for Romani.* Strasbourg: Council of Europe.

MacKenzie, Marguerite. 1980. Towards a Dialectology of the Cree-Montagnais-Naskapi Language. PhD thesis, University of Toronto.

McMillan, Alan. 1994. Canadian Native Distribution, Habitat and Demography. *The Native North American Almanac: A Reference Work on Native North Americans in the United States and Canada,* ed. by Duane Champagne and Cynthia Rose, pp. 223–243. Detroit: Gale Research.

Mitchell, Mary Louise, J. Randolph Valentine, and Lisa Valentine. 1988. *Introductory Ojibwe (Severn Dialect), Part One.* Thunder Bay, ON: Lakehead University.

Nichols, John, and Earl Nyholm. 1995. *A Concise Dictionary of Minnesota Ojibwe.* Minneapolis:

University of Minnesota Press.

Norris, Mary Jane. 2007. Aboriginal Languages in Canada: Emerging Trends and Perspectives on Second Language Acquisition. *Canadian Social Trends* 83(20):19–27.

O'Grady, William. 2018. Assessing Language Revitalization: Methods and Priorities. *Annual Review of Linguistics* 4:317–336.

Valentine, J. Randolph. 1994. Ojibwe Dialect Relationships. PhD thesis, University of Texas at Austin.

Ojibwe Obstruent Voicing

Richard A. Rhodes

The Ojibwean subfamily is one of the best studied of any branch of Algonquian.[1] The earliest documents are from the 17th century, but starting in the early 19th century documentation as well as extensive materials in multiple varieties were produced. This depth of attestation allows us to see the changes in various Ojibwe varieties that lead to the current state of the language and its dialects. In this paper I will discuss the development of the obstruent system of modern Ojibwean.

There are two types of obstruent systems found in Ojibwe dialects (Rhodes and Todd 1981). The first type is found in the western and northern varieties of Ojibwe, Saulteaux, Northwestern Ojibwe (Fiero 2013), and Severn/Oji-Cree (Nichols 2014), consisting of a set of simple voiceless obstruents that also occur in three types of clusters, nasal plus stop, /h/ plus obstruent, and sibilant plus stop.[2] The system is outlined in (1).

(1) a.	p	t	č	k
		s	š	

b.	i.	mp	nt	nč	nk	
			ns	nš		
	ii.	hp	ht	hč	hk	
			hs	hš		
	iii.	šp	št	šč	šk	sk

There is every reason to believe that this reflects the structure of the Proto-Ojibwe system. In the modern varieties of Ojibwe with this system, the simple obstruents are voiced or partly voiced intervocalically and in nasal clusters. A description of this kind of system is given in O'Meara (1996:xiii–xvi), the key part of which follows:

> When between vowels, the stops, affricate, or fricatives, may be partially voiced, and they are usually voiceless, or only partly voiced at the beginning or end of a word." (p. xiv)

O'Meara does not discuss nasal clusters, but his table of phonetic realizations (1996:xvi) gives only nasal plus voiced obstruent clusters, including sibilants.

The second type of obstruent system is found in all other modern varieties of Ojibwean, including Potawatomi. It features two series of simple obstruents, one voiced lenis, and one voiceless (and long) fortis. The lenes occur in two types of clusters, nasal plus obstruent, and sibilant plus stop. Following the general practice of students of Ojibwe, the lenes are represented by voiced symbols, because they are voiced in most contexts, and fortes by voiceless symbols. Fortes are uniformly voiceless and long. Fortes do not occur in clusters, but by long-standing convention the sibilant plus stop clusters, which are structurally lenis (with the stop sometimes partially voiced), are nonetheless written with voiceless symbols. The lenis-fortis system is outlined in (2).

(2)	a.	i.	b	d	ǰ	g	
				z	ž		
		ii.	p	t	č	k	
				s	š		
	b.	i.	mb	nd	nǰ	ng	
		ii.	šp	št	šč	šk	sk

This lenis-fortis type of system lacks nasal plus sibilant clusters, which developed

FIGURE 1. Example of lenis and fortis phonetics in contemporary Southwest Ojibwe

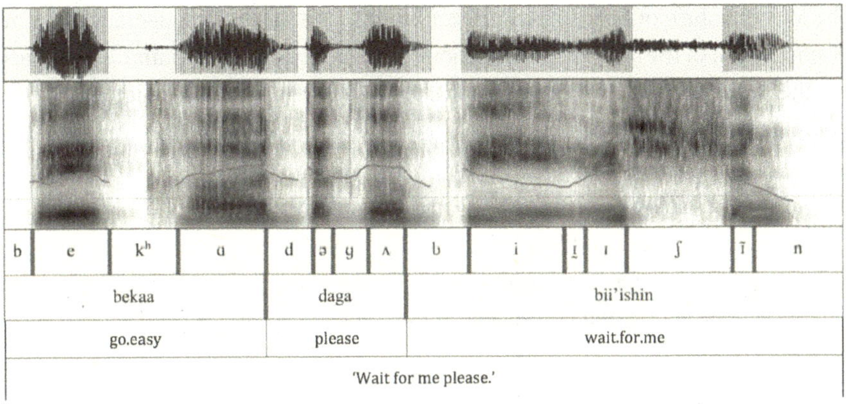

into nasalized vowel plus sibilant. An example of the phonetics of a lenis-fortis system can be seen in the spectrogram in Figure 1, which is a Southwestern Ojibwe sentence taken from the *Ojibwe People's Dictionary*, spoken by a consultant from Red Lake (Nichols 2015).[3]

In particular, notice that the fortis consonants are almost exactly twice as long as the lenis consonants in the same word. This is typical. There is no preaspiration at all associated with either fortis consonant. Rather, the fortis stop, a /k/, shows not only length, but significant VOT delay, i.e. has post-aspiration.

The main goal of this paper is to present evidence that the development of the modern lenis-fortis system is recent in at least some dialects, and to show that the trajectory of change has been consistent across a wide dialect area. The system only shifts to lenis-fortis when the pre-aspirated clusters become geminates, but when the system is lenis-fortis, there is a related shift in the simple obstruents from optionally voiced to obligatorily voiced. Although there is little direct indication of the shift to geminates in the nonlinguistic literature, there is ample evidence of ongoing changes in voicing. The 19th-century writers—francophone, anglophone, and Native—all heard voicing and transcribed it with surprising consistency. From the distribution of voiced obstruents we can infer when the system as a whole shifted.

We will start with direct evidence that Southwest Ojibwe developed a lenis-fortis system in the 20th century. The crucial text comes from the much cited volume of Ojibwe texts collected by William Jones between 1903 and 1905 (Jones

1917, 1919). It is number 43 in volume 1 (Jones 1917:363ff.). It is the sole text given by Maajiigaabaw of Leech Lake.[4] It stands out immediately as dialectally different from the rest of the texts in the collection by the lack of obviative plural, exemplified in the sentences in (3). (Both examples are cited only in original orthography for reasons that will soon be obvious.)[5]

(3) a. from Text 43 from Leech Lake (Southwestern Ojibwe)
Mīsa papimusät Nänabucu,
mī sa papimusä-t Nänabucu
EMPH EMPH RED.walk-3.AN Nenabush

ningutingigu pangi'tōwạn udōjimạn.
ninguting igu pangi'tō-w-ạn u-dōjim-ạn
once EMPH quiet.down-3-OBV 3.POSS-parallel.nephew-OBV
'And so, as Nänabushu went along, by and by his nephews ceased their noise.' (p. 370, line 17–18)

b. from Text 42 from Bois Fort (Border Lakes Ojibwe)
Nāgạtcigu māndāmina$^{\varepsilon}$ pisīgibisōwa$^{\varepsilon}$,
nāgạtc igu māndāmin-a$^{\varepsilon}$ pi-sīgibisō-w-a$^{\varepsilon}$
later EMPH corn-OBV.PL coming-pour.out-3-OBV.PL

uta'ki'kōwāng i·i·mā äcisībigisunit.
ut-a'ki'kō-wā-ng i·i·mā äci-sībigisu-ni-t
3.POSS-kettle-3.PL-LOC there CC.to-pour.out- OBV-3.AN
'After a while some corn came pouring out, into their kettle it poured.' (p. 362, line 8–9)

A close look at Jones's transcription practice shows that he marked preaspiration with significant regularity, but it seems that he heard Ojibwe with his Meskwaki ear and never marked it before sibilants.[6] A brief excerpt is given in (4) to show Jones's practice. He uses an open single quote (') to indicate preaspiration.

(4) Ạnipạpimusä kīwä^{n} Nänabucu; mägwāgu kīwä papimusät ogīwâbạndān sībawāsäyā'kwānig. Awägwāgi, kīwä^{n} päpā'ku·ạ·nk, awägwāgi kīwä 'i$^{\varepsilon}$i'^{u} a'ki kagwānisạgiunicicinini. "Mīsa o mackutä," i'kitu kīwä^{n}. Ucädināni kīwä^{n} imā kwaya'k äjät.

'On his way, they say, was Nänabushu walking and it is said that while walking about he beheld a vista opening out through the trees beyond. Really, so the story goes, when he broke through into the open, why, they say (what he saw) was a country marvellously [*sic*] beautiful. "This is a plain," he said, so goes the story. A ridge of high land, they say, lay exactly in the direction he was bound.'

By simple count Jones's transcription shows that he marked preaspiration about two-thirds of the time where it was to be expected. But then the history of Algonquian studies has shown that preaspiration is hard to hear, even for native speakers. Voicing, on the other hand, is marked by documenters from the earliest times, even when it is not contrastive, so there is every reason to believe that when

TABLE 1. Stop transcription in Jones's Text 43 (Southwest)

FEATURE OF INTEREST	% TRANSCRIBED	TIMES TRANSCRIBED/ NUMBER OF INSTANCES
marked preaspiration	66.2%	94/142
voicing in nasal clusters	81.7%	67/82
intervocalic voicing	52.1%	293/562
word final voicing (all *g*)	22.2%	28/126
word initial voicing	0.7%	1/155

Jones heard voicing, he indicated it. The statistics for preaspiration and voicing in the Leech Lake text, excluding sibilants, are given in Table 1.

Table 1 and all following statistical tables have three columns. The first column lists a property or property in context followed by a percentage of the times that property was explicitly transcribed. The last column has the raw numbers on which the percentage was calculated given as t/n, where *t* is the number of times the property was transcribed, and *n* is the number of times the property was expected based on proto-Ojibwe. For example, the last word in (3b) is transcribed as *äcisībigisunit*. The proto-Ojibwe form would be **eši-si·pi·kisonit*. Discounting the sibilants, as we do throughout the paper because they have complicating factors, the voicing score for this word would be 2/3, because there are three proto-Ojibwe simplex obstruents (n=3) and two are transcribed as voiced (t=2).

The array of facts in Table 1 indicates that the Leech Lake text represents a version of Southwestern Ojibwe prior to the shift in the consonant system, so the appropriate phonemic transcription of (4) is given in (5) above the original transcription.

(5) Ani-papimohse	kiiwenh	Nenaposhoo;	mekwaa ko	kiiwenh
Ạnipạpimusä	kīwä^{n}	Nänabucu;	mägwāgu	kīwä
he.walks.away	EVID	Nenabozho	while.EMPH	EVID

papimohset	okii-waapantaan	shiipaawaahseyaahkwaanik.[7]
papimusät	ogīwâbạndān	sībawāsäyā‘kwānig.
he.walks	he.sees.it	it.shines.through.the.trees

Awekwaaki,	kiiwenh	pepaahko’ank,[8]
Awägwāgi,	kīwä^{n}	päpā‘ku·ạ·nk,
behold	EVID	when.he.broke.through

awekwaaki	kiiwenh	i’iw	ahki	kakwaanihsaki-wanishihshinini.
awägwāgi	kīwä	‘i^{ɛ}i’^{u}	a‘ki	kagwānisạgiunicicinini.
behold	EVID	that	land	it.is.amazingly.beautiful

“Mii hsa	ow	mashkote,”	ihkito	kiiwenh.
“Mīsa	o	mackutä,”	i‘kitu	kīwä^{n}.
“it.is.EMPH	this	prairie,”	he.says	EVID

Ohshetinaani	kiiwenh	imaa	kwayahk	eshaat.
Ucädināni	kīwä^{n}	imā	kwaya‘k	äjāt.
it.is.a.ridge	EVID	there	right	where.he.goes

‘On his way, they say, was Nänabushu walking and it is said that while walking about he beheld a vista opening out through the trees beyond. Really, so the story goes, when he broke through into the open, why, they say (what he saw) was a country marvellously [*sic*] beautiful. “This is a plain,” he said, so goes the story. A ridge of high land, they say, lay exactly in the direction he was bound.’

Unfortunately, the other older materials available to us do not explicitly mark preaspiration. But they do mark voicing. For example, Cuoq, the lexicographer of the variety that is now recognized as the Nipissing dialect, published a dictionary in 1886. In it he has no indication of preaspiration, but marks voicing of etymologically simple stops with some frequency. There are some significant issues with pulling data from a lexicon, not the least of which is that lexicographers work out the spellings of words, so there is a danger of distortion of the statistics. To help minimize that effect, I collected random example sentences adding up to 616 words and analyzed the percentages of voicing in the same environments as in the previous text, realizing that the overall voicing percentage is not particularly meaningful. The results are given in Table 2.

Comparing the Cuoq statistics to the Leech Lake text statistics we see a pattern

TABLE 2. Stop voicing in Cuoq (Nipissing)

CONTEXT	% TRANSCRIBED	TIMES TRANSCRIBED/ NUMBER OF INSTANCES
voicing in nasal clusters	97.6%	82/84
intervocalic voicing	51.2%	106/207
word final voicing	12.8%	16/125
word initial voicing	6.3%	11/174

emerging. Simple stops voice more in some environments than in others. The scale of voicing is given in (6).

(6) Ojibwe voicing scale
after nasals > intervocalically > word finally > word initially

It must be noted that I have omitted sibilants from this study because there are philological difficulties about when to interpret written <s> as voiced or voiceless. The voicing of sibilants will need separate study.

Like Southwestern Ojibwe, the modern Nippissing dialect is a lenis-fortis dialect. Yet the pattern of voicing in Cuoq suggests that he was describing a dialect with an obstruent system very much like that of the Leech Lake text, i.e. one that still had preaspiration. It should be noted in passing that Nipissing (and Algonquin) differ from the other dialects with lenis-fortis systems in having word initial fortis consonants as reflexes of simple obstruents, as shown in (7) (Nipissing forms from McGregor 1994).

(7) Nipissing	Eastern	Odawa	Southwestern	
pejig	bezhig	bezhig	bezhig	'one'
tebwe	debwe	debwe	debwe	's/he tells the truth'
chìmàn	jiimaan	jiimaan	jiimaan	'canoe'
kìgònz	giigoonh	giigoonh	giigoonh	'fish'
sàgam	zaagham	zaagham	zaaga'am	's/he goes out'
shàbòmin	zhaaboomin	zhaaboomin	zhaaboomin	'gooseberry'

This is not surprising, given the voicing scale. If word initial obstruents are the last to voice, it explains why there can be two different outcomes when the systems restructure to lenis-fortis. One set of dialects flipped before the voicing became regular in initial position; the other set flipped after voicing became regular in initial position.

Now let us turn to Odawa. There are two good sources and I present both. The first are three letters home from a Michigan soldier, Charles Allen, written during the Civil War in 1863, discussed in detail in Rhodes 2017. Allen is a very fluent writer. His hand is impeccable, suggesting much practice, while variations in spelling suggest that he had not simply memorized the spelling for every word. Thus the forms in the letters he wrote are likely to be probative. For this study I analyzed the longest of the letters, 243 words. The statistics are given in Table 3.

What is striking with these numbers is that voicing is very advanced in this sample. If our assumptions are correct, this is already a lenis-fortis system, decades ahead of both Southwestern and Nipissing. This makes it worthwhile to check a second source. Sifferath's (1869) Catechism is a good exemplar (a fuller discussion of the language in the Catechism can be found in Rhodes 2010). It was developed in Michigan and approved for publication in 1864. This makes it exactly comparable with Allen's letter. A text excerpt of 728 words was examined and yielded the statistics found in Table 4.

TABLE 3. Stop voicing in Allen letter (Odawa)

CONTEXT	% TRANSCRIBED	TIMES TRANSCRIBED/ NUMBER OF INSTANCES
voicing in nasal clusters	100%	72/72
intervocalic voicing	96.9%	156/161
word final voicing	98.0%	50/51
word initial voicing	50.8%	30/59

TABLE 4. Stop voicing in Sifferath (Odawa)

CONTEXT	% TRANSCRIBED	TIMES TRANSCRIBED/ NUMBER OF INSTANCES
voicing in nasal clusters	100%	127/127
intervocalic voicing	89.9%	249/276
word final voicing	98.9%	89/90
word initial voicing	50.8%	125/248

Sifferath has numbers very similar to Allen, corroborating the state of voicing in Michigan Odawa in the mid-1800s. Both Allen and Sifferath have final voicing a little ahead of intervocalic voicing, but the numbers are very high for both positions, so they may not tell us as much as the varieties where voicing is less advanced.[9]

The earliest citations of Odawa dating from the 17th century (Racines de la langue 8ta8aise et algonquine, ca. 1669) show little voicing outside of nasal clusters and function words, as shown in the examples in (8).

(8) tá**nd**ibi 'where', but tá**nt**assìn 'how many'
mí sa**g**8h8 'It's them', but 8**k**8 'these (an.)'[10]

Because the manuscript is a grammar, the repetition of forms makes any statistical analysis meaningless. Nonetheless, given what we now know about the progression of voicing in Ojibwe varieties, it is reasonable to assume that the variety of Odawa in Racines de la langue 8ta8aise et algonquine (1669) has the conservative obstruent system.

Next we have Du Jaunay's *Dictionarium Gallico-Otaoaku[m]*, ca. 1740. It shows some intervocalic voicing and voicing in nasal clusters, but is less advanced than in Allen or Sifferath.

(9)	paſkiſſi**g**an	'gun'
	8tchi**b**ik	'root'
	ninch8aſſin**g**	'seven times'
	ni'8in**d**ama**gh**e	'I advise (people)'
	but **t**ipatchim8	's/he tells a story'

The main problem with du Jaunay is that it is a hodgepodge of dialects including Algonquin (probably Nipissing), so until an adequate analysis of the contents is made, no meaningful statistics are feasible. My first impression is that there is not enough voicing to think that the variety represented in du Jaunay has a shifted obstruent system, meaning that the shift happened between 1740 and 1860.

There is one point that needs to be raised regarding obstruent voicing in Odawa. Modern Odawa has phrase final devoicing, as can be seen in the close transcription of a 1969 Odawa text in Rhodes and Buszard-Welcher (1996). A sentence from that article is reproduced here showing the devoicing.[11]

(10) Aaniish mii sa iidig ddan'ziwaad go naa ziisbaakdokewaad.
.85P .5ħħ 1.2P ʔãĩš·mis·əidɪk
1.65P t·ʌnziwɒdɣʊnã̜z̥is·bɑk·d̥ə̥k·e·ɒ·d̥
'They used to stay in a certain place and make sugar.' (1996:356)

But the levels of voicing in auslaut shown in Tables 3 and 4 indicates that final devoicing in Odawa is recent. It cannot be a continuation of original voicelessness. Final devoicing is found in Bloomfield's (1958) description of the phonological content of Walpole Odawa based on data taken in 1939,[12] and also in the single text taken by Sapir in Sarnia in 1912. (See Rhodes 2012:360.)

Now let us turn to Eastern Ojibwe. The most copious 19th-century source is Wilson (1874), based on work done between 1865 and 1872 (Rhodes 2005). The breakdown of a 1,025 word sample is given in Table 5.

Wilson's transcription looks like it is close to modern Nipissing, with no initial voicing and all but complete voicing elsewhere. Again it is consistent with the pattern in (6), up to the point that, as in Ottawa, intervocalic voicing lags slightly behind word final voicing. The biggest surprise is how low the percentage of initial

TABLE 5. Stop voicing in Wilson (Eastern Ojibwe)

CONTEXT	% TRANSCRIBED	TIMES TRANSCRIBED/ NUMBER OF INSTANCES
voicing in nasal clusters	100%	89/89
intervocalic voicing	96.6%	542/561
word final voicing	100%	78/78
word initial voicing	19.4%	25/129

voicing is. Still the voicing pattern appears to reflect a dialect that has shifted to a lenis-fortis system.

This brings us to Baraga's seminal dictionary of Ojibwe (1853). Baraga came to Michigan in 1831, settled in an Odawa village, and began studying the local language. The dictionary he produced is clearly in Southwestern Ojibwe. He marked forms as being Odawa or Algonquin (probably Nipissing). However, voicing is very far advanced in the forms in Baraga's dictionary. In fact, the voicing pattern in Sifferath *is* the voicing pattern in Baraga. Sifferath uses Baraga's spelling, as can be readily seen by comparing words that are misspelled or where a sequence of segments presents a spelling challenge. Both authors make the same mistakes and solve the same challenges the same way. A particularly clear case is /s/. Baraga only writes <ss> for /s/ in some places, e.g. in negative, and Sifferath has the same asymmetry. These various types of irregularities in spelling show that the Sifferath, who followed Saenderl, who followed Baraga, as the priest at L'Arbre Croche, an Ottawa settlement dating back to at least 1750 (Tanner 1987:61), and who worked there in the 1850s and 1860s used Baraga's materials. Examples are given in (11).

(11)	manito	'spirit'
	kinawa	'you' pl.
	ka sa awiia o gashkıtossin	'no one is able'
	atchitchaii	'aside'

The fact that the Baraga/Sifferath transcription matches the Odawa pattern of the Allen letters and not the Southwestern pattern of the Leech Lake text means that Baraga represents a variety of Southwestern Ojibwe with an Odawa accent. This may sound far-fetched at first, but consider. It is well known that Southwestern Ojibwe was the trade language in Michigan in the 1800s (Rhodes 2012), based on direct historical evidence in a letter written in January 1837 by the Rev. Simon Saenderl, the Redemptorist priest who was successor to Baraga at L'Arbre Croche, to his bishop, the Rt. Rev. Frederick Rese, the bishop of Detroit. That letter includes the following passage:

> I am at great pains to learn Chippewa, as this is the official and diplomatic language of all Indians and the medium of communication between the various tribes. An educated Indian must speak Chippewa the way a man of breeding in Germany must speak French. (Saenderl 1837:4–6)

Given the influence Baraga's work has had on our view of what Ojibwe is like, the array of facts given above show it is time to rethink our view of 19th-century Ojibwe, and perhaps Ojibwe in general.

In conclusion, let us step back and think about the implications of the data presented here. Three things come to mind. First for Ojibwe dialectology, the thing to notice is that the lenis-fortis system arises in the dialects of Michigan and the adjacent region of southern Ontario (Wilson worked in Sarnia, Ontario, across from Port Huron, Michigan). The shift appears to be complete there by the middle of the 19th century, and only in the 20th century does it spread to adjacent varieties, Nipissing to the east, and Southwestern Ojibwe to the west. Specifically, contemporary work on Southwestern Ojibwe starting in the 1970s found it had a lenis-fortis system (e.g. Nichols 1980). From the date of the Leech Lake text, we can place the shift in Southwestern Ojibwe somewhere between 1910 and 1970. Similarly, modern work on the Nipissing dialect first at Golden Lake, also in the 1970s (Aubin 1979), shows a lenis-fortis system in modern Nipissing. So the spread of the lenis-fortis system must have taken place in the first half of the 20th century eastward, too.

There is a very real possibility that the shift started in Potawatomi. An 1843 vocabulary of Potawatomi shows full voicing, including both word initial and word final obstruents (Bourassa 1843). That puts Potawatomi ahead of all other varieties of Ojibwean.

Second, as just noted, we need to rethink what Ojibwe is really like. It has been a working assumption of scholars of Ojibwe that the lenis-fortis type of system is "core" Ojibwe. For example, the Baadwewedamojig project,[13] which seeks to make the Ojibwe texts collected by William Jones accessible for language revitalization purposes, retranscribes all of the texts in a transcription appropriate for a lenis-fortis dialect. As admirable and wonderfully useful as their editions are for pedagogical purposes, as we have just seen, all of the Jones texts are in varieties

TABLE 6. Intervocalic voicing by point of articulation in Jones's Text 43 (Southwest)

POINT OF ARTICULATION	% TRANSCRIBED	TIMES TRANSCRIBED/ NUMBER OF INSTANCES
labial	51.6%	79/153
apical stop	28.8%	63/219
apical affricate	27.1%	16/59
velar	53.6%	187/349

with a conservative obstruent system. For philological purposes, all those texts need to be retranscribed.

Lastly, there are potentially wider implications for language change implicit in these data. There is a well-documented typological tendency for voicing to be more favored the further forward in the mouth the articulation occurs (Ohala 1983:194–195). Breaking down the voicing data cited above in the varieties that have optional intervocalic voicing, the apicals and apical affricates lag, against this tendency. The data for the Leech Lake text are given in Table 6.

Ohala (1983:198) claims that the following vowel can have a significant impact. But given that the rate of voicing of the grave consonants is nearly double that of the acute consonants, it seems unlikely that adjacent vowels would have any effect. This is likely to be a fruitful line of inquiry in contemporary dialects with a conservative obstruent system.

NOTES

1. This paper benefited greatly from discussions with David Costa, David Pentland, John Nichols, and Chuck Fiero. David Pentland generously shared materials on Old Odawa with me. Both he and David Costa were helpful with pointers and insights into older manuscripts. All mistakes are, of course, my own.
2. Clusters with /w/ are omitted because they are not relevant to the structure of the system. A /w/ can co-occur with almost all of the consonants and clusters listed.
3. The speaker is the late Rose Tainter (Zhaangweshi).
4. The editor of the Jones texts, Truman Michelson, is uncertain about the authorship of Series 4 in volume 2. He thought they might have been given by Midaasoganzh. However, all but two of the 17 texts contain plural obviative forms, proving indisputably that the speaker is not a Southwestern Ojibwe speaker, and in the texts that do not contain a plural obviative form, no plural appears in a position to be obviated. Hence we can presume that they, too, were from a Border Lakes speaker.
5. The abbreviations are: 3 = third person, AN = animate, CC = changed conjunct, EMPH = emphatic, EVID = evidential, IN = inanimate, LOC = locative, OBV = obviative, POSS = possessive, PL = plural, RED = reduplication.
6. William Jones was raised by his Meskwaki grandmother (Johnson et al. 1928:205–206).
7. It is clear that the initial consonant must be /š/ and not /s/ as transcribed. There is no Ojibwe initial *siipaa-*/*ziibaa-*, but there is an initial *šiipaa-*/*zhiibaa-*. It most often means 'under', but it can imply a passageway, in contrast to *anaam-*, the more usual initial

for 'under'. The initial *šiipaa-/zhiibaa-* occurs in connection with vision in the verb *zhiibaayaabi* 's/he looks though a telescope/gun sight' cited in Nichols (2015). The image conjured up by *šiipaawaahseyaahkwaa* is of seeing something dazzling through the trees while still a ways from the edge of the forest.

8. This word is otherwise unattested. Etymologically, one would have expected *payaahkaahko'ang* or reduplicated *pepaahkaahko'ang* 'when he opened [something wooden]', which could refer to parting trees.
9. The development of voicing in final position is unexpected on typological grounds where devoicing generally develops. Noteworthy in that respect is the fact that both Potawatomi and Odawa, the first varieties of Ojibwean to shift to a lenis-fortis system, have subsequently developed word final devoicing. This development will be discussed below.
10. Cuoq, following the tradition of Francophone documenters of Indigenous languages in the 17th, 18th, and 19th centuries, represented <ou> with a handwritten symbol that looks like an <8> but with the top open—exactly a <u> on top of an <o>, but written with a single stroke. By typographic convention an <8> is substituted for that symbol. That <8> represents either [u] or [w] depending on context.
11. This example is excerpted from a very close transcription of an Odawa text. The notational practice indicates the timing of silence and audible breathing. xP means an x second pause (i.e. silence); xħħ means x seconds of audible inhaling.
12. The language of Walpole Island is Odawa, in spite of the fact that Bloomfield called it Eastern Ojibwe. See Rhodes (1976, 1985).
13. http://ojibweproject.weebly.com/.

REFERENCES

Aubin, George. 1979. Golden Lake Algonquin: A Preliminary Report. *Papers of the Tenth Algonquian Conference*, ed. by William Cowan, pp. 121–125. Ottawa: Carleton University.

Baraga, Frederic. 1853. *A Dictionary of the Otchipwe Language, Explained in English*. Cincinnati: Joseph A. Hemann.

Bloomfield, Leonard. 1958. *Eastern Ojibwa: Grammar, Texts, and Word List*, ed. by Charles Hockett. Ann Arbor: University of Michigan Press.

Bourassa, Joseph N. 1843. A Vocabulary of the Po-da-wahd-mih Language: with illustrative sentences and a translation of the first three chapters of the Gospel of Matthew, followed by a vocabulary of the Kaw language. National Anthropological Archives MS1740A.

Cuoq, J. André. 1886. *Lexique de la langue algonquine*. Montréal: J. Chapleau.

Du Jaunay, Pierre. ca. 1740. *Dictionarium Gallico-Otaoaku[m]*. https://archive.org/details/McGillLibrary-112143-491.

Fiero, Charles. 2013. An Ojibwe Word List: Vocabulary from Communities in Northwestern Ontario and Eastern Manitoba. Unpublished manuscript.

Johnson, Allen, Dumas Malone, and Harris Elwood Starr. 1928. *Dictionary of American Biography*. New York: Scribner.

Jones, William. 1917. *Ojibwa Texts*, ed. by Truman Michelson. American Ethnological Society Publications, vol. 7, part 1. New York.

Jones, William. 1919. *Ojibwe Texts*, ed. by Truman Michelson. American Ethnological Society Publications, vol. 7, part 2. New York.

McGregor, Ernest. 1994. *Algonquin Lexicon*. Maniwaki, QC: Kitigan Zibi Education Council.

Nichols, John D. 1980. *Ojibwe Morphology*. PhD thesis, Harvard University.

Nichols, John D. 2014. *Anihshininiimowin Oji-Cree Dictionary (Severn River and Winisk River)*. Sioux Lookout, ON: Kwayaciiwin Education Resource Centre.

Nichols, John D. 2015. *The Ojibwe People's Dictionary*. https://ojibwe.lib.umn.edu/.

Ohala, John J. 1983. The Origin of Sound Patterns in Vocal Tract Constraints. *The Production of Speech*, ed. by Peter J. MacNeilage, pp. 189–216. New York: Springer.

O'Meara, John D. (ed.). 1996. *Ninoontaan / I can hear it: Ojibwe Stories from Lansdowne House* written by Cecilia Sugarhead. Memoir 14, Algonquian and Iroquoian Linguistics. Winnipeg: Algonquian and Iroquoian Linguistics (University of Manitoba).

Racines de la langue 8ta8aise et algonquine. ca. 1669. MS. 302, Archives Indiennes, Notre-Dame de Montréal, Place d'Armes, Montréal, PQ.

Rhodes, Richard A. 1976. A Preliminary Report on the Dialects of Eastern Ojibwa-Odawa. *Papers of the Seventh Algonquian Conference*, ed. by William Cowan, pp. 129–156. Ottawa: Carleton University.

Rhodes, Richard A. 1985. *Eastern Ojibwa-Chippewa-Ottawa Dictionary*. Documentation, No. 5. Berlin: Mouton.

Rhodes, Richard A. 2005. The Dictionary in Rev. Edward F. Wilson's *The Ojebway Language*. Paper presented at the 37th Algonquian Conference, Carleton University.

Rhodes, Richard A. 2010. The Language of Sifferath's Ottawa Catechism. Paper presented at the 42nd Algonquian Conference, Memorial University of Newfoundland.

Rhodes, Richard A. 2012. Algonquian Trade Languages Revisited. *Papers of the Fortieth Algonquian Conference*, ed. by Karl Hele and Regna Darnell, pp. 358–369. Albany, NY: SUNY Press.

Rhodes, Richard A. 2017. A Civil War Soldier's Letter. Paper presented to the 49th Algonquian Conference, Université de Montréal, Montreal, October 29.

Rhodes, Richard A., and Laura Buszard-Welcher. 1996. An Intruder in a Sugar Camp Is Beaten Off: *nikotwâsik iskwâhtêm, pâskihtêpayih! Studies in Honour of H. C. Wolfart*, ed. by John D. Nichols and Arden C. Ogg, pp. 355–366. Winnipeg: Algonquian and Iroquoian Linguistics (University of Manitoba).

Rhodes, Richard A., and Evelyn Todd. 1981. Subarctic Algonquian Languages. *Handbook of North American Indians*, vol. 6: *Subarctic*, ed. by Ives Goddard, pp. 52–66. Washington, DC: Smithsonian Institution.

Saenderl, Simon. 1837. Letter to Rt. Rev. Frederick Rese. II-2-g A.L.S. (German). University of Notre Dame Archives, South Bend, IN.

Sifferath, N. L. 2006 [1869]. A Short Compendium of the Catechism for the Indians, with the Approbation of the Rt. Rev. Frederic Baraga . . . [By] Rev. N.L. Sifferath . . . Catholic Church Catechisms Ottawa. Ann Arbor: Michigan Historical Reprint Series.

Tanner, Helen Hornbeck (ed.). 1987. *Atlas of Great Lakes Indian History.* Norman: University of Oklahoma Press.

Wilson, Edward F. 1874. *The Ojebway Language: A Manual for Missionaries and Others Employed among the Ojebway Indians.* Venerable Society for Promoting of Christian Knowledge. Toronto: Roswell and Hutchison.

#Begish naa weweni bgosendmaan—I Hope I'm Hoping Properly

Hope and Wish Constructions in Nishnaabemwin

Mskwaankwad Rice

This paper is an investigation of optativity in Nishnaabemwin, observing constructions expressing sentiments of *wish* or *hope*.[1] In this paper I document a degree of variation in preferred strategies for making such statements by speakers from related communities and dialects. These optative strategies are: constructions with various lexical verbs of desire and emotion, an expression that translates as 'hopefully', and constructions utilizing the optative particles *begish naa*[2] and *gesnaa*. I will focus on the latter strategy as the breadth of syntactic variation in *begish naa* constructions as well as the use of *gesnaa* as an optative particle are both previously undocumented. A section on the semantics of optativity in Ojibwe is also included as a topic of ongoing study.

Preliminaries

Speakers, Dialects, and Communities

Six L1 Nishnaabemwin speakers from the Lake Huron communities of Waasaaksing, Gchi-mnising, and Wiikwemkoong were interviewed for this study.[3] Wiikwemkoong is considered to be of the Odawa dialect, with the other two communities typically considered Eastern Ojibwe. Valentine's discussion of dialect and variation in Ojibwe notes varied influences upon Nishnaabemwin in general, and intercommunity variation is to be expected considering the linguistic influences upon those speech communities (2001:1–18). Nonetheless, speakers of the same dialects and from the same communities were seen to exhibit a surprising degree of variation in their respective idiolects.

Data Collection

The majority of data was elicited via translation tasks in individual interviews. Back-translation and the verification of the many forms between speakers was undertaken as much as possible. Verification via storyboarding exercises is currently underway with the consultants in an attempt to minimize leading and to elicit natural speech.

Note on the Preterit Mode

A discussion of what is commonly known as the PRETERIT MODE in Ojibwe is important to the present discussion. Valentine notes that it is "used to express verbal predications that took place in the past and are no longer taking place, or in which the predication precedes in time some reference predication that also took place in the past" (Valentine 2001:1049). Nichols describes the preterit mode in the independent verbal order as functioning to contrast past occurrence of an event or state with a later non-occurrence of it (and vice versa in negative environments), while in the conjunct order the preterit can indicate something "contrary to fact" (Nichols 1980:121–123). While there is some debate over the accuracy of the label *preterit,* I will argue that it is also a marker of counterfactuality in the conjunct order and will label it as CF in glosses when utilized as such.

Optative Strategies

Overall, three main strategies were found to express wish and hope in Nishnaabemwin. These are: those containing optative particles (*begish naa* and *gesnaa*), lexical verb constructions, and a phrase meaning 'hopefully'.

Lexical Verb Constructions

This is the most broad and perhaps most diverse of optative strategies considering the wide range of lexical verbs and tense-aspect-mood configurations available. I group them into those using desiderative predicates specifically (which often contain the initials *bagos-* and *misaw-*) and emotive verbs generally. Simply speaking, lexical verb constructions combine an independent verb with one in the conjunct to convey an expression of hope, wish, desire, etc.[4]

(1) Desiderative predicate + plain conjunct DK.GM
Mbagsendam ji-gmiwang waabang.

mbagsendam	ji-gmiwang	waabang
1SG.hope/wish.that	FUT-it.rains.CONJ	tomorrow

'I hope it will rain tomorrow.'

(2) Emotive predicate + plain conjunct
Ndaa-kchinendam gmiwang waabang. GP.WA

ndaa-kchinendam	gmiwang	waabang
1SG.MOD-be.happy	it.rains.CONJ	tomorrow

'I hope it will rain tomorrow.'
(lit.: 'I would be happy that it rains tomorrow')

Hopefully

A lexicalized expression conveying a sentiment of 'hopefully', *aabdek sa naa gnamaa*, combined with an independent clause is another strategy used by some Nishnaabemwin speakers.[5] This expression is generally used with an independent verb, although *aabdek sa naa gnamaa* can be said on its own to mean simply 'hopefully' (Naokwegijig-Corbiere and Valentine 2015–2019).

(3) Aabdek sa naa gnamaa + independent verb
Aabdek sa naa gnamaa nga-waabmaa bi-zhaat maanpii. MC.WI

aabdek	sa	naa	gnamaa	nga-waabmaa
certainly	EMPH	EMPH	in.case	1SG.FUT-see.DIR.3SG

bi-zhaat	maanpii
hither-go.3SG.CONJ	here

'I hope I'll see h/ when s/he comes here.'

Optative Particles

Expressions with the optative particles *begish naa* and *gesnaa* are discussed in greater depth in what follows, as these particles exhibit a very wide range of syntactic configurations in their usage.

Begish naa

In my findings, this optative particle[6] combines with verbs in the specific contexts of plain conjunct, plain conjunct in preterit mode, and changed conjunct (specifically with the conjunct future tense *ji-* realized in the changed conjunct as *ge-*). This variation is of interest since most accounts of *hope* or *wish* in Ojibwe utilizing *begish* describe the construction as containing the particle plus a verb in the plain conjunct.[7] My data, however, shows that *begish naa* can appear with a conjunct verb in the preterit mode as well as with a verb in changed conjunct form.[8]

(4) *Begish naa* + plain conjunct

Begish naa wiiba bi-giiwet. MC.WI

begish	naa	wiiba	bi-giiwet
OPT	EMPH	soon	hither-come.home.3SG.CONJ

'I hope s/he comes home soon.'

(5) *Begish naa* + conjunct-counterfactual

Begish naa baatiintooyaambaan zhoonyaa. AP.WA

begish	naa	baatiintooyaambaan	zhoonyaa
OPT	EMPH	have.lots.of.it.1SG.CONJ.CF	money

'I wish I had lots of money.'

(6) *Begish naa* + changed conjunct

Begish naa ge-bkinaageyaan. AP.WA

begish	naa	ge-bkinaageyaan
OPT	EMPH	IC.FUT-win.1SG.CONJ

'I hope I will win.'

(7) *Begish naa* + independent verb

*Begish naa nga-pkinaage.

begish	naa	nga-pkinaage
OPT	EMPH	1SG.FUT-win

(Intended: 'I hope I will win.')

Notably, (7) indicates the ungrammaticality of *begish naa* with an independent complement, a judgment confirmed with all speakers interviewed.

Gesnaa

There are two apparent uses of the word *gesnaa*: as an adverb meaning 'ever', 'how', or 'what' (Naokwegijig-Corbiere and Valentine 2015–2019) and as an optative particle. Unlike *begish naa*, *gesnaa* takes complements with verbs in either the conjunct or independent orders, albeit with some apparent restriction. Below is an overview of some morphological combinations.

(8) Adverbial use

Gesnaa ngii-gchinendam.[9] MC.WI

gesnaa	ngii-gchinendam
ADV	1SG.PST-be.happy

'Was I ever glad!'

(9) *Gesnaa* + conjunct-counterfactual

Gesnaa niibna zhoonyaans yaamaambaa. MC.WI

gesnaa	niibna	zhoonyaans	yaamaambaa
OPT	lots	money	have.it.1SG.CONJ.CF

'I wish I were rich.'

(lit.: 'I wish I had lots of money.')

(10) *Gesnaa* + independent verb

Gesnaa oodenaang nwii-zhaa. DK.GM

gesnaa	oodenaang	nwii-zhaa
OPT	town.LOC	1SG.FUT-go

'I wish I could go to town.'

(11) *Gesnaa* + changed conjunct
*Gesnaa ge-zhoonyaamyaan.
gesnaa ge-zhoonyaamyaan
OPT IC.FUT-be.rich.1SG.CONJ
(Intended: 'I wish I were rich.')

(12) *Gesnaa* + changed conjunct-counterfactual
*Gesnaa ge-zhoonyaamyaambaan.
gesnaa ge-zhoonyaamyaambaan
OPT IC.FUT-be.rich.1SG.CONJ.CF
(Intended: 'I wish I were rich.')

(13) *Gesnaa* + plain conjunct
#Gesnaa zhoonyaamyaan.
gesnaa zhoonyaamyaan
OPT be.rich.1SG.CONJ
(Intended: 'I wish I were rich.')

It is of interest to note that for this particular strategy, conjunct complements appear with preterit/counterfactual morphology, and plain conjunct complements were dispreferred though not unintelligible. Moreover, *gesnaa*'s use as an optative particle is not previously described in the literature.

TABLE 1. Summary of strategies

		CONJUNCT IN PRETERIT MODE	CHANGED CONJUNCT	PLAIN CONJUNCT	PLAIN CONJUNCT
OPTATIVE PARTICLES	Begish naa	✓	✓	✓	×
	Gesnaa	✓	×	#	✓
LEXICAL VERB CONSTRUCTIONS		✓	×	✓	×
Aabdek sa naa gnamaa		×	×	×	✓

Summary of Strategies

Table 1 summarizes various optative strategies by acceptability. A check mark denotes a preferred strategy employed by one or more speakers while an 'x' indicates that it is ungrammatical. The hash (#) represents a form that was neither a preferred strategy nor considered unacceptable but was dispreferred by speakers.

Speaker Variation

Examples (14–17) illustrate the range of L1 speaker preferences in a translation task of the sentence "I wish I were rich."[10] Of five speakers, one used *begish naa*, two preferred *gesnaa*, and two preferred a lexical verb strategy.

(14) *Begish naa* + conjunct-counterfactual

Begish naa baatiintooyaambaan zhoonyaa. AP.WA

begish	naa	baatiintooyaambaan	zhoonyaa
OPT	EMPH	have.plenty.of.it.1SG.CONJ.CF	money

'I wish I had lots of money.'

(15) *Gesnaa* + conjunct-counterfactual

Gesnaa zhoonyaamyaambaan. DK.GM/MC.WI[11]

gesnaa	zhoonyaamyaambaan
OPT	be.rich.1SG.CONJ.CF

'I wish I were rich.'

(16) Desiderative predicate + plain conjunct

Ndaa-maswendaan niibwa zhoonyaa yaamaan. HC.GM

ndaa-maswendaan	niibwa	zhoonyaa	yaamaan
1SG.MOD-desire.it	a.lot	money	have.it.1SG.CONJ

'I'd be happy to have a lot of money.'

(17) Emotive predicate + conjunct-counterfactual

Ndaa-kchinendam chi-zhoonyaakeyaambaan. GP.WA

ndaa-kchinendam	chi-zhoonyaakeyaambaan
1SG.MOD-be.happy	great-make.money.1SG.CONJ.CF

'I'd be happy to make lots of money.'

Optativity and Counterfactuality in Ojibwe

Iatridou (2000) provides an in-depth analysis of ways in which various languages express counterfactuality. Expanding upon this, Bjorkman and Halpert (2017) construct a typology of counterfactual marking, noting that this is generally conveyed morphologically in two ways: with past tense or imperfective aspect marking. Though their and Iatridou's accounts are much more comprehensive than expressed here, I note that the generalization holds true for Ojibwe. The counterfactual morphology is bolded in example (18).

(18) Begish naa daabaan yaawagba. MC.WI/DK.GM[12]

Begish	naa	daabaan	yaaw-**agba**
OPT	EMPH	car	have.h/-1SG>>3SG.CONJ.**CF**

'I wish I had a car.'

I do not make the claim that the preterit mode in Ojibwe always expresses imperfective aspect, nor that it is the only means of expressing that aspect in Ojibwe. However, translations of verbs in the preterit mode in Ojibwe suggest that it is analogous to imperfective aspect.

(19) Ninibaanaaban gii-bi-mawadisheyan.[13]

ninibaanaaban	gii-bi-mawadisheyan
1SG.sleep.PRET	PST-hither-visit.2SG>1SG

'I was sleeping when you came to visit.'

I claim that the presence of the preterit in the conjunct order is a marker of counterfactuality, indicating the speaker's belief that a situation is untrue, not possible, or unlikely. The speaker noted that the sentence in (20) had a more "definite" feel while (21) implied a "wistfulness."

(20) Begish naa bkinaageyaan. MA.WI

begish	naa	bkinaageyaan
OPT	EMPH	win.1SG.CONJ

'I hope I win.'

(21) Begish naa bkinaageyaambaa. MA.WI

begish	naa	bkinaageyaambaa
OPT	EMPH	win.1SG.CONJ.CF

'I wish I would win.'

The variation in meaning between the two sentences is easily handled in English, whose lexical terms *hope* and *wish* carry lexical meaning regarding the speaker's belief in the possibility of an event coming true or not. *Hope* suggests possibility while *wish* implies counterfactuality. While *begish naa* is seen to convey both meanings in Nishnaabemwin, the nuance of counterfactuality in a sentiment of wishing is marked by preterit/counterfactual morphology on the conjunct complement. In contrast, *gesnaa* always appears with a conjunct verb in the preterit mode and moreover is typically translated in English as *wish*. Speakers utilizing *gesnaa* as an optative particle accept constructions with a plain conjunct verb in back-translation, though they do not produce such constructions unprompted. The intricacies of *begish naa* versus *gesnaa* is a topic of ongoing investigation.

The semantic implications discussed above are suggested, though not explicitly stated, in existing sources.[14] The presence or absence of preterit/counterfactual morphology on a conjunct complement in conveying *hope* versus *wish* is seen in Rhodes (1985:37): the entry for *begish* is translated as 'one hopes that,' with the example seen in (22), and as 'one wishes that', with the example in (23).[15]

(22) Begish naa mno-yaayan.

begish	naa	mno-yaayan
OPT	EMPH	good-be.2SG.CONJ

'I hope you feel better.'

(23) Begish naa waandiziyaabaan.

begish	naa	waandiziyaabaan
OPT	EMPH	be.rich.2SG.CONJ.CF

'I wish I were rich.'

These examples suggest a known semantic difference in hoping versus wishing in optative constructions that can be conveyed via CF/conjunct-preterit morphology, and also that existing sources do not describe *begish* with the degree of variation seen *bgojiing* (in the wild).

Next Steps

There is much work to be continued from this preliminary investigation. Origins of the variation in speaker preferences may be investigated as the variation observed suggests an age-gradation. While it was tested wherever possible, further interviews need to be done to determine precisely which strategies each speaker has in their particular grammars. The influence of varied dialects in contemporary community speech may also be a factor, though investigating this would require an in-depth survey of many individuals and communities.

The specifics of the syntax and semantics of these many strategies are also to be studied. Within a particular strategy, what semantic and pragmatic factors determine which verb forms a speaker chooses? It is seen that speakers generally do not mark tense (seen only in changed conjunct ge-) with optative particles, and especially with conjunct-preterit constructions.

Conclusion

This paper has presented an account of three overall strategies for making hope and wish constructions in Ojibwe, pointing out speaker preferences towards each strategy and their specific forms. Noting consultant dialect and home community is done for informational purposes only, and certainly no conclusions are hereby made regarding which strategies may be typical of a particular dialect. These data, however, contribute to the literature as both the extent of variation in optative strategies utilizing *begish* (*naa*) and the use of *gesnaa* as an optative particle are previously undescribed. In addition to the former point, this paper presents a preliminary investigation of optativity in Ojibwe, and with further work, it is hoped that my research can also provide insight into the interactions of tense, aspect, and mood in Ojibwe generally, which is of great import to linguists and language learners alike.

NOTES

1. As explained further below, <#> is used to mark dispreferred utterances. The term *Nishnaabemwin* is intentionally used in this paper to refer specifically to the dialects of Eastern Ojibwe and Odawa, in which fieldwork for this research was undertaken. The

terms *Ojibwe* and *Anishinaabemowin* are also used to indicate the language as a whole.

2. This particle is realized cross-dialectically as *ambegish*, *apegish*, *begish*, *bekish*, and *pesh*, among other forms, and the presence of *naa* varies. All forms are taken as equivalent and used at times interchangeably in this paper. Speakers interviewed in this study preferred *begish naa*, although other forms are recognized.
3. Communities are abbreviated as follows: Waasaaksing = WA; Gchi-mnising = GM, and Wiikwemkoong = WI. Consultant initials are given alongside their home community abbreviation in each example.
4. Abbreviations used in this paper are: 1 = first person; 2 = second person; 3 = third person; ADV = adverb; CF = counterfactual; CONJ = conjunct verbal order; DUB = dubitative mode; EMPH = emphatic particle; FUT = future tense; IC = initial change; LOC = locative; MOD = modal; OPT = optative particle; PL = plural; PRET = preterit mode; PRET/DUB = preterit-dubitative mode; PST = past tense; SG = singular; >> = indicates subject to object in transitive verbs.
5. Two speakers interviewed used this as a preferred strategy and it was recognized by others.
6. For the speakers interviewed in this research, *begish* always appears with the discourse marker *naa*, and this feature is not stated explicitly in the literature, though *naa* is present in *begish* examples in Rhodes (1985) and Corbiere (1997). Back-translations without *naa* were generally deemed acceptable, but its presence was strongly preferred. One consultant did consider it obligatory in all *begish* constructions.
7. Entries in Rhodes (1985); Nichols and Nyholm (1995); and Nichols (2015) note this feature. It is also described as such in Valentine (2001).
8. Both the *Nishnaabemwin Online Dictionary* and the *Ojibwe People's Dictionary* entries for *begish* also note that the particles can be used on their own as an expression meaning 'I wish!' and I have also observed this in conversation with many L1 speakers. This particular function of begish (naa) was however not explored in this study.
9. Example taken from the *Nishnaabemwin Online Dictionary* (Naokwegijig-Corbiere and Valentine 2015–2019).
10. Care was taken in elicitation sessions to ensure that the past-tense English morphology of *were* or *was* did not result in a past-tense interpretation of the sentence. In other words, it was verified with the speakers that one wishes to be rich at the present time.
11. This form was also attested by MC.WI, albeit with the lack of a final nasal as per MC's dialect.
12. Parallel to example (15), this example was given by both MC and DK, and MC's translation is given here (DK's included the final nasal as per their dialect).

13. Brendan Fairbanks, personal communication, 2019.
14. Nichols and Nyholm's dictionary glosses *apegish* as 'I wish that . . .', notably excluding the term 'hope' in the gloss, and the entry for 'wish' contains *apegish* in addition to desiderative verbs (Nichols and Nyholm 1995:12, 285). Moreover, the entry for 'hope' excludes *apegish* and rather contains desiderative verbs (Nichols and Nyholm 1995:197). Baraga describes *apêgish/apêdash* as adverbs expressing a wish, desire, or request and gives an example with a conjunct verb complement (Baraga 1992: Part II, 45).
15. These examples are transcribed from Rhodes (1985) and the absence of a nasal in the first-person conjunct preterit suffix in (23) may be attributable to dialect variation as the example is noted as originating from the community of Curve Lake.

REFERENCES

Baraga, Frederik. 1992 [1878, 1880]. *A Dictionary of the Ojibway Language*. St. Paul: Minnesota Historical Society Press.

Bjorkman, Bronwyn, and Claire Halpert. 2017. In an Imperfect World: Deriving the Typology of Counterfactual Marking. *Modality across Syntactic Categories*, ed. by Ana Arregui, María Luisa Rivero, and Andrès Pablo Salanova, pp. 157–178. New York: Oxford University Press.

Corbiere, Mary Ann. 1997. Gaawii wi kidwin miiksesnoo: Semantic Rules for the Selection of Some Ojibwe Adverbs. *Papers of the 28th Algonquian Conference*, ed. by David H. Pentland, pp. 71–84. Winnipeg: University of Manitoba Press.

Iatridou, Sabine. 2000. The Grammatical Ingredients of Counterfactuality. *Linguistic Inquiry* 31(2):231–270.

Naokwegijig-Corbiere, Mary Ann, and J. Randolph Valentine. 2015–2019. *Nishnaabemwin Online Dictionary*. https://dictionary.nishnaabemwin.atlas-ling.ca.

Nichols, John D. 1980. *Ojibwe Morphology*. Cambridge, MA: Harvard University.

Nichols, John D. 2015. *Ojibwe People's Dictionary*. https://ojibwe.lib.umn.edu.

Nichols, John D., and Earl Nyholm. 1995. *A Concise Dictionary of Minnesota Ojibwe*. Minneapolis: University of Minnesota Press.

Rhodes, Richard A. 1985. *Eastern Ojibwa-Chippewa-Ottawa Dictionary*. New York: Mouton.

Valentine, J. Randolph. 2001. *Nishnaabemwin Reference Grammar*. Toronto: University of Toronto Press.

Prosodically Conditioned Phonology in Cheyenne

Rachel Vogel and Sarah E. Murray

This paper investigates the prosodic conditioning of two phrase-level phonological processes in Cheyenne, phrase-final devoicing and tonal downstep.[1] Our investigation of these phenomena makes use of recordings from 1965 of Cheyenne stories from a single male speaker, Ed Riggs (published in Olson 1968; Leman 1980). Foundational work on Cheyenne described both processes as occurring within a phonological phrase, and the former before a pause (Leman 1981), but does not otherwise define the phonological phrase or other prosodic domains in Cheyenne. Our research therefore addresses the questions of what conditions each of these processes and whether the two processes are indeed governed by the same domain. More broadly, our work also provides a case study in how archival materials can be used for phonetic and phonological analysis, and in how prosodic organization manifests in naturalistic data.

After introducing background on Cheyenne phonology and on prosodic organization in the next section, we present our methodology for studying phrase-final devoicing and tonal downstep in the preexisting recordings, then look at both processes in a single story. Next, as a follow-up, we conduct a more in-depth investigation of just one of the processes, phrase-final devoicing, in a second, longer story. Finally, we conclude.

Background

Cheyenne is an Algonquian language currently spoken in Montana and Oklahoma (see Leman 2011). This section first provides an overview of Cheyenne phonology, including its phoneme and tone inventories, as well as some prominent phonological rules. These rules include the two focused on in this paper: phrase-final devoicing and tonal downstep. Given that the paper concerns the application of these processes within domains beyond the individual word, the second part of this section provides a brief introduction to prosodic organization in general, as well as what is known about prosodic organization in Cheyenne.

Cheyenne Segmental Phonology and Tone

Cheyenne contains a relatively small phoneme inventory with ten consonants (shown in Table 1 along with two allophones in parentheses) and three vowels (Table 2) (Leman 2011). The symbols in angle brackets are IPA versions of the Cheyenne orthography in the same cells. The rest of this paper follows the Cheyenne orthography.

All consonants in Cheyenne are voiceless, except for /m/, /n/, and /v/. Leman (2011) also notes that /v/ is variably realized as [w], [β], or [v]. The [x] in parentheses is an allophone of /š/ and /h/. It surfaces from /š/ when followed by /a/ or /o/ and from /h/ when followed by another /h/. The [ts] in parentheses is a palatalized allophone of /t/ that surfaces before [e]. As can be seen in Table 2, there are only two contrastive vowel heights. Cheyenne also has two contrastive tones, high and

TABLE 1. Cheyenne consonant inventory (based on Leman 2011)

	BILABIAL	ALVEOLAR	POST-ALVEOLAR	VELAR	GLOTTAL
STOPS	p	t		k	' <ʔ>
AFFRICATES		(ts)			
FRICATIVES	v	s	š <ʃ>	(x)	h
NASALS	m	n			

TABLE 2. Cheyenne vowel inventory (based on Leman 2011)

	FRONT	CENTRAL	BACK
MID	e		o
LOW		a	

low (Leman 2011). Following Cheyenne orthography, high tones are marked with acute accents and low tones are unmarked in this paper.

Cheyenne allows certain sequences of two or three consonants word-internally; however, word-finally, codas are not permitted. When a word ends underlyingly with a nasal consonant, the nasal deletes, as in (1). When a word ends with an underlying obstruent, an *-e* is epenthesized after it, as in (2) (Leman 2011).[2]

(1) /mó'kehan/ 'moccasin' → [mó'keha] (Leman 2011)

(2) /mótehk/ 'knife' → [motšėske] (Leman 2011)

Vowel devoicing, also referred to as "devocalization" in some literature, is found in a number of Algonquian languages including Miami-Illinois (Costa 2003), Shawnee (Greenberg 1969), Fox (Goddard 1991), Northern East Cree (Knee 2014), and Blackfoot (Frantz 2009; St. Goddard 2014; Prins 2019). The phenomenon is quite extensive in Cheyenne, resulting from several different processes, including two word-internal processes and one phrase-final one. In the Cheyenne orthography, word-internal devoicing is marked with a dot above the vowel (e.g. ȧ). Phrase-final devoicing is not marked in the orthography because it depends on the position of a word within an utterance, but below we use an IPA diacritic to identify relevant vowels in examples illustrating this process. All three devoicing processes are said to affect the whole syllable, so voiced onsets preceding a voiceless vowel can also devoice (Leman and Rhodes 1978).

The first process, prepenultimate devoicing, affects low tone vowels followed by a voiceless fricative in any syllable to the left of the penult, as shown in (3). Here and in later examples, the vowels of interest are shown in bold.

(3) épo'evo'**ȧ**sóho. 'He sliced him off.' (Fisher et al. 2017)

This process is blocked either when the vowel is preceded by [h] or when it is in the penultimate syllable of the word (Leman and Rhodes 1978).[3]

The second process, called penultimate devoicing, affects vowels in underlying word-final syllables that are followed by any voiceless consonant. This process occurs before *-e* epenthesis at the end of underlying obstruent-final words, so it appears on surface penultimate syllables (Leman and Rhodes 1978), as illustrated in (4).

(4) **aéstomevéestȯtse** 'false teeth' (Fisher et al. 2017)

The third process, referred to as phrase-final devoicing, targets word-final vowels at the end of a phonological phrase or before a pause (Leman and Rhodes 1978; Leman 1981). This is the devoicing process focused on in the rest of this paper and is discussed more thoroughly in the following sections.

Underlying tones undergo various processes resulting in different surface tones, and are involved in conditioning (or blocking) other phonological processes including vowel devoicing. Relevant for the present paper are the facts that (a) all word-final tones surface as low, and the underlying final tone shifts to the penultimate syllable (Leman 1981; Milliken 1983); (b) vowel devoicing only occurs on surface low tones (Leman and Rhodes 1978); and (c) the absolute pitch of tones lowers gradually within words and more substantially between words, while maintaining the relative contrast between high and low tones, in a process described as tonal downstep (Leman 1981). This may be somewhat different from downstep processes observed in West African languages and Japanese, in which tone lowering is triggered only by particular tonal environments, (e.g. Gussenhoven 2004); however, we follow previous authors (Leman and Rhodes 1978; Leman 1981) in referring to Cheyenne tone lowering as downstep. As in other languages, downstep in Cheyenne ends with reset, which raises the absolute pitch of tones at the start of a new phrase. Thus, the end of a downstep interval can be identified as the point at which pitch resets.

Prosodic Structure

The study of prosody includes both the hierarchical groupings of phonological material between the syllable and the utterance, and the prominence relations within these groupings (e.g. stress, phrasal accents). This paper focuses on the former aspect of prosody, specifically on the phrasal groupings that are relevant for Cheyenne phrase-final devoicing and downstep.

Prosodic groupings at all levels of the hierarchy may be the domain of phonological processes (Selkirk 1980; Nespor and Vogel 1986), and in fact the restriction of different processes to different domains provides major evidence for the constituents of the prosodic hierarchy. Phrasal groupings in the prosodic hierarchy often correspond to syntactic structure, though the mappings are not always one to one (e.g. Nespor and Vogel 1986; Truckenbrodt 1999; Jun 2005; Selkirk 2011). For instance, higher levels of the prosodic hierarchy are more flexible and can be influenced by factors such as constituent size, speaking rate and style, and information structure. In this paper, "prosodically conditioned phonology" refers to phonological processes restricted to particular prosodic domains. In Cheyenne, both phrase-final devoicing and tonal downstep have been said to take place within the phonological phrase, with the former particularly likely before a pause (Leman and Rhodes 1978; Leman 1981). However, the number and type of prosodic domains in Cheyenne have not been otherwise defined. Our goal in this paper is to explore this question, based on the use of naturalistic archival data.

Methodology

This paper investigates the prosodic domains that condition phonological processes in Cheyenne. In particular, we are interested in the relationship between phrase-final devoicing and downstep and what domain or domains condition these processes. Phrase-final devoicing and downstep have not been looked at together to determine whether they occur in identical prosodic environments, or whether they both simply occur at some prosodic domain above the word but not necessarily the same one. To address this, we first look at both processes in a single story (Study 1). We then look further just at phrase-final devoicing in a second, longer story (Study 2). Our materials are two preexisting recordings of naturalistic speech from an Oklahoma Cheyenne speaker, Edward Riggs. Both were recorded in 1965 by Donald Olson, transcribed and published by Olson (1968), and later transcribed, glossed, and published by Leman (1980). This section presents the hypotheses that our investigation addresses overall and the methodology we use for annotating the recordings. The annotated versions of both stories are provided in the supplementary materials.

Hypotheses

In order to address the question of what domain or domains condition two phrasal processes in Cheyenne—phrase-final devoicing and tonal downstep—this paper tests the following hypotheses. First, (1) downstep and phrase-final devoicing are phrasal processes; thus they will not occur on every word, but will occur at the end of every sentence, and in some sentences may occur multiple times. Second, (2a) if downstep and phrase-final devoicing are conditioned by the same domain, downstep intervals will end with phrase-final devoicing, and phrase-final devoicing will coincide with the end of a downstep interval. Alternatively, (2b) if one process is conditioned by a smaller domain than the other, the smaller domain process should occur more frequently. Given the hierarchical organization we assume for prosodic structure, and the fact that we are comparing two domain-final processes, Hypothesis 2b also predicts that the larger domain process should always coincide with the smaller domain process, because the right edge of a larger domain should also be aligned with the right edge of smaller domains.

Annotation Methods

In our analysis, we identified occurrences of both phrase-final devoicing and downstep based on listening and impressionistic transcription as well as visual inspection of spectrograms in Praat (Boersma and Weenink 2020). As can be seen in the figures in this section, the high quality of the archival recordings allows us to clearly identify voicing and pitch in most cases, despite the age of the recordings and the fact that they were not originally collected for phonetic analysis. Visual evidence for phrase-final devoicing came from absence of a voicing bar and minimal-to-no formant structure during a word-final vowel. Spectrograms showing versions of the same morpheme with voiced and voiceless word-final vowels are provided in Figures 1 and 2 below for comparison (examples from clauses 6 and 11 of Story 1 respectively; see supplementary materials).

As mentioned in the background section, downstep in Cheyenne refers to the gradual lowering of tone within a word and more substantial lowering across words. To identify downstep, we compared the pitch (F0) of high tones and looked for intervals in which each consecutive high tone was lower than the previous one. For this comparison, we used the pitch track in Praat. An example of a clear case of lowering high tones within and across several words is provided in Figure 3 (clause

FIGURE 1. Voiced word-final -o (in box) with formant structure and voicing bar present

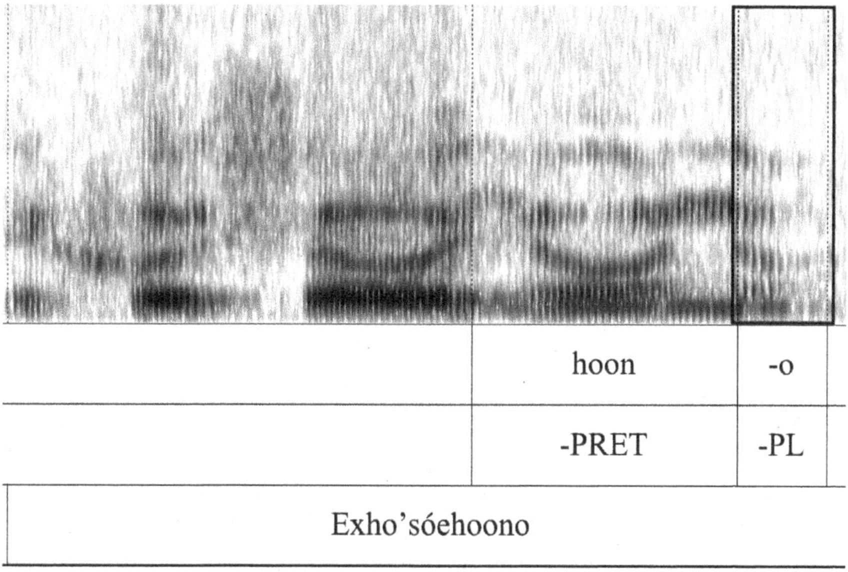

FIGURE 2. Voiceless word-final -o (in box) with minimal to no formant structure and voicing bar

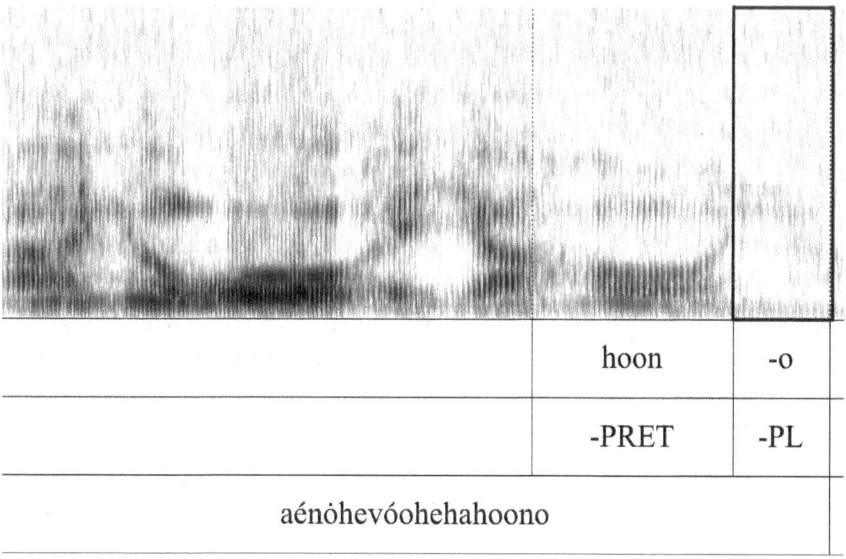

FIGURE 3. Pitch track showing downstep, with high tones marked as H on spectrogram.

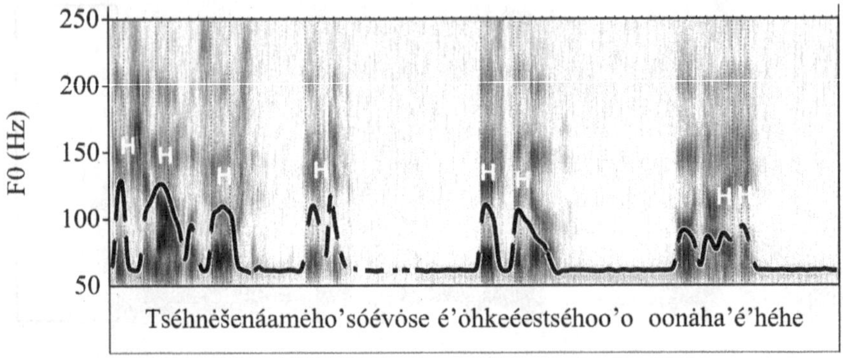

8, see supplementary materials). This figure shows a spectrogram and a black pitch track. 'H's written above the pitch track indicate where the high tones occur.

As can be seen in Figure 3, nearly every high tone across the phrase is somewhat lower than the preceding one. After the interval shown in the spectrogram, the pitch resets to roughly the same height as the start of the interval shown, indicating the beginning of a new period of downstep. Therefore, in our annotation of the recording, we counted periods of downstep as the intervals between pitch resets (plus two additional periods of downstep between silence and a pitch reset at the beginning and end of the story).

In order to compare the environments conditioning both processes, we looked at where the processes occurred with respect to word category, which can affect prosodic properties of a word (e.g. Lohmann and Conwell 2020 on English), and positions within a clause and sentence. For word boundaries, we used spaces in the orthography. Our word categories consisted of independent verb, dependent (conjunct) verb, noun, demonstrative, numeral, and other particles. For clause boundaries we used independent clauses, which contain an independent verb or can stand on their own, and for sentence boundaries we counted quoted speech as embedded within a sentence. As stated at the beginning of this section, the first study compares both processes within a single story, and the second study focuses on devoicing across two stories.

Study 1: Comparing Devoicing and Downstep within a Story

The first study compares the distribution of phrase-final devoicing and downstep in a story entitled "The Frog and her Brothers." The recording consists of 38 words, 13 clauses, and nine sentences, and is 1 minute and 15 seconds long.

Phrase-Final Devoicing Results

Of the 38 words in the story, 30 exhibited phrase-final devoicing. Nine of these occurred at the end of a sentence. The remaining 21 instances of final devoicing occurred in sentence-internal positions. These sentence-internal positions include before and after quoted speech, as in clauses 3–5 and 8–10 in the supplementary materials.

In both instances of quoted speech, final devoicing occurred at the end of the clause before the embedded quote, at the end of the quoted speech, and for a third time at the end of the sentence. The first and second occurrences of devoicing in each of the two cases of quoted speech together constitute four of the 21 sentence-internal cases of final devoicing. The remaining 17 were within a clause, including on independent verbs, dependent verbs, nouns, demonstratives, and other particles. These results by word category are summarized in Table 3 below, as proportions of the total occurrences of each category in the story (e.g. the count for nouns is 10/12 because there are 12 nouns in the story, 10 of which devoice). The results by position within a clause are summarized in Table 4 following the same format.

As can be seen in Table 4, all clause-final words exhibit phrase-final devoicing, as do the majority of clause-medial words, whereas clause-initial words rarely exhibit the process. In fact, of the eight words that were not devoiced in the story, six were clause-initial. (We counted single-word clauses as clause-final since the relevant syllable for devoicing was aligned with the right edge of a clause.) The

TABLE 3. Categories of words exhibiting phrase-final devoicing in Story 1

	INDEPENDENT VERBS	DEPENDENT VERBS	NOUNS	NUMERALS	DEMONSTRATIVES	OTHER PARTICLES
COUNT	9/11	6/8	10/12	0/1	3/3	2/3

TABLE 4. Positions within a clause exhibiting phrase-final devoicing in Story 1

	CLAUSE-INITIAL	CLAUSE-MEDIAL	CLAUSE-FINAL
COUNT	3/9	14/16	13/13

three clause-initial words with phrase-final devoicing were particles and a main verb (see the supplementary materials for detailed annotation).

A pattern that emerged from the data was that 9 of the 30 words with phrase-final devoicing ended in -he (e.g. *oonȧha'ĕ'héhe*, 'frog'), and in fact, every word in the story ending with *-he* exhibited final devoicing. Given that words ending in *-he* are so frequent (11 percent of verbs, 37.5 percent of nouns, and 100 percent of the demonstratives with phrase-final devoicing in the story), we keep track of them for the remainder of the paper.

Downstep Results

We identified 18 intervals of downstep in the story: 17 followed by pitch reset, plus the final interval at the end of the story, which was not followed by reset since there was no further speech. The ends of all nine sentences coincide with the end of a downstep interval. The remaining 9 of 18 intervals of downstep occur within a sentence. This includes the same four positions before and after quoted speech where we found phrase-final devoicing, which constitute all of the sentence-internal clause-final positions. Thus, the ends of all 13 clauses coincide with the end of a downstep interval. The remaining pitch resets are clause-internal, occurring after both verbs (clause 7, 11, supplementary materials) and post-verbal nouns (clause 7, 11, supplementary materials). Unlike devoicing, no instances of reset occurred after demonstratives.

We found that all instances of pitch reset co-occurred with phrase-final devoicing, but only 18/30 cases of phrase-final devoicing coincided with the end of a downstep interval, giving us a co-occurrence rate of 60 percent. Thus, the positions of reset constitute a proper subset of the positions of phrase-final devoicing. Interestingly, 8 of the 12 cases of phrase-final devoicing that occurred in the middle of a downstep interval were in word-final *-he*. If we exclude these eight cases of final *-he* devoicing from the comparison with downstep, the co-occurrence rate between the two processes would increase to 77 percent.

Summary and Discussion

This first study comparing patterns of phrase-final devoicing and downstep in a previously recorded Cheyenne narrative found phrase-final devoicing in 30 out of 38 words in the story. We also found 18 intervals of downstep. Table 4 above showed that not all words exhibit phrase-final devoicing or pitch reset, but both processes can occur multiple times within a sentence and even multiple times within a clause. This shows that the processes are conditioned by some prosodic domain larger than a word, but smaller than an utterance, supporting Hypothesis 1.

Rates of co-occurrence between the two processes offer insight into Hypothesis 2. There were 18 out of 30 (or 60 percent) instances of phrase-final devoicing that coincided with the end of a downstep interval. Downstep intervals did not end in any other positions, so the positions where downstep ended were a proper subset of those where phrase-final devoicing occurred. All 13 clauses and 9 sentences in the story ended with both phrase-final devoicing and the end of a downstep interval; additional instances of the two processes occurred within clauses. This suggests that there could be multiple phrase-final devoicing domains within a single domain of downstep. In other words, phrase-final devoicing occurs at a smaller domain than downstep, as predicted by Hypothesis 2b.

We also found that *-he* was always devoiced word-finally, which calls into question whether this is a result of phrase-final devoicing or another process. There is extensive word-level vowel devoicing in Cheyenne and a phonetic and phonological relationship between [h] and voiceless vowels (shared articulatory properties and laryngeal features), so one possibility could be an additional word-level devoicing process targeting these syllables.[4] Thus, it is possible that some (or all) of the nine words ending in voiceless *-he* are not actually affected by phrase-final devoicing. In fact, 8 of the 12 tokens of final devoicing that occurred in the middle of a downstep interval (66.7 percent) ended with *-he*. Excluding those words, the degree of overlap between cases of phrase-final devoicing and the end of a downstep interval would be substantially higher (77 percent) but still evidence for different domains. Given that different accounts of the *-he* devoicing might lead to different interpretations of the relationship between phrase-final devoicing and tonal downstep, a better understanding of *-he* devoicing is an important next step.

We also faced a methodological issue in identifying downstep, because in certain parts of the story, comparisons across high tones were difficult. One reason was that not all words have high tones, and even words that do can be very long and contain substantial stretches without any high tones to compare. The available definition of downstep in Cheyenne also does not specify whether downstep begins at the beginning of a phrase or only after a certain type or sequence of tones, making identification of reset particularly challenging when stretches without high tones occurred at the beginning of a word. It is unclear how exactly low tones are affected by downstep or reset, so comparison of low tones did not seem like a reliable option. A second difficulty for identifying downstep was that the data contains many instances of [h], which affect the pitch of adjacent vowels. Since the recording is of fairly fast naturalistic speech, vowels are not always long enough to find a reliable pitch track or distinguish F0 perturbations caused by adjacent consonants from the rest of the vowel. Therefore, a refined approach to defining downstep, and elicitation of utterances containing higher proportions of voiced segments and controlled distribution of high tones, would be valuable for our comparison between intervals of downstep and phrase-final devoicing.

Study 2: Phrase-Final Devoicing in a Second Story

This section presents a follow-up study, further exploring patterns of phrase-final devoicing in a longer story entitled "The Bat." Specifically, we investigate whether patterns emerge with more data to suggest that certain syntactic positions favor or disfavor phrase-final devoicing. We also consider the nature of final *-he*, since it was always devoiced in Study 1. Evidence to support a word-level devoicing process distinct from phrase-final devoicing would include devoicing on every instance of word-final *-he*, regardless of syntactic or prosodic position, as was the case in the first story. Although we are not comparing devoicing to downstep in this study, this further investigation of devoicing allows us to at least better understand the conditioning environment of one of the two processes.

"The Bat" is 2 minutes and 46 seconds long, and contains 84 words, 32 clauses, and 23 sentences. One three-word sentence contains a disfluency, with one word inserted into another. We exclude this entire sentence from our analysis and report only on the remaining 81 words.

Phrase-Final Devoicing Results

This section presents the patterns in phrase-final devoicing observed in the second story. We start by presenting results for final *-he* devoicing and then present rates of devoicing overall, broken down by syntactic category and by position in a clause, as was done for Study 1. This addresses the main question of what the domain is that conditions phrase-final devoicing. In the following subsection, we discuss the results further, including in comparison with the findings in Study 1.

Vowel devoicing was identified at the end of 62 out of 81 words, including at the end of all 23 sentences. The story contains 14 words ending in *-he*: six independent verbs, five nouns (all *mȯsėškanetsėnoonȧhe*, meaning 'bat'), two demonstrative particles, and one other particle. In the story, 13/14 of these words devoice; the one that does not is one of the tokens of 'bat.' Interestingly, the token that does not devoice occurs pre-verbally, whereas the other four nouns that devoice occur post-verbally. There are, however, other pre-verbal nouns that devoice (as will be discussed further).

Turning to the distribution of devoicing more broadly, of the 62 cases of final devoicing, 31 are clause-final and 31 are clause-internal. As there were 32 clauses in the story, all but one clause ends with devoicing. The one clause that does not end with devoicing is within a direct quote, as shown in (5) below, where independent verbs are underlined and devoiced final vowels are marked with the IPA diacritic below them (e.g. [ḁ]). The second word of the example is clause-final but quote-internal and does not devoice. The fourth word, which ends in the same morpheme, is also clause-final but does exhibit final devoicing.

(5)	naa	ná-me'-ta-tónėšévé-mȧse	tósa'e̥	ná-hó'xėstȧhé-mȧse̥
	and	1-should-HORT-what.do-RPT	where	1-belong-RPT
	'Well, what in the world should I do? Where do I belong?'			

Table 5 summarizes the devoicing results by syntactic category, and Table 6 summarizes the results by position within a clause. As in Study 1, the results are presented as proportions of each environment that exhibit devoicing.

As can be seen in Table 5, not all syntactic categories exhibit phrase-final devoicing at the same rate. Nearly all verbs do (97.6 percent), as do the majority of nouns (72 percent). In contrast, only 40 percent of the particles (and 33.3 percent of particles other than demonstratives) exhibit final devoicing. However, of the 18 particles, 8 are tokens of the word *naa*, which never devoices, perhaps because it is only one syllable. It can also be seen in Table 6 that while final devoicing does not occur on every word, it can occur multiple times within a clause, and in fact

TABLE 5. Categories of words exhibiting phrase-final devoicing in Story 2

	INDEPENDENT VERBS	DEPENDENT VERBS	NOUNS	DEMONSTRATIVES	OTHER PARTICLES
COUNT	31/32	10/10	13/18	2/2	6/18

TABLE 6. Positions within a clause exhibiting phrase-final devoicing in Story 2

	CLAUSE-INITIAL	CLAUSE-MEDIAL	CLAUSE-FINAL
COUNT	12/22	19/27	31/32

more than two thirds of the clauses in the story have at least two instances of phrase-final devoicing.

Next, we consider interactions between syntactic category and syntactic position. We focus on nouns and their position relative to verbs and clause boundaries. The 18 nouns in the story include eight in pre-verbal positions, eight in post-verbal positions, and two nouns further embedded within a disjunction, which both devoice. All of the post-verbal nouns devoice, but only two of the eight pre-verbal nouns devoice. In other words, post-verbal nouns always devoice, whereas pre-verbal nouns rarely do. The difference between pre- and post-verbal positions is illustrated in (6) and (7) below, which include the same noun *vé'kėseho*, 'birds' and verb *-móheeohtsė*, 'meet.' In the first example, 'birds' appears after the verb and devoices, whereas in the second it appears before the verb and does not devoice. In both, the noun is bolded and bracketed with its verb.

(6) naa máto hápó'ę [mó-h-móheeohtsė-he-vō-hę **vé'kėseh-o̥**]
and also likewise INF-PST-meet-NEG.SFX-3PL-INF.SFX bird-3PL
tséohkėhetaa'eame'hávȯse
CNJ-HAB-entire-fly.along-3PL-*3*
'And also likewise birds, those who fly, met.'

(7) ta-tsėhe'ōhtsė-stsę [**vé'kėseh-o** tsé-h-móheeohtsé-vȯ-sę]
TRL-go.to-IMPV bird-3PL CNJ-OBL-meet-3PL-3
'Go to where the birds are meeting!'

Two of the pre-verbal nouns appear clause-initially and six appear clause-medially. The two that devoice are clause-medial, suggesting that their position within the clause is a factor in whether they devoice. That is, nouns, like other syntactic categories (see Table 6), are more likely to devoice later in a syntactic clause than elsewhere. One possibility that follows is that the post-verbal nouns consistently devoice not due to their different position relative to a verb, but due to the fact that they tend to appear later in the clause than pre-verbal nouns do. Nevertheless, post-verbal nouns occur both clause-medially (three tokens) and clause-finally (two tokens) but devoice consistently in both positions.

In summary, both position within a clause and word category play a role in phrase-final devoicing. For nouns in particular, we also see that position relative to a verb is a relevant factor. Additionally, we see an interaction between word category and position within a clause, with verbs devoicing clause-initially, but never nouns.

Discussion and Comparison with Study 1

In the first study, all words ending in *-he* were devoiced, regardless of syntactic category or position, suggesting that devoicing on this syllable could be attributed to a different process. In the second study, most but not all words ending in *-he* devoice, demonstrating that final *he* devoicing does not occur 100 percent of the time, as we would expect for a word-level process. There is, however, only one case of word-final voiced *-he*, and this word is also the only *-he* final noun that occurs pre-verbally in either story. This leaves us with the question of whether the one instance of word-final voiced *-he* that we observed is an anomaly in the data, or whether it reflects a distinct pattern that would emerge with a larger dataset.

As for the devoicing patterns by syntactic category, the first story shows lower rates of devoicing on verbs than the second story does, but higher rates of devoicing on both nouns and particles. In Story 1, the rate of devoicing on nouns is slightly higher than on verbs (around 83 percent versus 79 percent), whereas in Story 2, verbs exhibit the highest rate of devoicing (97.6 percent). In Story 1, however, all categories had rates of devoicing roughly similar to each other. In the larger dataset of Story 2, on the other hand, more differences among syntactic categories emerge, with most verbs devoicing but few particles devoicing. It should be noted, however, that the high frequency of the particle *naa*, which never devoices, brings down the devoicing rate for particles overall. Both stories show similar effects of position within a clause, with initial position exhibiting the least devoicing and final position exhibiting the most.

These results suggest that factors influencing phrase-final devoicing include syntactic category, position in a syntactic clause, and for nouns, position relative to verbs. Furthermore, our more in-depth study of syntactic position in Story 2 suggests that position relative to a verb and position within a clause have interacting effects on devoicing rates for nouns.

Conclusion

This paper examines two phrase-level phonological processes in Cheyenne, phrase-final devoicing and tonal downstep. We used two previously recorded Cheyenne narratives from 1965 to study the processes in naturalistic speech. A comparison of the two processes in Study 1 showed that both can occur multiple times within a sentence, but not necessarily on every word. Broadly, this provides evidence for prosodic structure between the word and utterance levels in Cheyenne. Phrase-final devoicing occurs more frequently than downstep, but every interval of downstep coincides with phrase-final devoicing. This suggests that phrase-final devoicing is governed by a smaller domain than that of downstep.

Our second, follow-up study looked further at environments conditioning phrase-final devoicing and found that syntactic category and position within a clause both affect the process. Specifically, verbs are most likely to devoice, followed by nouns and then particles; clause-initial position also exhibits the least devoicing, and clause-final position exhibits the most. For nouns, we saw that clause position interacts with position relative to the verb.

Our study of downstep presented certain challenges due to both the nature of the archival recordings and some open questions about the definition of downstep in Cheyenne. Targeted elicitations of utterances containing more voiced segments and different distributions of high tones would be a valuable next step to better understand Cheyenne downstep in its own right.

Several questions about word-level phenomena also arose in our investigation of phrase-final devoicing. We found in both studies that words ending in *-he* exhibited a higher rate of phrase-final devoicing than other words. This raised the question of whether the devoicing of words ending in *-he* was in fact due to phrase-final devoicing or has some alternative explanation. Additionally, in Study

2, an issue emerged with the particle devoicing results: a high frequency word *naa*, which never devoices, constituted almost half of the particles in the data. We are therefore not able to tell whether the low rate of devoicing observed for particles reflects a property of that syntactic category as a whole or is simply skewed by a single lexical item.

Overall, this investigation provides insight into patterns of both phrase-final devoicing and downstep, as well as into prosodic structure in Cheyenne more broadly. The results from both processes provide evidence for multiple domains larger than the word, since the two processes occur at phrasal domains but not the same one. More specifically, the domain of downstep appears to be larger than that of phrase-final devoicing. Future work is necessary to better understand these phrasal domains, but this study has shown that with regard to phrase-final devoicing, multiple factors including word category, clause position, and the interaction between them are relevant in conditioning the process. More broadly, this paper adds to the case studies in how archival materials can be used for phonetic and phonological analysis, and in how prosodic organization manifests in naturalistic data.

NOTES

See supplementary materials online, https://algonquianconference.atlas-ling.ca/eng/supplementary-materials/.

1. Acknowledgments: Though all of our data came from archival sources, we would like to acknowledge the Cheyenne speakers and the Cheyenne language. We would also like to thank Wayne Leman, participants in the Cornell Linguistics Interface Seminar in Fall 2019, the audience at the 51st Algonquian Conference at McGill University, two anonymous reviewers, and the editors for their helpful comments and feedback. Any errors are our own.
2. CNJ = conjunct, HAB= habitual, HORT = hortative, IMPV = imperative, INF = infinitive, SFX = suffix, NEG = negation, OBL = oblique, PL = plural, PRET = preterite/narrative, PST = past, RPT = reportative, TRL = translocative.
3. The segmental environment in which this process occurs is never present in the final syllable of the word. Thus, while this process only occurs in "prepenultimate" syllables, it is only actively blocked in the penult.
4. High vowels (e.g. /i, u/) adjacent to boundaries or voiceless consonants are also

particularly prone to devoicing cross-linguistically, so a phonetic or phonological process targeting word-final /he/ would not be surprising from a typological perspective either. In Cheyenne, /e/ is written as a mid-vowel in the orthography and the Cheyenne grammar (Leman 2011), but since there is no other high front vowel, we may expect it to behave similarly to /i/ in other languages.

REFERENCES

Boersma, Paul, and David Weenink. 2020. Praat: Doing Phonetics by Computer. [Computer program]. Version 6.1.09. http://www.praat.org/.

Costa, David J. 2003. *The Miami-Illinois Language*. Lincoln: University of Nebraska Press.

Fisher, Louise, Wayne Leman, Leroy Pine Sr., and Marie Sanchez. 2017. *Cheyenne Dictionary*. Lame Deer, MT: Chief Dull Knife College. http://www.cheyennelanguage.org/dictionary/lexicon/index.htm.

Frantz, Donald G. 2009. *Blackfoot Grammar* (2nd ed.). Toronto: University of Toronto Press.

Goddard, Ives. 1991. Observations Regarding Fox (Mesquakie) Phonology. *Papers of the 22nd Algonquian Conference*, ed. by William Cowan, pp. 157–181. Ottawa: Carleton University.

Greenberg, Joseph H. 1969. Some Methods of Dynamic Comparison in Linguistics. *Substance and Structure of Language*, ed. by Jaan Puhvel, pp. 147–203. Berkeley: University of California Press.

Gussenhoven, Carlos. 2004. *The Phonology of Tone and Intonation.* Cambridge: Cambridge University Press.

Jun, Sun-Ah. 2005. Prosodic Typology. *Prosodic Typology: The Phonology of Intonation and Phrasing*, ed. by Sun-Ah Jun, pp. 430–458. Oxford: Oxford University Press.

Knee, Sarah. 2014. Vowel Devocalization in Northern East Cree. *Canadian Journal of Linguistics* 59(3):303–338.

Leman, Wayne (ed.). 1980. *Cheyenne Texts: An Introduction to Cheyenne Literature.* Occasional Publications in Anthropology: Linguistics Series No. 6. Greeley: Museum of Anthropology, University of Northern Colorado.

Leman, Wayne. 1981. Cheyenne Pitch Rules. *International Journal of American Linguistics* 47(4):283–309.

Leman, Wayne. 2011 [1980]. *A Reference Grammar of the Cheyenne Language*. Morrisville, NC: Lulu Press.

Leman, Wayne, and Richard Rhodes. 1978. Cheyenne Vowel Devoicing. *Papers of the Ninth Algonquian Conference*, ed. by William Cowan, pp. 3–24. Ottawa: Carleton University.

Lohmann, Arne, and Erin Conwell. 2020. Phonetic Effects of Grammatical Category: How

Category-Specific Prosodic Phrasing and Lexical Frequency Impact the Duration of Nouns and Verbs. *Journal of Phonetics* 78:1–22.

Milliken, Stuart. 1983. Vowel Devoicing and Tone Recoverability in Cheyenne. *Working Papers of the Cornell Phonetics Laboratory* 1:43–75.

Nespor, Marina, and Irene Vogel. 1986. *Prosodic Phonology.* Dordrecht: Foris Publications.

Olson, Donald. 1968. *Cheyenne Texts and Grammar Notes.* Mimeographed manuscript. Based on materials archived in the American Philosophical Society's Phillips Fund Collection, Philadelphia. https://search.amphilsoc.org.

Prins, Samantha Leigh. 2019. Final Vowel Devoicing in Blackfoot. MA thesis, University of Montana. https://scholarworks.umt.edu/etd/11363/.

Selkirk, Elizabeth. 1980. Prosodic Domains in Phonology: Sanskrit Revisited. *Juncture*, ed. by Mark Aronoff and Mary-Louise Kean, pp. 107–129. Saratoga, CA: Anma Libri.

Selkirk, Elizabeth. 2011. The Syntax-Phonology Interface. *The Handbook of Phonological Theory* (2nd ed.), ed. by John Goldsmith, Jason Riggle, and Alan Yu, pp. 435–484. Oxford: Wiley Blackwell.

St. Goddard, Rosalind. 2014. A Comparison of Japanese and Blackfoot Vowel Devoicing. *Calgary Working Papers in Linguistics* 28(Fall):81–96.

Truckenbrodt, Hubert. 1999. On the Relation between Syntactic Phrases and Phonological Phrases. *Linguistic Inquiry* 30:219–256.

Obligation and Restriction in Plains Cree

H. C. Wolfart

A philological review of the relationship between Plains Cree obligative and restrictive constructions showing the particle *piko*, this essay is intended to complement the formal treatment that Clare Cook outlined in her pioneering work on *The Clause Typing System of Plains Cree* (2014). What makes this case remarkable beyond the realm of linguistic analysis is the unexpected range of variation found for these constructions in the literary translations (1930, 1934) of the EARLY TEXTS Leonard Bloomfield recorded in 1925 and in the MODERN TEXTS prepared for publication since 1982 by Freda Ahenakew and H. C. Wolfart.[1]

The CLAUSE-INITIAL PREDICATIVE *piko* 'it is necessary that; it is proper that', which governs a verb in the conjunct order, defines the most prominent construction of obligation or necessity—and, of course, prohibition:

(1) a. **piko** ka-pê-kîwêyan, . . . (MT)
OBL ASP=hither=return.home.VAI2.CJ
'You have to come home, . . .'

b. **pikw** ân[i] êkâ ka-pakicîyahk, nôsisim! (MT)
OBL EMPH NEG ASP=give.up.VAI21.CJ grandchild.NDA.VOC
'We must not give up, Grandchild!'

The EMPHATIC RESTRICTIVE *piko* 'only, exclusively' FOLLOWS the constituent, commonly nominal or adverbial, over which it has scope:

(2) a. **nôcikwêsiw awa piko pîhtikwêw, . . .** (MT)
old.woman.NA3 this3 ENC.R enter.VAI3.IND
'Only this old woman went in, . . .'

b. **. . ., êkota mâna piko ê-kî-wâpamakik.** (MT)
then.RES habitually ENC.R CP=ASP=see.s.o.VTA1.3p.CJ
'. . ., only then did I see them.'

The INCONSEQUENTIAL CONCESSIVE CONDITIONAL is a construction based on *piko* as the initial member and a correlative like *itê* 'whither; where' as the final, as in *pikw îtê* 'wherever, whithersoever; everywhere, in every direction':

(3) a. **. . ., pikw îtê mawimoyani, môy nânitaw ka-kî-nâtamâkon, . . .** (MT)
CONC CORR.LOC cry.VAI2.SUBJ NEG in.some.way ASP=ASP=rescue.s.o.VTA0.2IND
'. . ., no matter where you might cry out, it will not be able to rescue you in any way, . . .'

b. **pikw îtê kî-papâmipicinâniwan, . . .** (MT)
CONC CORR.LOC ASP=camp.about.VAI.INDF.IND
'One used to camp about just any place, . . .'

In conditional constructions (as in (3a), with the subjunctive conjunct) such phrases serve as conjunctions, but they also occur adverbially (as in (3b), with the independent indicative).

While concentrating on these primary manifestations of *piko*, the present paper also touches on some distinct but structurally analogous particles, notably the necessity predicative *katâc, kâkatâc* 'it is necessary, it is opportune; of necessity, deliberately' and the phrasal *ohcitaw piko* 'it is necessary, it is appropriate; definitely, inescapably' along with the simple restrictive *nayêstaw* 'only', which precedes the constituent over which it has scope.[2]

In assembling the documentation on which this summary paper is based, we proceed on the hypothesis that at least the obligative and restrictive uses of *piko* constitute a case of polysemy.

The Necessity Predicative *piko*

In the most forceful of the necessity constructions, clause-initial *piko* governs a verb in the simple conjunct and showing the future/purposive preverb *ta*/*ka*. The deontic force of this construction is most unambiguously marked by the appearance of the negator *êkâ*:[3]

(4) a. . . ., **pikw** êkâ k[a]-âkayâsîmoyân ôm âya, . . . (MT)
OBL NEG ASP=speak.English.VAI1.CJ this0 HES
'. . ., I must not use English for this, . . .'

b. hâw, pikw ân[i] êkâ ta-wînêyihtaman, . . . (MT)
HES OBL EMPH NEG ASP=consider.s.t.dirty.VTI2.0CJ
'Well, you must not think of it as dirty, . . .'

Predicative piko *with the Simple Conjunct and the Preverb* ta/ka

The deontic function of clause-initial *piko* does not, however, depend on negation; in fact, there are several types of non-negated necessity constructions with *piko* and the simple conjunct. Its force seems amplified by the highly marked FUTURE/PURPOSIVE preverbs *ta*/*ka*.[4]

The necessity may be situational and immediate (5a, 5b) or more general, as in the sarcastic remark about the exalted expectations of today's children (5c):

(5) a. nôtokwêw, **piko** ka-nipâsiyân, . . . (MT)
old.woman-NA.VOC OBL ASP=sleep.DIM.VAI1.CJ
'I must have a little sleep, Old Lady, . . .'

b. "**piko** ta-nitaw-âyamihâyân," itwêw. (MT)
OBL ASP=go.and=pray.VAI1.CJ say.thus.VAI3.IND
'"I must go to church," she said.'

c. . . ., **piko** ka-wâpisk-ânâskâtihcik, . . . (MT)
OBL ASP=white=spread.mat.for.s.o.VTA.INDF.3p.CJ
'. . ., one has to make their beds up with white sheets, . . .'

Predicative *piko* often appears in the second clause of a contrastive sentence, with the first including a negative:

(6) a. êkây mâka êkos îsi pakitinihk,
NEG but thus.RES thus release.s.o.VTA2p.3IMVE
piko kîkway ta-wî-~ ta-tôtahk! (MT)
OBL something.0 ASP=ASP-~ ASP=do.s.t.thus.VTI3.0CJ
'But do not release her just like this, she will have to —~ she has to do something!'

It is also common as the apodosis of an explicit conditional, here with a subjunctive conjunct:

(6) b. êkw âwiyak miskwamâci êkon ânihi sôniyâsa,
now someone.3 find.s.o.VTA3.(3')SUBJ that.RES3' that3' coin.NA3'
piko ta-nîmihitowinihkêt, . . . (MT)
OBL ASP=hold.a.dance.VAI3.CJ
'then if someone found that coin [*sc.* baked in a cake] in his mouth, she/he had to hold the [next] dance, . . .'

Correlative constructions mark an implied conditional, with the protasis showing a conjunction like *iyikohk* 'so much, to such a degree, to such an extent':

(6) c. . . ., êkwa iyikohk ê-kaskihtâyahk
now CORR.to.such.an.extent CP=succeed.VAI21.CJ
piko ka-kakwê-wîcihâyahkik ôk âwâsisak, . . . (MT)
OBL ASP=attempt=help.s.o.VTA21.3p.CJ this3p child.NA3p
'. . ., and as much as we can we must try to help these children, . . .'

Predicative piko *with the Changed Conjunct and the Preverb* ê

The deontic force of predicative *piko* seems attenuated when it is construed with the changed conjunct and the preverb *ê*. By far the clearest differentiation between the two constructions is found in the context of negation: no cases have so far been encountered of *piko* with the changed conjunct and *ê* being negated.

While still deontic, *piko*-constructions with the unmarked preverb *ê* lack the highly marked future/purposive sense of the preverbs *ta*/*ka*; they are, in effect, ATEMPORAL. In (7a) the adverb *tâpitawi* 'all the time, at all times' covers the full tense/aspect spectrum:

(7) a. **piko** tâpitawi kîkway ê-tasîhkamân . . . (MT)
OBL always something.0 CP=be.engaged.in.s.t.VTI1.0CJ
'I must have something to do all the time . . .'

In (7b) the adverb *kîtahtawê*, which means both 'at a certain time, suddenly' and 'sometimes', is also neutral with respect to tense/aspect, as is the pragmatic situation in a passage explicitly introducted as an illustration by the exclamatory *îh* 'look, behold' and the personal pronoun *niya* 'I, me':

(7) b. îh niya, ê-~ môy ê-nihtâ-âkayâsîmoyân,
look I.myself NEG CP=competent=speak.English.VAI.1CJ
kîtahtawê, miton îta kâ-wanwêhkâkawiyân,
sometimes very.much CORR.LOC CP=confuse.s.o.VTA.INDF.1CJ
pikw ê-itwêstamâkawiyân; (MT)
OBL CP=interpret.for.s.o.VTA.INDF.1CJ
'Look at me, I cannot speak English, at times when I am seriously stumped [without English], I have to have someone interpret for me;'

Even the temporal adverb *anohc* 'now, today' is quite unspecific; in (7c) it gains its non-past value primarily from the contrast with the *kayâs* 'long ago, in the old days' of the preceding context:

(7) c. anohc êkwa kîkway, **piko**
today now something.0 OBL
ê-acâhcosihk wâwâc ôma
CP=buy.(it/them).from.one.another.DIM.VAI.T.INDF.CJ even this.0
kâ-nêhiyâwihk [*laughs*], . . . (MT)
CP-be.Cree.VAI.INDF.CJ
'Today now for any small thing, one has to buy it from one another even amongst Crees [*laughs*], . . .'

Atemporal clauses with *piko* and *ê* seem to be preferred in the context of a perfective domain established by the preverb *kî*:

(8) a. **pikw** ê-itwêstamâkêhk ôma kâ-kî-ati-ohpikiyâhk, . . . (MT)
OBL CP=interpret.for.people.VAI.INDF.CJ in.fact CP=ASP=ASP=grow.up.VAI.1p.CJ
'One had to interpret for people when we were growing up, . . .'

All the same, a long sequence of *kî*-verbs may be interrupted by an aside showing *piko* with the simple conjunct and *ta/ka*:

(8) b. (. . ., **piko** ta-pê-mostohtêt awiyak
OBL ASP=hither=simply.walk.VAI3.CJ someone.3
ta-pê-nâsit) (MT)
ASP=hither=fetch.s.o.VTA3.1CJ
'(. . ., someone had to come here on foot and fetch me there)'

The two constructions may even occur side by side within the same passage, preceded by the perfective preverb *kî*:

(8) c. "ê-asamacik, . . ., **piko** wîstawâw ê-asamacik,"
CP-feed.s.o.VTA2.3p.CJ OBL they.EMPH.3p CP.feed.s.o.VTA2.3p.CJ
itwêw. "anohc kâ-kîsikâk, namôy kîkway, . . ., **piko**
say.thus.VAI3.IND today CP=be.day.VII0'.CJ NEG something.0 OBL
k[a]-âtâwêyan," itwêw. (MT)
ASP=buy.(it/them).VAI.T2.CJ say.thus.VAI3.IND
'"You fed them, . . . , you had to feed them as well," she said. "Today there is none of that, . . . , you have to buy it [*sc.* from them]," she said.'

The *ê*-clause refers to a distant past, previously specified as *kayâs* 'long ago, in the old days'; the contrast with the present is made explicit by *anohc kâ-kîsikâk* 'today' and the future/purposive quality of the *ka*-clause.

Predicative piko *and the Focus Position*

Although predicative *piko* is structurally defined as clause-initial, it may in fact be preceded by constituents placed in focus, for instance the patient noun phrase:

(9) a. êwako piko ta-nâcinêhikêyan, . . .; (MT)
that.RES0 OBL ASP=request.things.by.payment.VAI2.CJ
'For THAT [curing] you have to make a formal request [along with payment], . . .;'

Locative expressions are common among preposed adverbials, e.g.,

(9) b. wâhyawês ohci piko ka-p-~ ka-pimitisahwâyêk, . . . (MT)
a.little.away from OBL ASP=-~ ASP=follow.s.o.VTA.2p.3CJ
You have to follow her from a little distance, . . .'

Most commonly, predicative *piko* is preceded by conjunctions like *êkwa* 'now, then; and' or *mâka* 'but; of course, to be sure' or phrases built upon them, which may be discontinuous, such as *mâk(a) êkwa* 'but now':

(9) c. . . ., mâk êkwa piko ta-wîcêwiyan, . . . (MT)
but now OBL ASP=accompany.s.o.VTA2.1CJ
'. . ., but now you must go with me, . . .'
d. . . ., mâka pikw êkwa ka-nêhiyawêyân, . . . (MT)
but OBL now ASP=speak.Cree.VAI1.CJ
'. . ., but now I have to speak Cree, . . .'

Adverbs expressing intensification are also often preposed to predicative *piko*. In this example, *mitoni* 'really, very much' modifies the cooking verb in both clauses:

(10) . . ., piko mitoni ka-kaskâciwasamihk aya, . . .,
OBL really ASP=cook.s.t.tender.VTI.INDF.0/0p.CJ HES
mitoni piko mîn êkoni ka-kaskâciwahtêki. (MT)
really OBL also that.RES.0p ASP=be.cooked.tender.VII.0p.CJ
'. . ., one has to really cook them until tender, . . . , those really also have to be cooked until tender.'

The mundane subject matter notwithstanding, the contrasting pair *piko mitoni* and *mitoni piko* may well constitute an instance of chiastic reversal, a classical form of high rhetoric in Plains Cree.[5]

Deontic Clauses without Predicative Particle

Not all deontic clauses, of course, need to exhibit *piko* or another overt predicative particle. The modal quality of constructions without an explicit necessity predicate, notably the hortative and the jussive, are most clearly identified by the choice of the deontic negator *êkâya*, which they share with the immediate and delayed modes of the imperative.

HORTATIVE clauses express a mild command; under negation, they show *êkâya* and the simple conjunct with the future/purposive preverb *ta/ka*:

(11) a.	. . ., mâk	**êkây**	cîk	ôhci	**ka**-pimitisahwâyêk, . . . (MT)
	but	NEG	close.up	from	ASP=follow.s.o.VTA.2p.3CJ

'. . ., but you should not follow her too closely, . . .'

In sentences that are not under negation, the only overt sign of the hortative is the optional adverb *mahti* 'let us, come on; please' (which also occurs freely with imperatives):

(11) b.	mahti	kisiwâk	kit-âyât. (ET)
	let.it.be	close.by	ASP=be.VAI3.CJ

'Let him get closer.'

JUSSIVE sentences, which are only identifiable under negation, show the deontic negator *êkâya* construed, strikingly, with a verb inflected in the independent indicative; they express a stern prohibition:

(11) c. . . .,	**êkây**	**wîhkâc**	**ka**-kisiwâhik	kôhtâwînaw, . . . (MT)
	NEG	ever	ASP=anger.s.o.VTA3.2IND	21PS.father.NDA.3

'. . ., never let yourself get angry at Our Father, . . .'

This construction seems to have gone unnoticed in modern studies of Plains Cree, although it is clearly documented in the dictionary and grammar of Albert Lacombe (1874a, b).

Necessity Predicatives Analogous to *piko*

Predicative katâc, kâkatâc

Predicative *piko* is never preceded by a negator; the sequence *môy piko* (or *namôya piko*) always represents the emphatic restrictive *piko*, which follows the constituent being restricted (cf. below). Predicative *katâc, kâkatâc* 'it is necessary, it is opportune; of necessity, deliberately', by contrast, in the vast majority of cases occurs with the epistemic negator *môy, namôya*, or the deontic negator *êkâya*.[6] In many instances, in fact, its function when negated seems very much complementary to that of predicative *piko*.

In the most common pattern, and analogously to *piko*, predicative (*kâ*)*katâc* is construed with the simple conjunct and the future/purposive preverb *ta/ka*:

(12) a. . . ., **namôy** **kâkatâc** miton âyamihêwikamikohk
NEG OBL really church.LOC
ka-nitawi-ocihkwanapiyahk, . . . (MT)
ASP=go.and=kneel-VAI21CJ
'. . ., it is not necessary for us to go and kneel in a formal church, . . .'

Unlike predicative *piko*, (*kâ*)*katâc* may be construed with the second position question marker *cî*; verbless clauses with (*kâ*)*katâc* may be either declarative, negated by *namôya*, or deontic, negated by *êkâya*:

(12) b. Q: **katâc** cî ka-kîwêyan anohc?
OBL INTERROG ASP=return.home.VAI2.CJ today
A: **môy** **kâkatâc**, mâka ninôhtê-kîwân. (MT)
NEG OBL but want.to=return.home.VAI1.IND
Q: 'Must you go home today?'
A: 'I don't have to, but I want to go home.'

c. hâw, êkwa kiya, **êkây** **katâc** mitoni cîki. (MT)
HES now you.yourself NEG OBL really close.up
'Well, now it is your turn, it is not necessary [to be] really close [to the microphone].'

Predicative ohcitaw piko

Unlike the other necessity predicatives, the phrase *ohcitaw piko* 'it is certain, it is appropriate, it is necessary; definitely, inescapably' also occurs as an adverbial. It is rare in the Bloomfield texts.

The phrase *ohcitaw piko* functions much like *piko* and (*kâ*)*katâc* when construed with a verb showing the simple conjunct with the future/purposive preverb *ta/ka*:

(13) a. **ohcitaw piko** ayisiyiniw **ka**-nipit. (MT)
OBL human.being.NA3 ASP=die.VAI3.CJ
'Man is mortal.' [*lit.* 'it is inescapable for humans to die']

b. **ohtitaw piko,** ta-nitotamâht kôhtâwînaw
OBL ASP=beg.s.o.VTA.INDF.3CJ 21PS.father.NDA.3
okisêwâtisiwin, . . . (MT)
3PS.blessing.NI0
'It is only proper that Our Father should be asked for his grace, . . .'

In verbless clauses, too, *ohcitaw piko* clearly functions as a necessity predicate:

(14) a. . . ., wiða nîð ê-nîmâskwêyân,
for I.myself CP=carry.a.weapon.VAI1.CJ
ohtitaw piko nîkân nîða. (MT)
OBL ahead I.myself
'. . ., for I carried the gun, I had to be in the lead.'

As an adverbial, the phrase *ohcitaw piko* is commonly translated as 'of course, still; definitely, inescapably.' In the absence of negation, however, verbless predicatives like (14a) are not always distinguishable from adverbials like (14b):

(14) b. . . ., mâk **ôhtitaw piko** mâna nikî-nôhtê-itohtân. (MT)
but OBL habitually ASP=want.to=go.there.VAI1.IND
'. . ., but I still wanted to go there.'

In (14c) the clause boundary indicated by the prosodic break is confirmed by Freda Ahenakew's informal translation: "it was a must, . . .":

(14) c. êkwa mîn **ôhtitaw piko,** kî-ayamihâwak ôm âyisiyiniwak
now also OBL ASP=pray.VAI.3p.IND in.fact human.being.NA3
wîstawâw kayâs. (MT)
they.EMPH.3p long.ago
'And it also was an obligation, people used to pray in the old days.'

The Emphatic Restrictive *piko*

As a second-position emphatic, putting the constituent that precedes it in focus, *piko* seems entirely analogous to emphatic *ani* (cf. Reinholtz and Wolfart 2001). Unlike *ani*, however, *piko* can occur in a sequence of postposed elements; thus, it is not a clitic in the strict sense.

The singulative and delimitative functions of postposed *piko* are independent of the category or word class of the item being highlighted. Paired with another clause, often including negation, the restrictive *piko*-clause is contrastive:

(15) a. . . ., namôy masinahikan ka-kî-nâtamâk;
NEG book.NI0 ASP=ASP=rescue.s.o.VTA0.3IND
kôhtâwînawa piko ka-nâtamâkot. (MT)
21PS.father.NDA.3' ENC.R ASP=rescue.s.o.VTA(3').3CJ
'. . ., a book will not be able to come to his rescue; **only Our Father** will rescue him.'

Predicative and restrictive *piko* may appear in one and the same sentence, e.g.,

(15) b. **piko** tâpitawi **pêyak-askiy piko** kik-âpacihtâyan, ... (MT)
OBL always one.year ENC.R ASP=use.(it/them).VAI.T2.CJ
'You always have to use them [*sc.* glasses] **for one year only,** . . .'

Restrictive piko *with Nominals*

A noun phrase that includes a determiner is treated as a unit, even when it is discontinuous:

(16) a. . . ., **awa piko iskwêw** êh-atoskêt, . . . (ET)
this.3 ENC.R woman.NA3 CP=work.VAI3.CJ
'. . ., **only the woman** worked, . . .'

Noun phrases showing constituent negation are typically discontinuous:

(16) b. **môy piko kêhtê-aya** ka-kitimâkisit,
NEG ENC.R old.person.NA3 ASP=be.miserable.VAI3.CJ
awâsisak ôki kâ-pê-nayawacikicik, . . . (MT)
child-NA.3p this.3p CP=hither=be.variously.grown.up.VAI.3p.CJ
'**not only** will **the old people** live in misery, but the children, too, who are coming after us in their various ages . . .'

c. . . ., êkwa aniki mîna mân âsikanak aya, **môy piko**
now that.3p also habitually stocking.NA.3p HES NEG ENC.R
pêyakw-âyak nôsîhânânak, . . . mihcêt mâna
one.set.PR.3p make.s.o.VTA.1p.3p.IND many habitually
kî-osîhêwak. (MT)
ASP=make.s.o.VTA.3p.(3').IND
'. . ., and also these stockings, we did **not only** make **one pair**, . . . they used to make lots of them.'

Demonstratives often carry contrastive focus; the resumptive deictic *êwako* 'that one, the selfsame' may occur by itself or combined with one of the demonstrative pronouns such as *anima* 'that one' (in (17a) with the future preverb *ka* appearing as *kê* under Initial Change) or with the emphatic clitic *ani*:

(17) a. **êwakw ânima piko** kê-âpacihikoyan. (MT)
that.RES0 that.0 ENC.R ASP=be.of.use.to.s.o.VTA0.2CJ
'**That is the only thing** that will sustain you.'

b. **êwakw âni piko** ê-wî-wîhtamâtakok, . . . (MT)
that.RES0 EMPH ENC.R CP=ASP=tell.s.o.about.(it/them).VTA1.2p.CJ
'**THAT is all** I am going to tell you about, . . .'

Personal pronouns, inherently emphatic in Cree and often preceded by the negator *môy, namôya*, are favored loci of contrast:

(18) a. **kiya** **piko,** kê-pîkonamâsoyan, kitasotamâkowin. (MT)
you.yourself ENC.R ASP=break.(it/them).for.oneself.VAI2.CJ 2PS.promise.made.NI0
'**Only you yourself** will be able to break the promises made to you.'

b. **niya** **piko** nitawâsimisak niwâpamâwak. (MT)
I.myself ENC.R 1PS.child.NDA.3p see.s.o.VTA1.3p.CJ
'I see **only my own** children [NOT yours].'

c. **môy** **niya** **piko,** nîtisâna mîna mâna
NEG I.myself ENC.R 1PS.sibling.NDA3' also habitually
kî-kitahamawêw. (MT)
ASP=warn.s.o.about.(it/them).VTA3.(3').IND
'and **not me alone**, she also used to warn my siblings against it.'

Restrictive piko *with Verbs, Adverbs, and Resumptive Deictics*

Ordinary verbs are rarely construed with restrictive *piko*; it is more typical with those expressing time of day or, most commonly, number:

(19) a. aya, **ê-pâsikâtêki** **piko** – (MT)
HES CP=be.dried.VII.0p.CJ ENC.R
'Ah, they **were only dried** –'

b. . . ., **têpiskâki** **pikoh** êh-pimohtêyâhk, . . . (ET)
be.night-VII0.ITER ENC.R CP=walk.along.VAI.1p.CJ
'. . ., walking **only at night**, . . .'

c. . . ., **nîsiwak** **pikoh** wîkiwâhk. (ET)
be.two.VAI.3p.IND ENC.R 3p.PS.lodge.NI.LOC
'. . ., the two, alone, in a tipi.' [*lit.* 'they **only were two** in their tipi']

Numerals, whether bare or the first element of a discontinuous noun phrase, are common as the restricted constituent under contrastive focus:

(20) a. **nîso** **piko** nitayâwâwak, . . . (MT)
two ENC.R have.s.o.VTA1.3p.IND
'I have **only two** of them, . . .'

b. **nîso** **piko** **mistatimwa** ê-âpacihât, . . . (MT)
two ENC.R horse.NA3' CP=use.s.o.VTA3.(3').CJ
'using **only two horses**, . . .'

c. **pêyak piko** nipahâw **nêhiyaw**, . . . (ET)
one ENC.R kill.s.o.VTA.INDF.3IND Cree.person.NA3
'**Only one of the Cree** was slain, . . .'

Numeral adverbs range from the basic type, e.g., *nêwâw* 'four times' or its phrasal counterpart *môy pêyakwâw* 'not once' (in this example discontinuous), to the adverbial quantifier *tânitahtwâw* 'how many times; so many times, many times':

(21) a. . . ., **nêwâw piko** kik-âh-ayiwêpin. (ET)
four.times ENC.R ASP=RED.rest.VAI2.IND
'. . ., **only four times** are you to stop and rest.'

b. – **môy piko pêyakwâw**, tânitahtwâw êkos îsi mâna
NEG ENC.R once many.times thus.RES thus habitually
nikî-âcimostâkonân – (MT)
ASP=tell.s.o.about.(it/them).VTA3.1p.IND
'– **not just once** but many times he used to tell us about these things –'

More fully specified sets are derived by a suffix identifying the object being counted; the latter include both unit words like *niyânanwêwipêhikan* 'five dollars' with the suffix *-pêhikan* 'bill, note, ticket, playing-card' and compounds (the members of which are separated by external sandhi) with an adverbial like *kîsikâw* 'so many days' worth':

(21) c. . . ., **niyânanwêwipêhikan piko** êyâpic ê-miyikawiyâhk. (MT)
five.dollars ENC.R still CP=give.(it/them).to.s.o.VTA.INDF.1p.CJ
'. . . , we are still given **only five dollars**.'

d. . . ., **nîso-kîsikâw pikoh** aniki kâ-nîmihitocik nipiy êkâ
two.days ENC.R that.3p CP=dance.VAI.3p.CJ water.NI0 NEG
ê-minihkwêcik, . . . (ET)
CP=drink.VAI.3p.CJ
'. . ., **for two days and no longer** the dancers drink no water, . . .'

The resumptive deictic base *êwakw-* (or *êkw-*) also appears in a range of further adverbs, for instance *êkwa* 'then; now', *êkota* 'there, at that place; then, at that time', *êkotê* 'thither, there', *êkospîhk* 'then, at that time', *êkotowahk* 'of that kind', *êkotowihk* 'in that place', and especially, *êkwayihkohk* (or *êkoyikohk*) 'that much, to that degree, to that extent'; all of these are readily placed in focus by means of enclitic *piko*:

(22) a. . . ., **êkota** **pikw** êyiwêhk ê-pêhtamihk
there.RES ENC.R still CP=hear.s.t.VTI.INDF.0CJ
êkotowi-kîkway, . . . (MT)
that.kind.RES=something.0
'. . ., **that** [the Sundance] **is the only place** where one still hears that kind of thing, . . .'

b. **êkwayikohk** **piko** ê-kî-nisitawêyimakik, . . . (MT)
to.that.extent.RES ENC.R CP=ASP=understand.s.o.VTA1.3p.CJ
'**That is as much** as I knew of them, . . .'

In the vast majority of instances where *piko* is construed with an adverb, it is the resumptive deictic manner adverb *êkosi* 'thus' which serves as antecedent for the correlative preverb *isi* 'thus' or for verb stems based on the unpalatalized variant of the same root, e.g. *it–* VTA 'say thus to s.o.':

(23) a. . . ., êkosi pikw ê-is[i]-âstê-ayâyan. (MT)
thus.RES ENC.R CP-thus-recovered-be.VAI2.CJ
'. . ., **that is the only way** for you to recover.'

b. **êkosi** **piko** ê-wî-isi-wîhtamâtakok êwak
thus.RES ENC.R CP=ASP=thus=tell.s.o.about.(it/them).VTA1.2p.CJ that.RES0
ôma. (MT)
this.0
'**That is all** I am going to tell you about that.'

c. **êkosi** **piko** ê-ititakok, . . . (MT)
thus.RES ENC.R CP=say.thus.to.s.o.VTA1.2p.CJ
'**That is all** I say to you, . . .'

The Unmarked Restrictive *nayêstaw*

Besides the enclitic *piko*, Plains Cree also has a preposed delimitative, *nayêstaw*; the two appear to be largely synonymous, as suggested by implication in the illustrative phrases in Lacombe's dictionary (1874a):

(24) a. (i) nipiy piko 'rien que de l'eau' [nothing but water]
(ii) nayestaw nipiy 'rien que de l'eau' [nothing but water]

The claim that their meanings are, at least in some contexts, indistinguishable is supported by the laboratory illustrations of Freda Ahenakew, which parallel the evidence of Lacombe:

(24) b. (i) kiya piko 'only you'
nayêstaw kiya
(ii) ôki piko 'only these'
nayêstaw ôki
(iii) kiya piko kik-êtohtân. 'Just you will go there [no one else].'
nayêstaw kiya kik-êtohtân.

In the texts, the translations for *nayêstaw* range from 'only, exclusively, merely' all the way to 'always, all the time'.[7]

Restrictive nayêstaw *with Nominals*

The unmarked restrictive *nayêstaw* is common with every kind of noun phrase:

(25) a. …, **nayêstaw** **mînisah** êh-mîcicik. (ET)
PRE.R berry.NI.0p CP=eat.(it/them).VAI.T.3p.CJ
'…, and they ate **only berries.**'

b. …, **nayêstaw** **pêyak** **napakikamikos** mân êkota
PRE.R one log.house.DIM.NI0 habitually there.RES
ê-kî-cimatêk. (MT)
CP=ASP=stand.erect.VII0.CJ
'…, **only a single little log-house** used to stand there.'

c. **nayêstaw** anima, ana wayân ana. (MT)
PRE.R that0 that3 skin.NA3 that3
'It was **only that**, the skin.'

The conjoint nouns under the scope of *nayêstaw* in the first clause of (25d) are in the second resumed by the deictic *êkoni*:

(25) d. . . .; **nayêstaw** **askiya** **êkwa** **pasêkâna,** **nayêstaw**
PRE.R moss.NI0p and cattail.NA3' PRE.R
êkoni ka-sikicikêcik, . . . (MT)
that.RES0p/3' ASP=wet.things.down.VAI.3p.CJ
'. . .; **only moss and cattails**, so that they would wet **only those**, . . .'

Restrictive nayêstaw *with Verbs and the Resumptive Deictic*

Unlike enclitic *piko*, preposed *nayêstaw* is common in constructions with verbs:

(26) a. . . ., kahkiyaw kîkway **nayêstaw**
all something.0 PRE.R
ê-kakwê-sôniyâhkâtamihk. (MT)
CP=attempt=earn.money.by.s.t.VTI.INDF.0CJ
'. . ., you **only try to make money** from everything.'

b. . . ., êkwa ôtênawa ôhi, **nayêstaw** **kahkiyaw** **ta-pihkowiwa,** . . . (MT)
and city.NI0p this.0p PRE.R all ASP=be.ashes.VII.0p.IND
'. . ., and all the cities will be nothing but ashes, . . .'
[*lit.* 'and the cities, **they will all of them be ashes only**']

The restrictive clause is often contrastive, with a negative clause preceding:

(26) c. nama kêkway kotak atoskâtam, **nayêstaw**
NEG something.0 other.0 work.VTI3.0IND PRE.R
êh-tâpakwêt . . . (ET)
CP=set.snares.VAI3.CJ
'She worked at **nothing but snaring rabbits** . . .'

Instances of *nayêstaw* with quantifiers and adverbials seem rare:

(27) . . ., **nayêstaw** **êkotowahk** ôta kâ-kî-aya-cimatêki
PRE.R that.kind.RES here CP=ASP=HES=stand.erect.VII.0p.CJ
mistikokamikwa; (MT)
log.house.NI.0p
'. . ., there were **only that kind**, log houses, standing here;'

The Co-occurrence of piko *and* nayêstaw

It is not uncommon to find *piko* and *nayêstaw* in successive clauses; here the first shows two nouns under the scope of *nayêstaw*, while in the second they are collectively referred to by the resumptive deictic *êkoni*, emphasized by *piko*:

(28) a. . . ., **nayêstaw** **ôm** **âya** **wâsaskocêpayîs** **êkwa** **pimiy**
PRE.R in.fact HES electric.heater.NI0 and oil.NI0
kâ-pônamihk, **êkoni** **pikw** ê-wâpahtahkik; (MT)
CP=make.fire.VTI.INDF.CJ that.RES.0p ENC.R CP=see.s.t.VTI.3p.0p.CJ
'. . ., [the young see] **only electric heaters and kerosene** when one makes a fire, they see **only those**;'

The two clauses may be parallel, with the second typically elaborating upon the first:

(28) b. . . ., **niyanân** **piko** **ninîsinân,** nititohtânân
we.ourselves(EXCL) ENC.R be.two.VAI.1p.IND go.there.VAI.1p.IND
awa **nayêstaw** **ê-manâ-tôtawâyâhk** awa . . . (MT)
this.3 PRE.R CP=sparingly=do.thus.to.s.o.VTA.1p.3CJ this.3
'. . ., **it was only the two of us**, and we went in with him **only as a courtesy to** him . . .'[8]

It is the most striking aspect of the singulative and delimitative system of Cree that *piko* and *nayêstaw* actually co-occur in a phrasal restrictive, combining the preposed *nayêstaw* with the enclitic *piko*:

(29) a. . . ., **nayêstaw** **piko** **ê-otakohpiyân,** mihawêsâkay mêton
PRE.R ENC.R CP=have.a.blanket.VAI1.CJ fur.coat.NI0 really
ê-mêstatapêkipayik, . . . (MT)
CP=be.worn.to.bare.skin.VII0.CJ
'. . ., **the only thing I had for a blanket** was a balding fur-coat, . . .'

b. kahkiyaw ayîsiyiniwah kîh-mêscihêw.
all human.being.NA3' ASP=annihilate.s.o.VTA3.(3').IND
nayêstaw **pikoh** **kôhtâwiyinaw** pimâtisiw. (ET)
PRE.R ENC.R 21PS.father.NDA.3 be.alive.VAI3.IND
'She has exterminated the people. **Only our father** is alive.'

When the two elements occur in the opposite order, the *piko* is clearly predicative:

(30) a. . . ., piyê-takohtêci **piko** **nayêstaw** **êh-kîhkâmât**, . . . (ET)
ASP=arrive.walking.VAI3.ITER OBL PRE.R CP=scold.s.o.VTA3.(3').CJ
'. . ., every time she came back, **she would do nothing but scold them**, . . .'
[*lit.* 'predictably she would do nothing but scold them']

While this might be dismissed as accidental, another instance found in Bloomfield's historical texts suggests that it may be deliberate:

(30) b. êkwah **pikoh** awâsisah **nayêstaw** **piko** **êh-mêtawâkêt,**
now OBL child.NA3' PRE.R ENC.R CP=play.with.people.VAI3.CJ
êko **piko** **nayêstaw** êy-isi-atoskêt. (ET)
that.RES0 OBL PRE.R CP=thus=work.VAI3.CJ
'He **only played with** the children, **that was the only work he did.**'
[*lit.* 'predictably he would play with the children exclusively, . . .']

This sentence gives every appearance of a chiastic construction, based on the reversal of constituents in successive clauses and a key element of high literary style in Cree.

The Bloomfield Translations

In the editions of the Modern Texts recorded since 1967 the deontic constructions defined by predicative *piko* are fairly consistently translated by English modals like *must* and *have to* or *should.* In the Early Texts of Bloomfield, by contrast, such plainly deontic translations are rare. Instead, we find fairly convoluted turns of phrase, with considerable variability from one instance to the other.

The "conventional" translation (from the perspective of the Modern Texts) is of course also found in the Bloomfield texts:

(31) a. **piko** ta-nipâyahk! (ET)
OBL ASP=sleep.VAI21.CJ
'We shall have to sleep out!'

b. **piko** ta-piciyahk! (ET)
OBL ASP=move.camp.VAI21.CJ
'We must move camp!'

But Bloomfield's translations seem to vary quite dramatically from the modern practice when *piko* is construed with *ê*-verbs:

(32) . . ., **pikoh** mistik ohci ê-saskahohtêt, . . . (ET)
OBL stick.NI0 by.means.of CP=walk.with.cane.VAI3.CJ
'. . ., he hobbled along leaning on a stick, . . .'
[*lit.* 'he had to walk with a stick as cane']

The *ta/ka* examples in the Bloomfield texts consistently indicate the future while those with *ê*-verbs generally indicate the past. With the verb in the *ê*-conjunct, Bloomfield remarkably also tends to translate the deontic clause temporally, by *always*:

(33) a. nama wîhkâc pêtamâsôw
NEG ever bring.(it/them).for.oneself.VAI3.IND
ta-mîcit, **pikoh** êh-pêtamâht. (ET)
ASP=eat.(it/them).VAI.T.3.CJ OBL CP=bring.(it/him).for s.o.VTA.INDF.3CJ
'Never did he need to fetch his food, for always others brought it to him.'
[*lit.* 'one had to bring it to him']

In fact, the same translation is also found in the Modern Texts, in this case with the future/purposive *ka*:

(33) b. kêhtê-aya kâ-wâpamat, sâsay ôsisima
old.person.NA3 CP=see.s.o.VTA2.3CJ already 3PS.grandchild.NDA.3'
piko ka-pimi-wîcêwât; (MT)
OBL ASP=along=accompany.s.o.VTA3.(3').CJ
'When you see an older person, she will always have her grandchildren along; . . .'
[*lit.* 'already it is inevitable that she have them along'][9]

Bloomfield, however, also employs this translation for the restrictive postposed *piko* 'only', which here follows the verb *ê-nikohtêt* 'she gathered fire-wood':

(34) êkwah mâna kah-kapê-kîsik êh-nikohtêt **piko**
now habitually RED.all.day CP=gather.fire.wood.VAI3.CJ ENC.R
awa oskinîkiskwêw, nama wîhkâc kêkway otinam, . . . (ET)
this.3 young.woman.NA3 NEG ever something.0 take.s.t.VTI3.0IND
'Then, when the young woman always gathered wood all day, she never picked up anything, . . .'
[*lit.* 'she only gathered wood']

The most tantalizing examples are those where Bloomfield translates the obligative by English *only* (regardless of the preverb):

(35) a. hâ, namoya! **pikoh** **ka**-mêtawêyahk! (ET)
HES NEG OBL ASP=play.VAI21.CJ
'Oh, don't say that! **Only** do let us have a contest!'
[*lit.* 'Well, no! It is necessary for us to have a contest!']

b. **pikoh** **kita**-kakwêyâhoyin ta-tapasiyahk. (ET)
OBL ASP=hurry.up.VAI2.CJ ASP=flee.VAI21.CJ
'The **only** thing for you to do is to hurry preparations that we may flee.'
[*lit.* 'it is necessary for you to hurry']

c. . . .; kiya namoya: **pikoh** **kita**-wîhtamôwacik
you.yourself NEG OBL ASP=tell.s.o.about.(it/them).VTA2.3p.CJ
tânisi kit ês âtoskêcik, . . . (ET)
how ASP=thus=work.VAI.3p.CJ
'. . .; not you: you are **merely** to tell them what to do as they work, . . .'
[*lit.* 'you have to tell them how to do their work']

d. nama wîhkâc êh-tipiskâyik êkwah pimohtêw,
NEG ever CP=be.night.VII0'.CJ now walk.along.VAI3.IND
pikw **êh**-kîsikâyik. (ET)
OBL CP=be.day.VII0'.CJ
'Now he never walked at night, but **only** in daytime.'
[*lit.* 'it was necessary that it be day']

The suggestion of a link between necessity and restrictiveness is especially striking where Bloomfield combines the deontic—'have to', 'need to', 'there is nothing to do but'—and the restrictive—'all'—in his translations of *ta/ka* sentences:

(36) a. **piko** mâka **kita**-pakamahwak, êkâ wî-pakitiniski! (ET)
OBL but ASP=strike.s.o.VTA1.3CJ [*sic*][10] NEG ASP=release.s.o.VTA3.2SUBJ
'But all you have to do is club her, if she will not let go of you!'
[*lit.* 'but it is necessary that you club her']

b. ê-ma-môminêt niwâpamâw,
CP=RED.eat.berries.from.bush.VAI3.CJ see.s.o.VTA1.3IND
piko mâka ta-tôtamahk, ntâyîm. (ET)
OBL but ASP=do.s.t.thus.VTI.INDF.CJ 1PS.co-wife.NDA.VOC
'I saw him eating berries from the bush, and that is all we need to do, my sister-wife.'
[*lit.* 'but it is necessary that we do so']

In sum, Bloomfield's treatment of the *piko*-sentences is highly suggestive: unless he viewed all instances of *piko* as an undifferentiated whole—which seems implausible in light of the elegance and consistency of his translations—his choices seem to reflect a gradual progression from necessity and predictability to emphatic restriction, culminating in a blend of deontic and restrictive elements. The evidence of translations, however, is never conclusive with respect to the original text, nor can we be certain of the extent to which the unexpected range of variation in the translations of *piko*-sentences in the Early Texts is Bloomfield's own: since we have neither his field notes nor any preliminary versions of the translations, none of the variants can be identified with one or another of the Cree speakers on whom he relied in his analysis of the texts and in preparing his translations—among whom he singles out Baptiste Pooyak as "the only person . . . who can with any consistency tell in English the meaning of a Cree expression" (1930:2).

In the Modern Texts, by contrast, which have been appearing in print since 1982, all the translations reflect the native control of a single Plains Cree speaker, Freda Ahenakew, and her long experience in the preparation of critical editions, so that the observed variation can more confidently be ascribed to the original text.

A fairly robust test is provided by sets of overtly ambiguous sentences, where *piko* is (1) FOLLOWED by a verb in the simple conjunct and with the future/purposive preverb *ta/ka* and (2) PRECEDED by a nominal, typically a resumptive deictic or a numeral phrase. For instance:

(37) . . ., êkos âyisk **piko** t[a]-êsi-pônihtâyân
thus.RES for ENC.R ASP=thus=cease.of.(it).VAI.T.1.CJ
minihkwêwin, . . . (MT)
drinking.NI0
'. . ., for this was the only way in which I might put an end to the drinking, . . .'

This sentence might also be interpreted as predicative, with *êkosi* and the causal conjunction *ayisk* 'for, because' preposed, resulting in a reading: 'for I had to put an end to the drinking in this way'; it is in fact translated as restrictive, with *êkosi* 'thus' under the scope of *piko*.

The first test set comprises four ambiguous sentences, (38a)–(38d), taken from the discourses of a single speaker, *kâ-pimwêwêhahk*/Jim Kâ-Nîpitêhtêw, and showing the same syntactic structure; yet the published translations vary: two interpret *piko* as predicative and two as restrictive.

The translation of (38a) is predicative, with preposed *êwako* resuming a preceding *kisêyinîw-âcimowin* 'the traditions of the old men':

(38) a. . . ., êwako **piko** kik[a]-âpacihtâyân, . . . (MT)
that.RES0 OBL ASP=use.(it/them).VAI.T.1.CJ
'. . ., THAT is what I will have to use, . . .'
[cf. restrictive 'for me to use that exclusively']

In (38b) the resumptive deictic *êwako* 'the selfsame' does not preclude an analysis of *piko* as predicative but the published translation is restrictive:

(38) b. êwakw âni **piko** ka-kiskinowâpahtahk
that.RES0 EMPH ENC.R ASP=learn.by.watching.s.t..VTI3.0CJ
oskayisiyiniw. (MT)
young.person.NA3
'That will be the only thing for the young people to watch and learn from.'
[cf. predicative 'THAT the young must watch and learn from.']

With the conjunction *cikêmô* 'of course, evidently' treated as extra-clausal and *piko* preceded by the full patient noun *kêhtê-aya* 'the old people', the translation of (38c) is predicative:

(38) c. . . ., cikêmô kêhtê-aya **piko** k[a]-âspitonâmoyahk; (MT)
of.course old.person.NA3 OBL ASP=place.reliance.VAI21.CJ
'. . ., for of course we must put our faith in the testimony of the old people;'
[cf. restrictive 'of course for us to rely on the old people exclusively']

In (38d) the extraposed subject noun phrase *matotisân ôma* 'this sweat-lodge' is separated by a prosodic break and resumed by the deictic phrase *êwak ôma* 'that one'; the translation is restrictive:[11]

(38) d. matotisân ôma, êwak ôma **piko**
sweat.lodge.NI0 this0 that.RES0 this0 ENC.R
ka-pimohtahikoyêk ôtê nîkân, . . . (MT)
ASP=take.s.o.along.VTA0.2p.CJ over.there ahead
'This sweat-lodge, that is the only thing which will guide you there in the future, . . .'
[cf. predicative 'THAT must guide you']

Unless the choice of translation of these four parallel sentences were to be viewed as random, or as depending on a lexical or rhetorical feature yet to be identified, could we reasonably appeal to ambiguity?

The second test case is a formal passage quoted from the Treaty Six discourse of *kâ-pimwêwêhahk*/Jim Kâ-Nîpitêhtêw. It begins and ends with parallel clauses built on *piko* and the simple conjunct form of the same stem with the future/purposive preverb *ka*:

(39) kîkway **piko** **k**[a]-âspitonâmot ayisiyiniw,
kitayânânaw kîkway k-âspitonâmoyahk kâ-nêhiyâwiyahk;
êwak ôma 'oskiciy' k-êsiyîhkâtêk,
êwako **piko** **ka**-kî-aspitonâmoyahk. (MT)
'The people must have something to rely upon as testimony,
and we who are Crees do have something to rely upon as testimony;
that which is called 'the pipestem',
that is all upon which we can rely as testimony.'

The variation in the published translations—the opening line is rendered as predicative, the closing one as restrictive—invites experimental reversal or, indeed, attempts at translating both the same way.

In relying on the choices or, at least, preferences of Freda Ahenakew, we defer to the native speaker and her *sprachgefühl*. But the analytical argument remains incomplete.

Necessity and Restriction

The case of predicative *piko* and its postposed counterpart presents an obvious challenge: if we are dealing with polysemy, can we isolate and define the common element and arrive at a *gesamtbedeutung*?

All matters of translation aside, the necessity construction with *piko* and the emphatic restrictive construction with *piko* both are defined by an ABSENCE OF CHOICE.

While the coercive force may range from an appeal to authority or a cultural norm to blind necessity (at the extreme, human mortality itself), it permits no choice. In a slightly attenuated form, the same is true of the restriction to a single person or object, time or place, manner or number: there is no alternative.

Ironically, there is a third major construction with *piko* (briefly mentioned in the Introduction) that stands in opposition to both the first two. As the initial member of compounds with pronouns and adverbs, *piko* forms universal concessive conditionals (and also general indefinites). It is mostly construed with correlative conjunctions:

(40) a. **pikw** **îyikohk** nitawêyimaci,
CONC CORR.to.such.an.extent want.s.o.VTA2.3SUBJ
ka-miyitin. (MT)
ASP=give.(it/them).to.s.o.VTA1.2IND
'No matter how much [money] you want, I will give it to you.'

In an analogous fashion, it also serves to render completely general and indefinite the reference of verbs of saying built on the correlative root *it-* 'say thus':

(40) b. **pikw** **êh-itwêyan** nka-tôtên, . . . (ET)
CONC CP=say.thus.VAI2.CJ ASP=do.s.t.thus.VTI1.IND
'Whatever you say I will do, . . .'

In this function, which John Haiman (1974, 1989, writing about Hua, Latin, and several other languages) has characterized as INCONSEQUENTIAL, the meaning of *piko* is the very opposite of necessity and restriction: it leaves open all possible outcomes equally.

It is not unheard of in the languages of the world for one and the same term to denote polar opposites. In the case of Plains Cree *piko*, it is their common opposition to the limitless choice expressed by the inconsequential that unites the necessity and restrictive constructions defined by the absence of choice.

NOTES

1. While the inspiration of John Haiman and Clare Cook will be obvious throughout this essay, all errors of fact or interpretation are mine alone. For critical comments at the conference I am also grateful to Rose-Marie Déchaine, Marie-Odile Junker, and Connor Quinn.

   All sentential illustrations are cited from spoken texts, identified as ET for Early Texts and MT for Modern Texts (published over the past three decades by Wolfart and Ahenakew; cf. F. Ahenakew ed. 1986, Vandall and Douquette 1987, Bear et al. 1992, Whitecalf 1993, Minde 1997, kâ-pimwêwêhahk / Kâ-Nîpitêhtêw 1998, A. Ahenakew 2000, kêkêk / Masuskapoe 2010, kâ-mimikwatowêt / Greyeyes 2014). Other abbreviations are as follows: NA = animate noun, NDA = dependent animate noun, NDI = dependent inanimate noun, NI = inanimate noun, s.o. = someone, s.t. = something, VAI = animate intransitive verb, VAI-T = syntactically transitive verb of the VAI class, VII = inanimate intransitive verb, VTA = transitive animate verb, VTI = transitive inanimate verb; person-number-obviation categories: 3, 3p, 3', 2, 2p, 21, 1, 1p; stems are marked with a trailing en-dash, and compounds with an internal hyphen.

   In the interlinear representation (line 2) the compound boundary is marked with the symbol =. The verb stems are identified as to their paradigmatic class quâ their syntactic and semantic potential rather than showing their actual manifestation in each case.

   Transitive stems of the VTA and VTI classes are glossed with 's.o.' and 's.t.', respectively, while those of the VAI-T class have the patient, which may be of either gender or number, indicated by (it/them).

   The following additional abbreviations are used to elaborate on verbal, nominal, pronominal, and numeral forms; except for the latter, all particles are simply glossed.

   Boldface is used to highlight items being discussed; the symbol || indicates parallel clauses.

Verbal: ASP = aspectual preverb, CISLC = cislocative preverb, CJ = (changed) conjunct, CP = complementizer, CONAT = conative preverb, IMVE = imperative, IND = independent, INDF = indefinite agent, SUBJ = subjunctive conjunct, TRANSLC = translocative preverb.

Nominal and pronominal: LOC = locative, PS = possessor, RES = resumptive, VOC = vocative.

Elsewhere/passim: CONC = concessive, CORR = correlative, DIM = diminutive, EMPH = emphatic, ENC.R = enclitic restrictive, EVID = evidential, FACT = factive particle, HES = hesitation particle, INTERROG = interrogative, NEG = negator, NUM = numeral, NUM.ADV = numeral adverb, OBL = obligation/necessity predicative, PRE.R = preposed restrictive, QUANT = quantifier, QUANT.DIM = quantifier diminutive, RED = reduplication.

2. Adverbial phrases with *piko* as the final member, for instance *âhci piko* 'still, nevertheless, despite it all' or *nawac piko* 'sort of, kind of, approximately; more or less; even a little; not fully' will be set aside for separate treatment. Only the briefest of mention is made here of such particles as *sapiko* 'actually, as a matter of fact', *(pi)konita* 'in vain, without reason, without purpose, for nothing; without further ado; anywhere, at random, in a random place' or *kîhkîhk* 'of necessity'.
3. While the unmarked negator *namôya* (and its variants *nama* and *môya*) is found in matrix clauses, the highly marked deontic negators *êkâ* and *êkâya* are used not only in subordinate but also in jussive and hortative clauses and with verb forms of the imperative order.
4. The distribution of *ka* and *ta* (and *kita*) is highly variable; in particular, it does not follow the distinction between the third person (in some previous studies thought to be limited to *ta* or *kita*) and the first and second persons (at times seen to favour *ka*). Though *ta* sometimes seems to have a greater deontic force than *ka*, this hypothesis is not borne out by the evidence of the texts.
5. Cf. Wolfart 2002, especially p. 245, and Wolfart 2014:173–174.
6. No distinction has been established between the variants *katâc* and *kâkatâc*. Bloomfield on occasion writes *kâ-katâc* although the final devoicing of the heavy reduplication syllable has not been observed in the Modern Texts. *(kâ)katâc* is much less common in the Early Texts recorded by Bloomfield than in the Modern Texts.
7. Unlike *piko*, moreover, *nayêstaw* recurs as part of the stem in verbs like the following, with illustrations also provided by Freda Ahenakew:

   (i) *nayêstawam-* VTA 'eat s.o. (e.g., bread) exclusively'
   e.g., ninayêstawamâw pahkwêsikan 'I eat nothing but bread'

(ii) *nayêstawaht-* VTI 'eat s.t. (e.g., meat) exclusively'
e.g., ninayêstawahtên wiyâs 'I eat nothing but meat'

(iii) *nayêstawisi-* VAI 'be alone, be by oneself'

8. Note the comitative construction of the intransitive verb form *nititohtânân* 'we went there' with *awa* 'this one'.
9. This example shows both the adverb *sâsay* 'already' and the patient noun *ôsisima* 'her grandchildren' preceding the necessity predicative, evidently without affecting the principle of its clause-initial status.
10. Note that the first verb in this example shows the suffix *-ak* VTA1-3CJ, while the translation appears to reflect a verb ending in *-at* VTA2-3CJ. The analytical point at issue here is not affected by this discrepancy, presumably due to a clerical error, between the Cree text and the English translation.
11. Note that the published interpretation of (38d) may also be expressed by the changed future preverb *kê* (rather than the unchanged *ka*):

(i)	hâw,	êwak	ôma	**piko**	kê-pimohtahikoyahk;	(MT)
	HES	that.RES0	this0	ENC.R	ASP=take.s.o.along.VTA0.21.CJ	

'Indeed, this is the only thing that will guide us;'

REFERENCES

Ahenakew, Alice. 2000. *âh-âyitaw isi ê-kî-kiskêyihtahkik maskihkiy/They Knew Both Sides of Medicine: Cree Tales of Curing and Cursing Told by Alice Ahenakew*, ed., trans., and with a glossary by H. C. Wolfart and Freda Ahenakew. Publications of the Algonquian Text Society. Winnipeg: University of Manitoba Press.

Ahenakew, Freda (ed.). 1986. *kiskinahamawâkan-âcimowinisa/Student Stories, Written by Cree-speaking Students*, ed., trans., and with a glossary by Freda Ahenakew. Algonquian and Iroquoian Linguistics Memoir 2. Winnipeg.

Bear, Glecia, Irene Calliou, Janet Feitz, Minnie Fraser, Alpha Lafond, Rosa Longneck, and Mary Wells. 1992. *kôhkominawak otâcimowiniwâwa/Our Grandmothers' Lives as Told in Their Own Words*, told by Glecia Bear et al., ed. and trans. by Freda Ahenakew and H. C. Wolfart. Saskatoon, SK: Fifth House Publishers.

Bloomfield, Leonard. 1930. *Sacred Stories of the Sweet Grass Cree*. National Museum of Canada Bulletin 60. Ottawa: King's Printer.

Bloomfield, Leonard. 1934. *Plains Cree Texts*. American Ethnological Society Publication 16.

New York: G.E. Stechert and Co.

Cook, Clare. 2014. *The Clause-Typing System of Plains Cree: Indexicality, Anaphoricity, and Contrast.* Oxford: Oxford University Press.

Haiman, John. 1974. Concessives, Conditionals, and Verbs of Volition. *Foundations of Language* 11:341–359.

Haiman, John. 1989. Inconsequential Clauses in Hua and the Typology of Clauses. *Clause Combining in Grammar and Discourse*, ed. by John Haiman and Sandra A. Thompson, pp. 49–69. Amsterdam: John Benjamins.

kâ-mimikwatowêt/William Greyeyes. 2014. *The Travelling Companion, told by kâ-mimikwatowêt/William Greyeyes*, ed. and trans. by H. C. Wolfart and Freda Ahenakew. Appendix to H. C. Wolfart, Two Plains Cree Performances of a pre-Victorian *Kunstmärchen*, pp. 177–215. *Anthropological Linguistics* 56(2):159–218.

kâ-pimwêwêhahk/Jim Kâ-Nîpitêhtêw. 1998. *ana kâ-pimwêwêhahk okakêskihkêmowina/The Counselling Speeches of Jim Kâ-Nîpitêhtêw*, ed., trans., and with a glossary by Freda Ahenakew and H. C. Wolfart. Publications of the Algonquian Text Society. Winnipeg: University of Manitoba Press.

kêkêk/Cecilia Masuskapoe. 2010. *piko kîkway ê-nakacihtât: kêkêk otâcimowina ê-nêhiyawastêki* [There's Nothing She Can't Do: Kêkêk's Autobiography Published in Cree]. mitoni ê-âh-itwêt mâna Cecilia Masuskapoe, itasinahamiyiwa ôhi nîso, H. C. Wolfart êkwa Freda Ahenakew [Exactly as told by Cecilia Masuskapoe, in a critical edition by H. C. Wolfart and Freda Ahenakew]. Algonquian and Iroquoian Linguistics Memoir 21. Winnipeg.

Lacombe, Albert. 1874a. *Dictionnaire de la Langue des Cris.* Montréal: C.O. Beauchemin et Valois.

Lacombe, Albert. 1874b. *Grammaire de la Langue des Cris.* Montréal: C.O. Beauchemin et Valois.

Minde, Emma. 1997. *kwayask ê-kî-pê-kiskinowâpahtihicik/Their Example Showed Me the Way: A Cree Woman's Life Shaped by Two Cultures*, told by Emma Minde, ed., trans., and with a glossary by F. Ahenakew and H. C. Wolfart. Edmonton: University of Alberta Press.

Reinholtz, Charlotte, and H. C. Wolfart. 2001. The Syntax of Emphatic *ani* in Eastern Swampy Cree and in Plains Cree. *Actes du Trente-Deuxième Congrès des Algonquinistes*, réd. par John D. Nichols, pp. 427–454. Winnipeg: L'Universite du Manitoba.

Vandall, Peter, and Joe Douquette. 1987. *wâskahikaniwiyiniw-âcimowina/Stories of the House People*, told by Peter Vandall and Joe Douquette, ed., trans., and with a glossary by Freda Ahenakew. Publications of the Algonquian Text Society. Winnipeg: University of Manitoba Press.

Whitecalf, Sarah. 1993. *kinêhiyâwiwininaw nêhiyawêwin/The Cree Language Is Our Identity: The*

La Ronge Lectures of Sarah Whitecalf, ed., trans. and with a glossary by H. C. Wolfart and Freda Ahenakew. Publications of the Algonquian Text Society. Winnipeg: University of Manitoba Press.

Wolfart, H. C. 2002. Cree Literature. *Encyclopedia of Literature in Canada*, ed. by W. H. New, pp. 243–247. Toronto: University of Toronto Press.

Wolfart, H. C. 2014. Two Plains Cree Performances of a Pre-Victorian *Kunstmärchen*. *Anthropological Linguistics* 56:159–218.

Contributors

Maral Aguilera-Moradipour recently completed her PhD in the Department of English and Writing Studies at Western University and is presently a sessional instructor at King's University College. Aguilera-Moradipour's research develops an interdisciplinary examination of literary and visual cultures that brings together the fields of Indigenous theory, diaspora cultural studies, and Asian thought.

Jerome Biedny is a former graduate student of the University of Wisconsin–Madison in the language sciences program. He remains a passionate supporter of the perpetuation and self-sufficiency of indigenous languages and cultural practices.

David J. Costa is the program director for the Language Research Office at the Myaamia Center at Miami University of Ohio. He grew up in northern California and completed his PhD in linguistics at University of California, Berkeley in 1994. He has been studying the Miami-Illinois language since 1988.

Andrew Cowell is professor of linguistics at the University of Colorado, where he specializes in linguistic anthropology. His work focuses primarily on Algonquian languages, especially Arapaho. He recently completed an ethnography of language shift and efforts at language maintenance among the Northern Arapaho (*Naming the World: Language and Power among the Northern Arapaho*, 2018), as well as an anthology of *Gros Ventre/Aaniiih Narratives* with Terry Brockie (2017). He is continuing work on an online Lexical Database of Arapaho.

Andrea Cudworth is an Algonquianist specializing in the phonetics and phonology of Menominee. She also works with language education programs in support of indigenous language revitalization.

R.-M. Déchaine is associate professor at the University of British Columbia.

M. Dufresne is an associate researcher at Queen's University, Kingston, Canada. A specialist in historical linguistics and the theory of change, she conducts research on the syntax and morphology of Medieval French (based on corpus data) and has authored numerous articles on prepositions, particles, and aspect. Her current work on Algonquian and Iroquoian languages focuses on using her expertise in theoretical and corpus linguistics.

S. Frazier is an incoming graduate student at the University of British Columbia, in the Department of Linguistics. Her work thus far has primarily focused on experiential linguistics and the syntax-prosody interface of Ojibwe.

Erik D. Gooding is a professor of anthropology in the Department of Anthropology and Earth Science at Minnesota State University Moorhead. His current linguistic research centers on Meskwaki and Sauk, with other research interests in Plains/ Western Great Lakes music and dance.

Sarah Holmstrom is a graduate student at the University of Wisconsin–Madison in the Language Sciences Program. Her research focuses on phonetics and phonology, sound change, and Algonquian languages.

Marie-Odile Junker is a full professor of linguistics at Carleton University, in Canada. She is active in Indigenous language documentation, maintenance, and revitalization. She uses a participatory-action research framework to work with communities and individuals interested in seeing their language thrive in the 21st century. Exploring how information and communication technologies can help Indigenous languages, she has developed several websites and online dictionaries for languages of the Algonquian family (Cree, Innu, Atikamekw). She is leading the co-creation of the Algonquian Linguistic Atlas (www.atlas-ling.ca), a large collaborative project that is building a digital infrastructure for Algonquian dictionaries and other resources. In 2017, she received a Governor General's innovation award for her Indigenous language work.

Robert E. Lewis Jr. is an assistant professor in the Department of Anthropology at the University of Winnipeg and is on the board of Bodwéwadmimwen Ėthë ték, Inc. (The Center for the Potawatomi Language), a Wisconsin-based nonprofit organization that seeks to preserve and facilitate the use of Bodwéwadmimwen (the Potawatomi language).

Angela Mesic is associate lecturer of the first-year Anishinaabemowin courses at the University of Wisconsin–Milwaukee. She obtained her bachelor's degree in the field of psychology and is currently working on a Masters of Community Psychology. Angela has a strong interest in research focused on psychology of learning and curriculum development. At the Electa Quinney Institute for American Indian Education she is a project manager for several projects in language revitalization with regional partners including the Indian Community School, several tribal nations, and universities throughout the United States.

Cherry Meyer is a member of the Sault Ste. Marie Tribe of Chippewa Indians and an LSA Collegiate Fellow in the Department of American Culture at the University of Michigan. She received her PhD in linguistics from the University of Chicago in 2020 and works on the Ojibwe/Nishnaabe language, focusing on noun categorization.

Gabrielle Mistretta is a language sciences graduate student at the University of Wisconsin–Madison.

Sarah E. Murray is an associate professor of linguistics at Cornell University, as well as a graduate field member in American Indian and Indigenous studies, cognitive science, and philosophy. Since 2006, she has been working with Chief Dull Knife College and the Cheyenne community in Montana on a variety of language projects.

John O'Meara is professor in the Faculty of Education at Lakehead University. He has taught in the Indigenous Language Teacher Certification program at Lakehead University and has been involved in documenting Anishinaabemowin and Munsee Delaware and in supporting Munsee language revitalization initiatives.

Claire Owen is a research associate and instructor at Carleton University in the School of Linguistics and Language Studies. She is assistant director of the Algonquian Linguistic Atlas (www.atlas-ling.ca) and has worked closely with Junker and various Indigenous partners since 2012 to help create practical resources for language learning, teaching, and revitalization.

Cécile Planchon's research interests lie primarily in sociolinguistics and Indigenous lexicography. She focuses mainly on languages in minority contexts, language assessment, language use and variations, as well as language attitudes. She is an adjunct professor at Carleton University and has worked as a researcher in Marie-Odile Junker's team for three years.

Richard A. Rhodes is professor emeritus of linguistics at UC Berkeley. He has studied Ojibwe, especially the Ottawa dialect, intensively throughout his career. He has also contributed significantly to the documentation of other endangered languages: Métchif and the Mexican language Sayula Popoluca. The focus of his work has ranged from morphology and descriptive syntax to lexical semantics and lexicography. Currently he is working on historical linguistic questions in Algonquian and on 19th century documents in Ojibwe.

Mskwaankwad Rice is an L2 speaker/learner of Nishnaabemwin from Waasaaksing First Nation. He is a cofounder of the Eshki-nishnaabemjig immersion program and is currently undertaking a PhD in linguistics at the University of Minnesota.

Joseph Salmons is Lester W. J. "Smoky" Seifert Professor of Language Sciences at the University of Wisconsin–Madison. He works to understand language change and sound systems, increasingly in Algonquian languages.

Charlotte Vanhecke is a PhD student in language sciences at the University of Wisconsin–Madison, where she also teaches Dutch. Her research focuses on phonology and language change, especially of heritage languages.

Rachel Vogel is a linguistics PhD student at Cornell University. She is interested in Cheyenne phonology and phonetics as well as broader issues in phonology and the phonetics/phonology interface.

H. C. Wolfart is professor emeritus of linguistics at Manitoba. He has long concentrated on the analysis of spoken texts. For Plains Cree, the results of this work include a variety of grammatical, lexical, historical, and literary studies and, most importantly, a series of text editions prepared jointly with Freda Ahenakew.

Bo Zhan is currently a PhD dissertator in Chinese linguistics at the University of Wisconsin–Madison. Her research interests are Sino-Japanese phonology and the teaching and perception of pragmatics. In addition to her research, she has taught various levels of Chinese and Japanese at different institutes.